WINNER TAKE ALL

WINNER TAKE ALL

How Competitiveness
Shapes the Fate of Nations

RICHARD J. ELKUS JR.

BASIC
BOOKS

A Member of the Perseus Books Group
New York

Published by Basic Books,
A Member of the Perseus Books Group

Books published by Basic Books are available at special discounts
for bulk purchases in the United States by corporations, institutions, and
other organizations. For more information, please contact the Special Markets
Department at the Perseus Books Group, 2300 Chestnut Street, Suite 200,
Philadelphia, PA 19103, or call (800) 810-4145, ext. 5000, or
e-mail special.markets@perseusbooks.com.

Designed by Brent Wilcox

A CIP catalog record for this book is available from the Library of Congress.
ISBN: 978-0-465-00315-0

10 9 8 7 6 5 4 3 2 1

To Helen

Anyone can win, unless there happens to be a second entry.

—GEORGE ADE

Contents

PREFACE

At the end of 2001 the U.S. trade surplus in advanced technology products turned negative. It had done this once before, in 1986, turning positive again in 1987. But in 2001, after the deficit returned, it didn't go away. "Advanced technology products" is a U.S. Census Bureau category that includes new or leading-edge technologies such as biotechnology, life science, optoelectronics, information and communications, electronics, aerospace, and nuclear technology. These critical technologies have been at the very core of America's economic growth.

The United States is in danger of losing its competitive position in a significant portion of these vital areas. In some, America is virtually out of the business. During the last forty years, Asia has become America's most aggressive competitor in the world of technology. The increase in Asian competitiveness at the expense of the United States is not a temporary phenomenon. It is the result of years of effort on the part of Asian industry devoted to national and corporate strategies of competition against which the United States has been unwilling or unable to rally a significant defense.

Should America worry? Many say no, asserting that the genius of America lies in innovation, creativity, and imagination, and that any product or market the United States loses will be replaced by another. "Innovation" is a popular word, associated with new and exciting products, high-paying jobs, and a high standard of living. But all these things can be fleeting when innovative products are produced by others, who control not only price but availability. The typical response to this concern is that the consumer will be protected since competing suppliers will always try to offer the right product at the right time and the right price in order to gain market share. But this assumption only works when it is to the seller's advantage or when another suitable supply is available. Often, neither of these circumstances exists. And the notion that innovation in America will happen when it is needed ignores a fundamental fact: the evolution of an idea into a product does not occur in a vacuum.

Innovation is based on an ongoing infrastructure of knowledge and experience in both product development and manufacturing. When the infrastructure goes away, innovation goes with it. A nation that loses its ability to translate technological development into successful products will ultimately lose its ability to innovate. Low-priced foreign products can in no way compensate for the cost America will pay for those losses. As advanced technologies, along with their industrial base, are lost to America's global competitors, there will be few new technologies to replace them anytime soon. Moreover, future technology will find its basis in what exists today—nothing comes out of the ether.

The United States over time developed an infrastructure of products and markets in advanced technology that was once second to none. The technologies on the Census Bureau's list have been the source of America's economic, military, and political strength. They are important, in one way or another, to virtually every product and market on Earth. The transfer of those technological and manufacturing assets to others may soon diminish America's economic and political leadership.

Global competitiveness today goes far deeper than our current discussions about national debt, currency valuations, and cheap labor—factors that are more result than cause. Ultimately it is about strategy based on a set of principles. When these principles are violated in the face of competitors who understand them, it is tough to win. For the last forty years this has been the plight of America. This book is about changing the course of any nation's global competitiveness before rather than after a crisis. It is also about the future of the United States.

Introduction:
The Great Giveaway

Look around. Note all the electronic and electromechanical devices that you see—TVs and set-top boxes; computers, printers, and monitors; cell phones, CD and DVD players, digital cameras, printers, PDAs, iPods, MP3 players, and fax machines. These all-pervasive products have at least two things in common: they use digital electronic technology to record, process, and distribute information, and most of their components and final assemblies originate outside the United States, primarily in Asia.

Not only are the vast majority of the electronics we buy manufactured in Asia, but more and more of the initial design and related R&D is being done by Asian companies as well. As these outsourced manufacturing entities gain expertise, moving up the food chain from mere assembly to design for manufacturing to overall product design, once dominant American companies are finding themselves no longer able to compete. By the time the outsourced design and manufacturing house decides to brand its own products, it is often too late for the U.S. competitor. This is not an unfamiliar story: the Asian competitors that have overtaken American domination of the consumer electronics industry include such household names as Sony, Samsung, Matsushita (Panasonic),

LG Electronics, Pioneer, Sharp, and Toshiba. And in the onslaught, organizations like RCA, Motorola Quasar (Motorola's television division), Magnavox, Sylvania, Polaroid, and Zenith have been absorbed by the competition.

These circumstances did not come about by accident. They are the direct result of strategic planning and industrial policy within Asian countries since the end of World War II. America as a nation has no such strategy or policy. A U.S. industrial policy is implicit in laws and taxes, but it tends to govern individual circumstances with little consideration given to the nation's global competitiveness. Individual companies are left to fend for themselves. This may have been manageable in the predigital age, when Japan was the only competitive threat. But today the United States is also contending with China, Korea, Taiwan, Singapore, Malaysia, Indonesia, and India—to name a few—countries where there abound intercompany cooperation and partnerships that are vertically and horizontally integrated and committed to similar and allied products and markets.

These Asian-made digital electronic products are extremely sophisticated, the result of research, development, and investment that today run into multibillions of dollars per year. The rate of growth of this investment is staggering, outrunning similar investment in the United States. In some markets, such as displays, investment by Asian companies and governments substantially exceeds that of the United States. In many instances the initial technology came from creative efforts of individuals, companies, and government agencies in the United States, but this is rapidly shifting. Original technology is being implemented in Asia and elsewhere at breakneck speed.

A TALE OF TWO COUNTRIES

In the late 1960s, IBM dominated the computer industry. Having introduced the "360" family of mainframe computers in 1964, IBM was at that time considered the only safe decision when purchasing computers for one's company. Problems with a second-tier brand would put the purchaser's job at risk, and it was a cliché that "nobody ever got fired for buying IBM." This market dominance was the result of a huge financial and technological bet made years earlier. Prior to 1964, most computers were custom designed, with specific modifications for particular customers. IBM had essentially bet the company that there was a market for a line of standardized mainframes that all ran the same user instruction set. With the introduction of the 360, IBM changed the computer business forever. Standardization built around a family of products allowed the customer to meet a variety of computer needs with one company while offering a faster learning curve than the competition and substantially fewer service and support requirements. As a result, IBM captured more than 75 percent of the global computer market before the competition knew what had happened.

Competition in the computer industry was based almost entirely in the United States, financed by U.S. companies and the U.S. government. One of IBM's closest competitors was Control Data Corporation, which claimed to have a more powerful machine. Control Data's model 7600, introduced in 1970, utilized 1.8 million transistors, filled a ten-foot-square room, was purported to be substantially faster, and cost $15 million. The computer industry was driving the development of the semiconductor, software, and electronic display industries. American dominance of computer manufacturing easily put the United States at the top of the food chain of information technology—technology that was fundamental to the nation's economic growth and political power. To lose that industrial base was unthinkable.

Yet in spite of IBM's glorious past, its future was far from certain. Because of its near monopoly of the computer business and a constant fear that it would be broken up by the U.S. Department of Justice, IBM became insulated from the rest of the world, an island unto itself. The company lost touch with its marketplace, the competition, and finally itself. It lost control of its assets, its liabilities, and its ability to compete. In 1993 Lou Gerstner was brought into IBM to reorganize what many felt was a failing company. When he took over, there was cash enough for only one hundred days. Every facet of the company's business was put under review. By the time IBM was reorganized, it had nearly two hundred thousand fewer employees but was once again a successful company.

In the ensuing years, IBM concentrated resources in those areas deemed essential to its future. Product emphasis shifted from personal computers and workstations to information management, consulting services, and related software, with support from its servers and mainframe computers. IBM shed much of its computer operations over the next few years. Its state-of-the-art hard drive business went to Hitachi in 2002. Even the personal computer, a product that was unimaginable in 1964 but was brought to market by IBM in 1981 (and that in turn put Microsoft on the map), was sold in 2004 to Lenovo, a Chinese company. By 2007, IBM, once the largest manufacturer of semiconductors in the world, was no longer in the top twenty.

What happened? How did IBM manage to become a lesser player in the computer business it once dominated? How did *America* become a lesser player in the computer business it once dominated? Does it matter?

In 1986 a commission of MIT faculty and staff was established to study the competitiveness of American industry, and two years later its results were released in a book called *Made in America*. Arguing that manufacturing was essential to a successful American economy, the commission noted that many strategic and structural changes in American industry were needed if the United States was to remain competitive. "The United States," the report warned, "needs to make a major new commitment to technical and organizational excellence in manufacturing after years of relative inattention."[1] As many industry leaders would confirm, it's very hard to separate manufacturing from innovation. If you aren't manufacturing products, your technological base can become limited, substantially reducing your ability to understand the interdependent evolution of the design and manufacturing processes that are fundamental to the commercialization of the product. For an economy like America's, which depends on innovation for its growth, manufacturing is not optional, the commission argued, it is a necessity—and we were letting it slip away.

In the late 1980s the competitive threat to the United States seemed limited to Japanese electronics; Korea, Taiwan, Singapore, India, and China were not yet on the radar screen. Not long after the publication of *Made in America,* two events conspired to suggest that MIT's concerns might not be that serious. In 1990, the real estate bubble in Japan burst, and the resulting financial cost to that country was monumental. Much of the value of the land within the city boundaries of Tokyo, said at one point to equal the entire value of all the land in America, disappeared virtually overnight. The nation had racked up enormous debt against its real estate, and while the value of the assets plummeted, the debt remained. The Nikkei index dropped by 80 percent, and the country went into a recession that lasted fifteen years. Japan as a competitive threat appeared to melt away.

The second event was the American commercialization of the internet. For a time it seemed the United States had struck an endless supply of gold that no other nation could touch.

But Japan had not gone away. It remained the second-largest national economy on Earth, and the largest with a trade surplus. Throughout its prolonged recession, its trade surpluses continued to grow as America's trade deficits deepened. And when the supply of internet gold ran out in 2000, it was apparent that much of America's investment during the 1990s had been opportunistic—aimed more at generating speculative profits than at producing real growth. When the speculators grew uneasy, businesses failed; the NASDAQ, like the Nikkei before it, dropped 80 percent.

Despite the financial problems caused by the collapse of its real estate market, Japan's desire for a world-class microprocessor had never diminished. Even before they had any high-tech industry to speak of, the Japanese clearly understood the importance of computer technology and such related areas as displays and semiconductors. For over a decade in the 1980s and early 1990s they attempted without success to design their own computer operating system (called Tron). But by the 1980s their overall attempt to build a high-tech industrial base had begun to pay off. The Japanese were propagating their electronic products across the globe, usually at the expense of entrenched competition. In 2001, Sony and Toshiba entered into a joint R&D relationship with IBM to design and manufacture what IBM called the Cell processor, a new multicore semiconductor processor to be used in IBM's servers and mainframe computers. IBM felt that the Cell processor's unique capabilities would give it a technological lead. But for IBM to design its own processor was a huge financial and technological undertaking. IBM initiated the joint project because it needed both the resources to help fund its multibillion-dollar effort and the technological expertise that resided with the Japanese companies.

For Sony and its partner, Toshiba, the joint R&D project was a gamble similar to IBM's bet on the 360 forty years earlier. Sony and Toshiba needed a new processor for the PlayStation 3 to follow on the heels of the PlayStation 2, the most successful game console ever. They wanted, in effect, a microprocessor with supercomputer properties that not only would provide stiff competition to Microsoft's Xbox, but could ultimately be incorporated into their myriad consumer and computer products. The Cell processor seemed just the right product. The Sony/Toshiba joint R&D effort with IBM was a continuation of the need, originally expressed in the Tron program, for a Japanese company able to produce its own microprocessor with its own operating system to support Japan's rapidly growing position in end-use electronic products. Whether Sony is successful in its venture or not, the outcome of this bet could have significant implications for the balance of power between the United States and Asia. In theory, the Cell processor could be Asia's answer to Intel and AMD.

PlayStation 3, with the Cell processor inside, debuted in late 2006. With 234 million transistors, the Cell processor has substantially more capacity and is several thousand times faster than the Control Data 7600. Moreover, this processor neither occupies a hundred square feet nor costs $15 million; it resides on a half-inch-square chip inside a PlayStation 3, which includes a Blu-ray high-definition video player and a sixty-gigabyte hard drive and retails for a few hundred dollars. The Cell processor has the potential to transform the computing business just as profoundly as the IBM 360 did a generation earlier. It is Sony's hope not only that the Cell processor will be propagated across its entire product line, but that the PS3, powered by the Cell processor, will evolve into something far more than a game box, becoming a central computing facility for the home. With Japan's strength in consumer electronics, displays, and semiconductors, the Cell processor could become a key component in a national strategy for global competitiveness.

There are four key points to be understood here. First, a major technology bet this time is being made in Japan. Second, the PS3 has the technological power of a supercomputer coupled with a Blu-ray high-definition video player and hard drive at a tiny fraction of the cost one would have imagined only a few years ago. Third, this console is intended to be the data-processing centerpiece of an array of related products including computers, displays, sound systems, and information storage devices. Fourth, the bulk of these products will not be manufactured or even designed in the United States. Most important, perhaps, is the fact that the rest of Asia, resolved to rival the success of Japan, has been watching and learning with the potential to be an enormous competitive threat to America's technological base.

In addition to its collaboration with Sony and Toshiba in the Cell processor design, IBM has recently developed a semiconductor manufacturing consortium that includes Samsung in Korea and Chartered Semiconductor in Singapore. The purpose of the consortium is to exchange process and manufacturing know-how among its partners in order to provide a common semiconductor design platform. This, in turn, offers consortium partners without manufacturing facilities the ability to design their own devices with unique specifications that can be manufactured by any member of the consortium at relatively low prices and with fast delivery. IBM gains additional design, manufacturing, and financial resources from the consortium while the other members gain IBM semiconductor design and manufacturing technology. The problem for

America is that the majority of the semiconductors produced by the consortium will more than likely be manufactured in Asia. And most of those devices will go into end-use products—consumer electronics, displays, and computers—that are also made in Asia.

The joint development of the Cell processor is not an isolated example of the transfer of technology from America to other nations. One of the first major transfers of seminal technology and related products occurred in the 1960s, when U.S. companies licensed and outsourced to Asia and Europe the technology to design and manufacture magnetic recorders.

As a result, the U.S. current account deficit, the financial worry of the entire world for good reason, now includes a negative balance of trade in advanced high-tech products. It appears these products will increasingly be designed and manufactured in Asia unless something consequential is done to bolster American competitiveness. The loss of ascendancy in computer technology and related products and markets—unthinkable a few years ago—is today a stark reality. The MIT commission sent a clear warning twenty years ago. But nobody listened.

The decline in the design and manufacture of high-tech products in the United States is a symptom of two corrosive myths that are confounding the American economy. First is the belief that the value of the manufactured products, intellectual property, and services the United States is now producing can continue to decline from current levels and still support America's political, economic, and military objectives. It cannot; those objectives—and the dominant position in the world that they support—must be scaled back unless the United States finds a way to produce more value. The second myth is that to the extent that America is losing its competitive position in products and markets, it is because the dollar is unfairly valued relative to other currencies and should be substantially reduced. If this were done soon, America's trade deficits would disappear, and everything would be fine. But the fact is that the relative value of the dollar is much less important to America than the drain of intellectual property and manufacturing expertise.

At an ever-increasing rate the ability of the United States to create real and lasting value for its goods and services is being transferred to other nations in pursuit of short-term profits and a way to invest on the cheap. America is not just outsourcing; it is exiting critical businesses that are fundamental to its long-term future. As a result, the worth of America's goods and services is becoming highly transitory and increasingly dependent on fundamental value created by others. It is not a weak dollar that gives the United States its economic strength. It is the value of its infrastructure of technology, products, and markets that keeps America competitive. That infrastructure requires massive capital investment and a solid long-term strategy. Faith in quick fixes is a way of denying the harsh truth: America's economic problems are much deeper than that. They took decades of shortsighted opportunism to develop and will take extraordinary effort and sacrifice to remedy.

In the mid-1980s, along with Ed David, former president of Exxon Research and science advisor to the president of the United States, I met with the senior officer of the venture capital arm of Japan's Nomura Securities, at that time the largest securities firm in the world. He pointed out that in 1968 the yen had an exchange rate of 360 yen to the dollar. He then told us, with great determination in his voice, that the yen would ultimately increase in value to 100 yen to the dollar—a 72 percent increase—and when it did, Japan would be the most competitive nation on Earth. Japan would win, he argued, not because of low-cost products and services but because it was creating products whose compelling value was more important than the value of its currency. The yen did exactly what he said, and Japan's manufacturing base has been the core of its export-driven economy ever since.

This concept must be fundamental to the competitiveness of the United States. America will not win because of cheap labor. It will win because of technological excellence and resulting products that represent the best the world has to offer in areas strategic to American objectives. With dedication, savings, investment, and a national strategy, the United States should be able to turn the tide in a decade. The alternative represents undue hardship for all Americans and an uncertain future for the rest of the world.

WHO CARES?

No industry has been more important to America's long-term economic health over the past fifty years than electronics. It is the largest manufacturing industry on Earth, growing at nearly double-digit rates annually, and is progressively suffusing *all* industries. Electronics manufacturing requires the support of significant software and electromechanical design expertise and infrastructure. Digital home entertainment electronics, just one segment of the overall industry, represents approximately $200 billion in annual world revenues. Semiconductors, the core element of all electronics products, generate a $260 billion annual market. Displays, the primary means by which digital information is presented, represent roughly $100 billion and computers, another $400 billion. In 2007, the total electronics market worldwide amounted to about $2 trillion.[2] The technology of information and image processing has become the lifeblood of postmodern society. At an ever-increasing rate, the design, development, and manufacturing of key components of the digital age—a direct outgrowth of infrastructure totally dominated by the United States after World War II—are shifting to Asia to the great detriment of U.S. competitiveness.

American technological expertise was not, for the most part, stolen; it was given away. The United States sold or licensed the technologies. It sold or outsourced infrastructure that would become necessary to maintain a competitive position in related businesses. In the wake of myopic opportunism, the once dominant American enterprise no longer functions adequately. Attempts to justify this situation in the context of U.S. competitiveness ride on the expectation that the United States will be able to purchase products that are much cheaper, more innovative, and more reliable than could be made in America.

Why should America care about this trend? Haven't the American consumer and economy benefited from it? The answer is that the benefit was temporary and is beginning to run out. Now that the United States has been operating this way for nearly forty years, the problem is becoming too widespread and is accelerating. It was one thing when America was simply outsourcing certain manufacturing operations; now it is literally exiting critical businesses. These product and market losses are fundamental to basic image and data processing, storage, and communication in a digital world, and as such, they impact every last industry on Earth. Any waning of American expertise in information and image processing relative to other nations will have a negative effect on the ability of the United States to be competitive in many industries, but primarily those that are laden with electronic content, such as networking and telecommunications, automobiles, aircraft, biotech, defense, pharmaceuticals, films, and publishing.

In large part because of early losses in consumer electronics, the United States is suffering from a competitive disadvantage in the automotive industry and losing ground in semiconductor fabrication. Electronics technology is increasingly used in support of service industries, including finance, accounting, inventory control, distribution, medical care, education, research, and the legal profession. In short, no industry is left untouched by electronics.

The United States is rapidly and unwittingly losing its competitive position in the world of information and image processing. What once was total domination of world computer markets is no more. IBM sold its entire PC business to Lenovo in China. Related areas in image processing, such as displays, recorders, cameras, and cell phones, which in one form or another affect the entire U.S. communications industry, are being usurped by Asia. Software, which is enabled by these electronic platforms, will ultimately be at risk as well.

The most strategic piece of equipment used in the manufacturing of semiconductors is called the stepper, which imprints the digital circuit patterns on a chip. Having once made half the world's steppers (scanners), America now produces almost none. Approximately 90 percent of new and technologically advanced semiconductor plants are now being built offshore, most of them in Asia.[3] Information and image processing is utterly dependent on the semiconductor industry. If this drain continues much longer, America's competitiveness in the global community will be extremely difficult to rebuild.

There is another dimension. The digital age enables products to evolve rapidly in ways that are difficult to predict. Consider the convergence of cell phones, computers, cameras, and television. As we participate less and less in the design and manufacture of these products and the vertical integration of their related components, old-line producers that depended on one market—personal computers, for example—are being forced to compete in markets where America's position is weak at best and lacks the critical infrastructure to maintain its competitive edge.

Intel is beginning to alter its strategic positioning as the personal computer gives ground to competing wireless devices that result from a combination of notebooks, cell phones, cameras, new processors and memory devices, and vast changes in display technology largely manufactured in Asia. In this new environment Microsoft cannot count on being the operating system of choice as it begins to compete in earnest with new operating systems developed for cell phones and other portable wireless devices. Kodak's film business is rapidly losing ground as digital cameras made in Asia take over. Polaroid went bankrupt. RCA is gone, along with every other American television manufacturer. Studies suggest that technology related to information processing, storage, and analysis related to defense may well be at risk for lack of domestic supply of critical items.

Why is it so vital for the United States to stay in the design and production of electronic products and systems including consumer electronics, displays, and semiconductors? The creation of digital information—for example, software development—is of no value without a platform to enable its use, such as a semiconductor, or an end product like a cell phone, television set, or computer. To get maximum benefit from its own advancements in designs that utilize digital information, America must at least produce those components that enable the use of that information. And considering that the ultimate benefit will show up in the final product that embodies those improvements, the United States should be in the business of producing those products as well. If not, the design expertise will leave the United States and congregate where the demand resides.

Set aside for the moment the fact that the design and manufacture of products associated with the storage, processing, and distribution of digital information maximally affect the development of intellectual property, which in turn contributes to further improvements; or the fact that losing positions in these markets reduces the demand for R&D and an environment that supports creativity and innovation; or the fact that if the engineering and professional careers associated with these products are in less demand, the brightest will go elsewhere. The fundamental fact is that information technology and its resulting products are prerequisites for America's competitive industrial base. Lacking those prerequisites, the United States will be forced to depend on its competition for much of the strategic infrastructure essential for advancement in information technology. If that support is denied, America suffers. If the cost of the competitor's product and services goes up, America suffers. If the United States has to borrow because it doesn't produce its fair share and no one wants dollars relative to other currencies, prices go up even further, and America suffers. Then you get stagflation. Stagflation is the worst of all worlds because prices go up, the economy deteriorates, employment drops, and the nation's standard of living enters into a period of protracted decline. Under these circumstances the ability of America to control its economic and political future will certainly be diminished as U.S. economic power quietly passes to those who produce and own the resources America needs most.

PANDERING TO SHAREHOLDERS

In November 1970, Ampex Corporation introduced the VCR to the world. Based upon Ampex's proprietary technological expertise, the

VCR had a profound effect on audiovisual communications. It became the most successful consumer electronics product in terms of gross revenues ever introduced up to that time. It was called "IC Hog" because it used more integrated circuits (semiconductor devices) than any product of its day. The fundamental driving force behind the development of image processing, television, displays, and microelectronics, the VCR helped make Japan the second-largest national economic power in the world. Learning to mass-produce the various components of the VCR helped create a whole new concept of robotics and automation in manufacturing. It was one of the preeminent factors in the development of digital cameras. Prerecorded tapes not only became the largest market for Hollywood movies but also exposed Eastern Bloc countries to the free-world standard of living, ultimately contributing to the destruction of the Berlin wall.

What the VCR wasn't was "made in America." The product was dropped by American industry and fervently appropriated by Japan. This was a major turning point in American international competitiveness. The full effect of this loss has not yet been felt but is becoming a major problem, affecting America's industrial base across the board. It is now nearly forty years later, and the United States has done little to recover its position. On the contrary, the U.S. industrial base has continued to decline along with its ability to create and innovate.

The following news release from the Associated Press in November 1988 illustrates the mind-set of the time:

> Glenview, Ill. (AP) A battle over America's industrial future is being fought in this Chicago suburb, where the nation's last major manufacturer of televisions is under siege from Wall Street. The struggle for Zenith Electronics Corp. is being watched closely by Washington, Silicon Valley, and foreign capitals because of what it could mean for the future of the United States in high technology. Two New Yorkers who ordinarily specialize in stock market speculation are asking Zenith shareholders to decide by Dec. 4 whether to dump the company's chief executive from

the board of directors and install them. The Wall Street arbitragers say they want to get rid of Zenith's money-losing television business.[4]

As it turned out, Zenith was one of the participating companies that helped establish the standards for high-definition television in the United States, contributing significant technology for the potential development of the industry. But when those major contributions were brought to fruition and HDTV and the digital revolution became a reality, Zenith as an American company was gone; it had been sold to LG Electronics of Korea in 1996 for a fraction of what it now costs to build a single display manufacturing facility. Today no television sets are made in America.

The Associated Press story made some other interesting points. Zenith, it said, was the "world's 13th largest color TV maker, tied with a Finnish company called Nokia Corporation." It also noted that "for an outsider, jumping into the TV business would be like trying to hop onto a speeding train," which is "why giants such as IBM have not started making TVs in spite of their public statements about the importance of a U.S. presence in the industry." And commenting on another U.S. company attempting to fund such an endeavor as television manufacturing, Stephen Balog of Shearson Lehman Hutton said it all: "For the good of the country, yes. For the good of their shareholders, no. The stock would go straight down."

But there is another side to the same story. In a brief history of the company, Nokia noted that the evolution of its consumer products, including computers, TVs, and radios, was a long and winding road that proved to be very expensive. But the electronics industry, it added, "paved the way for the telecommunications business." Largely because of Nokia's success in cell phones, its market capitalization was $140 billion in January 2008. In that same month, the market capitalization of Motorola, formerly the world's number-two supplier of cell phones—a company that had cut its teeth on wireless communications and until recently was one of Nokia's most formidable competitors—was only $23 billion.[5]

The events surrounding Zenith's and Motorola's lack of competitive strength mirrored much of what has happened to America's competitive position during this period. In 1974, long before Zenith went out of the television business, Motorola sold its Quasar television operations to Matsushita of Japan.

Partly in support of its communications and television business, Motorola had made significant investments in semiconductor manufacturing. By 1989 it had become the fourth-largest semiconductor manufacturer in the world. But in 1999, wanting to reduce its holdings in its highly cyclical and capital-intensive semiconductor operations, Motorola spun out its semiconductor components group in a management buyout, largely funded by the Texas Pacific Group, a private equity firm. As a result, ON Semiconductor began operations as a leading manufacturer of analog and standard and logic components. Then in 2003 Motorola decided to separate itself from the remainder of its semiconductor operations. It established Freescale Semiconductor, which became a public company in 2004. Two years later, Freescale was purchased by a private equity group. Many of the fabrication facilities for Freescale's newly established semiconductor operations are now owned and operated by Asian foundries.

Finally, in the first quarter of 2008, after experiencing turmoil and setbacks in its cellular phone business, coupled with intense pressure from investors looking for better returns, Motorola indicated its intent to sell those operations, exactly thirty-five years after Martin Cooper, manager of Motorola's communication systems divisions and inventor of the cell phone, placed the first-ever cellular telephone call.

For years both Zenith and Motorola had felt pressure from investors to generate acceptable margins in businesses that were considered problematic in America. Consumer electronics, displays, and semiconductor manufacturing had developed the reputation of commodity industries with inherently low margins and manufacturing capital investment requirements that were not conducive to satisfactory financial returns. So when U.S. companies reached the conclusion that they should divest themselves of activities in these areas, few other American companies were interested in entering the field. In the main, Asian companies developing infrastructure in these industries were there to pick up the slack. In the case of some products, such as semiconductors, they were interested in the manufacturing side of the business. In others, including consumer electronics and displays, they wanted the entire enterprise.

GM NEVER HAD A CHANCE

In "The Seamless Product," a 1991 article for *Automobile* magazine, I attempted to predict what I thought would be a major problem for the automobile business in the next few years.

> A seamless product is one so well integrated that you can't discern its beginning, middle, or end; the user and the product become one. The seamless automobile is not yet real, but Japan is hard at work to make it so. In the fall of 1989, an ad for Matsushita Corporation, a major Japanese supplier of consumer electronics, ran in *Fortune* magazine, presenting an exciting view of the future. "Put eyes in the back of your head, a navigation system in front of your nose, a telephone and a fax in the middle of everything." The ad listed a myriad such products that would be part of the future car.[6]

Matsushita was not an automobile company; it was one of several major consumer electronic companies located in Japan. Nothing like Matsushita existed in the United States. Most people would know it by its brand name, Panasonic. "There is no question," I concluded, "that seamless products will attract and satisfy consumers, but that could turn out to be a nightmare for the U.S. automobile industry, because today American industry simply can't provide Detroit with the necessary resources. And if America can't support its automakers, there are other industrious nations poised to take up the slack."

In September 2006, the *Wall Street Journal* put it this way: "Toyota Motor Corp. has a message for its struggling rivals in Detroit: We will bury you."[7] The comment was prompted by Toyota's sophisticated array of sonar distance-finding devices linked with the navigation system to provide virtually unassisted parking of a vehicle, climate control systems linked to sensors that detect when an occupant is overheating, and the robotic capability within the factory that can provide, among other things, an automotive finish substantially better than that available on American vehicles. This has nothing to do with price and everything to do with the rapid integration of the technological system called an automobile.

In 1981 the American automobile industry was beginning to wake up to the fact that Japan was challenging their dominance. Roger Smith, the new chair and CEO of General Motors, had a "consuming vision" of what GM had to achieve to compete. He was prescient in seeing that the car would become an "electromechanical system including onboard computers and electronic circuitry that would become as important as the actual engine."[8] He wanted a fully automated factory, similar to those operating in Japan. These "lights out" facilities (so called because of the limited lighting required by the few operating personnel) were common in the semiconductor industry and in certain consumer electronic fabrication facilities. He wanted to "block the Japanese from using their superiority in microelectronics to dominate the car market as they had the consumer electronics market."

Over the next ten years, GM spent $90 billion in an attempt to reinvent itself.[9] The effort was a total failure. In a 1986 management conference report, Executive Vice President of Finance F. Alan Smith pointed out that GM projected to spend $34.7 billion between 1986 and 1989.[10] That sum, he argued, was equal to the market capitalization of Nissan and Toyota combined. Theoretically, GM could buy out both companies, increasing its worldwide market share to 40 percent. What could an additional $34 billion investment give General Motors that would be worth that kind of sales increase? In any case, GM spent the money.

In January 2008, the combined market capitalization of Ford and General Motors was approximately $30 billion, one-sixth that of Toyota alone, which had a market capitalization approximating $165 billion. Toyota surpassed Ford in 2007 and General Motors in 2008, becoming the largest automobile company in the world in terms of sales. Chrysler, the other member of America's original big three automakers, was long ago sold to Daimler-Benz and then sold again to Cerberus, an American private equity firm, for just over $7 billion.

As several articles on GM pointed out, the company made many mistakes in strategy and management. But there is another factor that is little discussed. In many ways the cards were stacked against GM. The industrial alliances that form an integrated web of cooperation and support in Japan do not exist in the United States. America has become so opportunistic that there is no real strategic understanding of the relationship between products and markets, the need and the investment required to build market share, and the kind of infrastructure necessary to be competitive as a nation in a global economic community. There is no Matsushita in America that can integrate its expertise in an automotive infrastructure guided by GM. There is one in Japan, and Toyota and other Japanese automobile companies are the beneficiaries. The level of investment in time, money, technology, and equipment necessary to achieve what Roger Smith had in mind was billions and years more than was available to GM even as it represented the largest corporation in America. *What GM was trying to do on its own was what Japan was doing as a nation.* GM never had a chance.

In the late 1990s I spoke with a member of a Ford engineering team assigned to analyze a disassembled Lexus. She explained the team's concern when they compared the Lexus to a similar American vehicle. The Lexus, she said, was a totally integrated system. The information systems, engine, brakes, and control mechanisms were designed to make the passenger and the vehicle a complete operating unit, and they were seamless. Ford's vendor relationships were built largely on price and performance, while the Lexus reflected an integrated team organized as a virtual company—one expected to remain intact over the long term, with shared responsibility for the success of the final product.

If the United States continues to abandon the design and manufacture of products related to digital information technology, as it has over the past thirty-six years, its economy and way of life could ultimately face a very serious problem. This is not just because America faces global competition but because, as GM and Ford are finding out, it is losing the national resources necessary to give its best a fighting chance. The competition is usurping critical infrastructure of related technologies and products. It has taken nearly forty years to arrive at this point. But with the transferability between products of both digital technology and functionality, the pace of convergence is speeding up. Another fifteen to twenty years like this and the U.S. can bid its present way of life good-bye.

THE PRINCIPLES OF COMPETITION IN A TECHNOLOGICAL WORLD

In 1968 I presented the CEO of Ampex Corporation with the initial product plan for the VCR. As a result of my experience with the VCR, I was asked in 1985 to make a presentation to the American Electronics Association. I felt then, as I do now, that the complete abdication of that product and related markets to Japan was a serious blow to American competitiveness. I was later asked to give a similar talk to Sematech, a recently established organization of major American manufacturers of semiconductor devices in cooperation with the U.S. government. The purpose of Sematech was to reinvigorate America's competitive stance in the global community, particularly as it related to the semiconductor industry. I testified on the same subject before the Senate Banking Committee in conjunction with Don Petersen, retiring chair of Ford Motor Company, and Henry Shacht, CEO of Cummins Engine. I am convinced that competitiveness follows a systematic pattern. It is subject to laws every bit as much as is economics or, for that matter, physics.

In 1991, the Economic Strategy Institute, under the guidance of Clyde Prestowitz, published my testimony, including those laws, or principles, of competitiveness. If these principles are understood, a nation can devise a strategy to remain viable as a globally competitive economy. When they are violated, as they have been by the United States for nearly forty years, the nation is likely to experience a decline in its political and economic power and standard of living, particularly when the competition understands the rules of the game.

The ten principles listed below are expanded on in individual chapters:

(1) *As end-use products, markets, and related technologies evolve, they become increasingly interrelated, interdependent, and integrated.* They support one another as individual components of a system, often becoming integrated, as in the semiconductor business, when individual components become a complete system on a chip, or in consumer electronics, when a video recorder, camera, and cell phone become a single unit. This *convergence* leads to rapid and often unexpected innovation of additional products and technologies as well as an exponential increase in competitive advantage. Increasing the compactness, reliability, and capabilities of VCRs, video cameras, displays, and computers led to the complexity and versatility of today's digital cameras, HDTV, broadband telecommunications, and multifaceted cell phones. These convergent industrial infrastructures in turn integrate into the larger competitive infrastructure of the nation.

(2) *Growth of products and markets is always evolutionary, never revolutionary.* The idea that a company or economy can innovatively leapfrog the competition without the requisite base infrastructure is unrealistic. Imagine the internet developing in the United States without the hundreds of billions of dollars invested in telecommunications equipment and transmission lines. Yet to anyone missing the importance of that telecommunications infrastructure, the internet explosion looks like a revolutionary leap. Over time, products converge in ways no one expects, and seemingly overnight you have a new product, a new market, even a new industry. But the belief that these things grew out of thin air—or somehow mark a "revolutionary" step forward—is an illusion. The importance of this point for America lies in the time and cost

needed to develop this infrastructure of products, markets, and related technologies and the resultant power of their convergence. When that underlying network of relationships is lost, more often than not the game is over. Without that underlying network, it's difficult to recognize existing opportunities, let alone take advantage of them.

(3) *As the cost of building an infrastructure rises exponentially, the price of reentry to those who have lost that infrastructure becomes overwhelming.* Since 1970 the cost of building a semiconductor plant has risen from $10 million to $5 billion.[11] In the 1970s, manufacturing facilities to build displays in the United States cost $2 to $3 million. Today, factories that manufacture only the panels for flat panel displays cost $3 billion or more each, and there are no display manufacturers of significance left in America.[12] To regain lost technological infrastructure, when the current infrastructure has deteriorated to the point that it no longer provides an adequate basis for national competitiveness in that field, is extremely difficult and expensive. The one historical exception, the conversion to a wartime economy at the onset of World War II, suggests the level of economic sacrifice and discipline that may be required. And even that conversion was built on a formidable manufacturing base.

(4) *The nation's political and economic strategy is primary in establishing its educational agenda. The educational agenda seldom establishes the nation's political and economic strategy.* The quality and effectiveness of the educational system in the United States are largely dependent upon the development of a domestic, globally competitive, strategic infrastructure of products and markets—not the other way around. When you lose an industry, the demand for people with skills important to that industry evaporates. It's hard to persuade someone to pursue study in a field in which neither the industry nor the nation sees any future.

(5) *Certain technologies, products, and markets are strategic to a nation's industrial base and ability to compete.* What these are depends on the political, economic, and military objectives of the country and on what resources are available. It is hard, for example, to imagine America succeeding in its geopolitical goals without a competitive semiconductor

and display industry. The future of almost every other industry and market is influenced by these two areas.

(6) *Weakness in one sector may cause weakness in dependent sectors.* Abandoning positions in strategic products and markets may affect the long-term viability of dependent product and market infrastructure and thus a nation's ability to remain competitive. For example, since displays are a focal point for the dissemination of information in the digital world and no display manufacturers of note remain in the United States, American companies that require displays as a critical component in their product are at a disadvantage to competitors who have closer relationships with display manufacturers in their own country or who build both the display and other critical components.

(7) *A substantial loss of strategic infrastructure will ultimately impair a nation's ability to develop meaningful economic and political relationships with other nations.* When a nation loses its infrastructure of strategic products and markets, its competitiveness in those and related markets is impaired. Its remaining products and services become less competitive and thus less valuable as tools for economic and political negotiation and partnership.

(8) *Significant losses in the infrastructure of strategic technologies, products, and markets reduce a nation's ability to influence its economic and political destiny.* Flying from San Francisco to Hawaii is the longest over-the-water flight in the world without a safe landing spot between. There is a point of no return past which, if a problem occurs, the pilot has no choice but to continue the flight and hope to land safely. A nation's loss of economic power to negotiate can reach a similar point. Lacking the resources to further its cause, and thus at the mercy of the competition, it is forced to stay the course and above all conserve what resources it has left. At this point the weaker nation takes what it can get, often with severe strain to political relationships. As the limited strategic resources of a nation are reduced, its ability to produce the competitive products and services required to maintain a reasonable balance of trade disappears, and the value of its currency drops. In extreme circumstances, the dependence of the

weaker economy on the stronger can result in severe instability as the weaker nation surrenders much of its political and economic control.

(9) *If the nation as a whole is not competitive, it is difficult for any business or industry within that nation to remain competitive.* If the competition values market share over margin, and you have to fight your own system to win—pressured, for example, to show quarterly profits—chances are that you will ultimately lose. The long-term determinations of management as to what it takes to remain competitive must be supported by investor expectations. For a business to remain viable in a globally competitive market, employees, management, investors, and the country need to be on the same team.

(10) *To be competitive, a nation must have a national strategy for competitiveness.* There must be a plan in place—supported by laws, policies, and procedures—to leverage the nation's economic and political resources to its advantage throughout the world. In a globally competitive economic environment, the interests of businesses and other factions within the country diverge widely from each other and are not always in line with the nation's long-term interests. Thus, in matters of strategic importance, political and economic decisions at the highest levels are necessary to encourage competitive practices that serve the long-term interests of the country. Lack of a strategy is also a strategy—but one doomed to failure. America's leaders should understand the importance of long-term strategy over short-term opportunism.

America's concern over the rising competitiveness of other nations is in the end a concern about the decline of its own ability to compete. To focus on China, India, or any other nation as if it were somehow the cause of these problems is a great mistake. Japan developed a strategy based on a clear understanding of the canons of competition. If Japan could do it, so can China, India, Korea, Taiwan, or, for that matter, the European Union. For many reasons, America either doesn't understand the principles or feels that they don't apply. As a result, the United States has no cohesive strategy, and its competitive decline continues. Meanwhile, as America continues to consume billions more than it produces and the rest of the world produces billions more than it consumes, the global economy teeters on a precarious balance.

To grasp the principles of competition is to know that a reversal of America's competitive decline is undeniably possible but may require a long period of time and a radical change in the thinking of not only government and business but every American citizen. It will not happen overnight, but America has the will and strength of character to persist and succeed. The ethics, transparency, and stability of its economic system are the envy of the world. Reflecting its Enlightenment roots, America's political system is fundamentally rational, balanced, and just. As an open society and the largest free nation on Earth, the United States is truly the land of opportunity, but there is a difference between opportunity and opportunism. The greatest achievements in our history— whether building industries or winning wars—have always demanded time, extraordinary effort, and, most important, a well-conceived strategy when the outcome was uncertain.

The ten principles listed above, the DNA of competition, are in a specific order. Each principle is the foundation for the next. If one understands the principles, a national strategy and the policies to implement it can be formulated, and the nation can succeed. America's desire to play a major role in bringing peace, freedom, and prosperity to the world requires a grand strategy emanating from the office of the president, supported by Congress, and understood and accepted by the public. This is not a small task. But neither is it a small problem. The substance of the principles is simple to state but difficult to execute. The United States must determine what technologies, products, and markets are strategic to the nation and its aspirations. Where it is a player, it must stay in the game. To leave the field and then try to return are extremely difficult and very expensive. And where the United States is not a player in a strategic market, it must reenter the game and stay there. There are many ways to accomplish this, but the important thing is to fully understand the logic behind the principles. To see the logic is to grasp the problem; and understanding the problem is 90 percent of the solution.

In the end, the competitive problems of America are not based upon the low-cost labor of other nations. The cost of labor is relative. There will always be someplace cheaper. What is important is the degree to which Americans participate in markets that count and that can differentiate their products—not just by price, which can be altered at the stroke of a pen, but by technical superiority. This differentiation only comes from massive investment in research, development, and manufacturing technology, including capital equipment, not only to develop new products but to enhance the competitiveness of existing products and markets. The nation's manufacturing base provides a foundation for innovation, imagination, and creativity that can be achieved in no other way.

Globalization should not be considered a zero-sum game. The economics of global competition should ultimately lead to winners, not losers, as innovation resulting from the acceleration of convergence, infrastructure, and investment forces economies to expand and cooperate. The competitive issues faced by the United States can be expressed in one thought: as a nation, the United States does not have a viable competitive strategy; its most successful competitors do. America's dominant political, military, and economic world leadership is not guaranteed—to the contrary, it is at risk. There is no inherent condition or endowment ensuring that America's standard of living will remain the same, let alone improve. To compete globally, America must have an economic strategy. The best and the brightest know one thing: strategy is everything.

CHAPTER 1

Replay

September 2, 1970: No battle was fought; no treaty was signed; no disaster was recorded. Yet it was one of those days in whose wake the world was quietly transformed. I was in New York, standing at a podium on a stage in the Americana Hotel, looking out on an audience of some three hundred reporters, investors, and industry people—twice the number we had expected. We had rehearsed the presentation time after time. As general manager of the Educational and Industrial Products Division of Ampex Corporation, I hoped that the introduction of our new video recording system would rejuvenate us. We had suffered repeated setbacks. Ampex itself was in trouble. We needed not just a recognized win with investors, but a radical breakthrough that would capture the world. And that was exactly what we had.

"In 1956," I began, "Ampex Corporation invented the world's first practical videotape recorder. Now we are proud to announce Instavideo—the smallest, lightest, self-contained video system in the world!" The first video recorder constructed for both home and commercial use, Instavideo was also the first to feature automatic cartridge loading as opposed to manual reel-to-reel. A compact, portable system that ran on batteries or household current, it included such advanced features as slow motion, stop action, and stereo sound. Recording off the air or with the camera, it had better color and sound quality than any recorder of its day selling for thousands of dollars more. And Instavideo would do it all for about $1,000.

Until that day, a completely integrated home video recording system had been only a dream. Black-and-white television sets were still a major segment of the home entertainment market. Prerecorded tape was unknown. Color recording and playback systems for anything other than broadcast applications were a very small business. Approximately fourteen thousand video recorders were produced in 1970, with total sales less than $300 million. Up to that time, Ampex had produced high-end, closed-circuit systems for about $10,000 apiece, and broadcast recorders that occupied many cubic feet, used large reels of two-inch tape, and cost upwards of $100,000. Ampex also made cumbersome portable broadcast recorders that weighed nearly fifty pounds. But this was state-of-the-art. In 1970 Ampex made the best video recording equipment in the world, controlling nearly 100 percent of the world's video recording patents and more than 70 percent of the market.[1] There were smaller, inexpensive reel-to-reel recorders made in Japan and elsewhere that could be used in closed-circuit television, but their picture quality was poor, the sound inadequate, and the operation complicated.

CATBIRD SEAT

All of us participating in the announcement of Instavideo were hoping to astonish the world. When I saw the typical large, empty room at the Americana, it seemed out of synch with that expectation. I began wondering if anyone was really going to show up. Looking for ways to make the demonstration more exciting, I had hired an attractive model who worked for Marlboro cigarettes. As it turned out, the room filled beyond capacity; it was a wonder the fire marshal didn't shut us down.

On cue, the "Marlboro Girl" walked across the stage, the spotlight following her to a small round table. There, under a red velvet cloth, was a four-inch-high video recorder the size of a sheet of binder paper. As I completed my introduction, the model handed me a cartridge no larger than the palm of my hand, took the velvet cover off the recorder, and sauntered slowly off the stage. As the room darkened, I dropped the cartridge into the recorder and pushed the button. A clip of extreme skiing flashed onto monitor screens mounted every few feet along the Americana's walls, followed by a short clip of Sergio Mendez and Brazil '66 playing their version of the Beatles' "Fool on the Hill," demonstrating both color and stereo sound. Carlos Kennedy, the product manager, then picked up the recorder with camera attached and walked around the stage taping the audience. Replayed with sound, the newly recorded material was so striking in quality that one spectator jumped from his chair, exclaiming, "I wouldn't have believed this if I hadn't seen it with my own eyes," and rushed from the room to call his paper.

The audience was astounded. The reviews were exuberant; not one was negative. "In one bold stroke," wrote the publisher of *ETV Newsletter,* "the Ampex Corporation has shown why the reel-to-reel videotape recorder would never have made video playback a popular tool of the teacher, communicator, industrial supervisor, nurse, and housewife. By introducing its simple, portable, compact cartridge magnetic videotape system, Ampex is eliminating the hardware hangup for the user and guaranteeing that the videotape marketplace next year will be far different than it is today."[2] At the close of the presentation, a representative of *Life* magazine took me aside and asked if we could come to a photo shoot at 2 A.M. so that Instavideo could be included in their next issue.[3] The result was Instavideo's appearance in a two-page center spread. A representative from a major pharmaceutical firm asked if we would consider an order for ten thousand units. Had we been able to fill it, it would have amounted to more than 70 percent of expected video recorder sales for the year.

On the wave of good press, the stock of Ampex climbed 50 percent in the next few days. Our demonstration had been successful beyond our expectations. Yet I was concerned. With the exception of one group vice president, no other members of the Ampex board or top management had attended the presentation. This signaled that top management priorities were elsewhere. It was not a good sign.

Home video recording was in the mind's eye of every company on the globe familiar with the technology. If we did our job right, Ampex was in the catbird seat. We owned virtually every key video-recording patent in the world. Every player in the game had to license their video-recording technology from Ampex. In 1970 the world acknowledged that Ampex had the best understanding of video-recording technology. It dominated the broadcast market, the principal users of video recording at that time.

What Ampex owned and developed, in fact, was the technology that would become a key to the foundation of the information age. The VCR would ultimately have a greater influence on the uses and manufacturing process of semiconductor devices and display technology than any other product at that time. Moreover, the dependence of the VCR on cameras, lenses, displays, robotics, small motors, television sets, automated manufacturing, and other components necessary to its evolution created a massive, integrated industrial base. In time this new industrial base became the foundation for products and markets that were in many cases unforeseen and would then generate a new cycle of innovation. But this industrial base was not built in America. It was built in Japan.

Though Ampex in effect owned all the video-recording patents, none of which were ever successfully challenged, it was not about to follow through on its commitment to Instavideo. Under CEO William Roberts, top management faced problems that eclipsed any thought they might have given to resources necessary for the success of their newest product. What Roberts desperately needed was the appearance of profitability to thwart a denial of credit from the banks. The result was a series of opportunistic and highly questionable management decisions, most of which would not pass today's regulatory scrutiny. These decisions led finally to the demise of Ampex and the end of the video-recording industry in America. While the loss of this industry was a serious blow to the U.S. economy, the real problem lay in the resultant transfer to Asia of a major segment of America's industrial base, the taproot of which had been the development of video recording at Ampex. Central to that strategic American enterprise was image processing, which would become fundamental to the entire infrastructure of audiovisual communication in America.

The market for video recorders subsequently grew so large that the VCR became the driving force for all consumer electronics in Japan, representing at one point roughly half of that industry and two-thirds of its profits. Japan rode the VCR, the largest user of semiconductor devices prior to the PC, to world dominance in television, displays, image processing, and nearly all consumer electronics. I can think of no product outside of weaponry that has so massively reshaped the future of a country. As a result of its success with the VCR, which had a significant impact on its entire technological base, Japan became the world's second-largest national economy.

The conditions that led to America's loss of consumer electronics trace directly back to those events surrounding the introduction of Instavideo—that is, to Ampex. Ampex, a very small corporation with a large negative net worth, filed for bankruptcy on March 31, 2008. The companies that developed their own video-recording capability, most of them in Asia and originally under license to Ampex, have revenues in the multibillions of dollars, several between $50 and $100 billion, and are now household names. While fourteen thousand video recorders were sold in 1970, somewhere between forty and fifty million units were sold annually by the end of the 1980s, most produced in Japan.[4] No video recorders are manufactured in the United States today.

The introduction of Instavideo set in motion a long chain of events, resulting not only in the explosion of consumer electronics into nearly every facet of daily life but in a global shift in economic power to Asia. The loss of the video-recording industry, which began with the loss of the technology behind Instavideo, led to the United States losing the industries that produce televisions, HDTV systems, information displays, cameras, recorders, cell phones, sound systems, and DVD and CD players, as well as a major part of its computer industry. These losses account for a significant portion of America's trade deficit, which in 2007 was approaching the trillion-dollar mark.

How could Ampex have let this happen? More important, how could Japan have *made* this happen? The first question is the subject of this chapter; the second belongs to the next.

STAYING AFLOAT

The wonder of Ampex is that it survived inept management as long as it did. That it did so was a credit to the cornucopia of cutting-edge technology that flowed from the brilliance of its engineers. Fourteen years before the introduction of Instavideo, Ampex had astounded the world with its invention of the first practical video recorder. The application of this technology would prove almost limitless, radically changing the world of broadcasting along with the future of Ampex.

Ampex had proven time and again that its technological prowess was superb. Its management, however, could not keep up. In April 1960, *Fortune* magazine ran a story, "Five Little Ampexes and How They Grew," emphasizing the rapid growth of Ampex into a collage of entities that tried to capture the combinations and permutations of all the businesses sprung from this base of recording technology.[5] Management was overwhelmed by this multitude of technological riches, a case, perhaps, of too much, too soon.

The year 1959 saw a significant slowdown in the sale of broadcast video recorders, consistently the most profitable product in the Ampex line. Their consumer audio products, though sought after for their high-quality sound, had consistently lost money because of competitive pricing and inefficient manufacturing. And though Ampex was the world's largest manufacturer of audio- and video-recording tape—until the founding of Memorex by a group of former Ampex employees—the tape division, located in Opelika, Alabama, was neither well managed nor making a profit. Other divisions—broadcast audio recorders, instrumentation, computer recording equipment—were unable to compensate. Internal operating controls never matched the complexity of the business. The excitement surrounding the public perception of a great stock play, based on what seemed an endless stream of superb and highly marketable technology, took precedence over management expertise and due diligence. The result was a complete breakdown in control and a large financial loss.

In 1960, Ampex management was completely reorganized, and William Roberts replaced George Long as CEO. Roberts came from Bell and Howell Corporation, which served markets similar to those of Ampex. Having departed Bell and Howell abruptly after a change in top management, Roberts arrived at Ampex bent on proving two things. One was his management skill at turning Ampex around. The other was to beat what in his mind was an ungrateful former employer at its own game.

By coincidence, the market for broadcast video recording began to expand soon after Roberts arrived at Ampex. The resulting high margins gave a much-needed boost to the short-term future of the company. Roberts then decided to split the Ampex video engineering group into two parts. The segment devoted to broadcast recording remained at the corporate headquarters in Redwood City, California. The other group, which Roberts named the Educational and Industrial Products Division, was developing a relatively new technique called helical scan recording; it was packed up and moved to Chicago along with an organization that distributed a bevy of consumer audio products, mostly imported from Europe or Asia. At that time, helical scan video recording was considered suitable only for lower performance closed-circuit recording and potentially a home recorder. The relocation to Chicago was ostensibly to take advantage of that city's central location, but there was another reason. Roberts wanted to put an Ampex consumer products operation within a stone's throw of Bell and Howell, leaving the latter almost literally in the shadow of ranking competition. Flaunting that presence in the face of his former employer, Roberts was determined to get even.

The unfortunate result was the creation of two competing video engineering operations that should have become highly complementary as video-recording technology evolved. Instead, Ampex now had to fund both engineering groups at a much higher expense, never developing a cooperative relationship between them. Lacking knowledge of the business, the board of directors didn't question the decision. In the end, aside from all the other strategic and financial mistakes, the relocation was probably the most damaging blow to the competitive advance of video recording in America. Using the same helical scan technology that enabled the creation of the VCR, broadcast video recorders were ultimately designed and manufactured in Japan. The Japanese recorders performed as well or better and were more reliable, more portable, and easier to operate than the American competition. With limited resources applied too late, Ampex's position in video recording collapsed, leaving Japan the only dominant player in the game.

When I made my presentation in September 1970, Ampex was already in troubled waters. At the end of 1969, when I completed my recommendations and product plan for a home video recorder, Ampex led the world in professional audio and video recording, the result of years of successful innovation in mechanical and electronic design. It was the world leader in audio tape duplication, then in high gear as vinyl records gave way to prerecorded tape. But it was rapidly losing the race in the sale of consumer audio recorders. Ampex, like many other companies, had decided to outsource the tape decks to Asia—principally Japan—where rugged, reliable, consumer-oriented decks were produced in high volume at a substantially lower cost. Though American companies knew how to produce the decks, the Japanese products were far less expensive, and the manufacturing was financed in Asia, allowing U.S. firms to concentrate their capital elsewhere. Moreover, while the manufacture of the tape deck itself was not considered high technology, its American-grown electronics were. So Ampex and other American firms differentiated their products by the expertise involved in their electronics and signal processing and bought the low-cost "commodity" deck from Japan.

The assumption was that the Japanese would never have the technical expertise to match the quality of Ampex's audio output. But the level of investment required to design and manufacture these audio decks in highly automated factories would soon far exceed that which Ampex and others were investing in their electronics. This was because the tape decks they outsourced had to be manufactured in large quantities to exact specifications so that tapes would be interchangeable. Though Ampex's signal processing might differ from others, the decks had to be exactly the same. For Ampex and other U.S. manufacturers, this approach seemed to make financial sense. They got the products they wanted at relatively low prices without any heavy investment in plants and equipment. Outsourcing solved a multitude of issues for companies that were incurring losses not only in the consumer audio products they still made, but in mounting service problems with less reliable decks still manufactured in the States.

At this time professional audio, broadcast video, instrumentation recording, and tape duplication were profitable and appeared to keep the company afloat. But because of inadequate controls, often the result of opportunistic management, Ampex had limited understanding of its manufacturing activities, inventory, receivables, and profit margins. As a result, the company was burning through cash and financing its monetary needs with borrowing and highly questionable accounting. A close examination of the books would have revealed that, contrary to published figures, the company's financial condition during the ten years of Roberts's tenure as CEO was in constant decline. Its future was much less secure than was thought by the public or the banks. Yet no one in management or on the board seemed to understand or care. Roberts's stern and unyielding manner created an organization of people motivated to tell him what he wanted to hear. This unhealthy condition continued for longer than anyone would have thought possible. Ampex had always been a company known for producing blockbuster technology with huge financial potential, making it a darling of the stock market and a public relations dream. But management turned that dream into a nightmare.

In 1970 the Educational and Industrial Products Division was in particular trouble. It was losing large sums of money, had serious morale problems, and, like the rest of the company, was draining cash. I had been sent by Roberts to Chicago in 1969 to try to turn the division around. More important, because the helical scan video technology being developed there appeared suitable for a home video recorder, it was logical to use it as a platform for the design and manufacture of what was to become the VCR.

The division suffered from many of the same problems I'd seen while serving in various management capacities in other parts of the company. The division had been ill conceived and was managed accordingly. By the time I took it over, it was apparent that quality control was appalling; the division had shipped untold numbers of defective closed-circuit video recorders. The inventory contained millions of dollars of obsolete product. Some of it had been purposely produced in quantities larger than any supporting sales forecast in order to reduce the apparent manufacturing cost of the much smaller number actually sold. Some of the excess was sold to distributors and then simply returned in the next fiscal quarter, giving the appearance of profits in one period at the expense of another; this occurred with the approval of Ampex management.

Defective product continued to find its way into the marketplace in the form of goods either stolen from the warehouse or shipped for revenue regardless of condition. This threatened not only the status of the division but the reputation that Ampex had achieved as the finest producer of quality broadcast video recorders in the world. To stop these practices, I finally sent someone into the warehouse—like one of those ax-wielding Prohibition agents—to smash the defective recorders with a sledgehammer so they couldn't be resold.

Receivables disputed and unpaid for by many distributors were reported as good when in fact they were not. Eventually at least one-third of all receivables were bad. The result was a massive buildup of excess inventory, a tremendous drain on cash, and a dearth of information on how the division was actually doing. Until the costs became unbearable, top management never questioned these practices, which plagued other parts of Ampex as well and would finally bring down the company.

"WE DON'T NEED ANOTHER
COMPETITOR ON U.S. SOIL"

In 1970, with limited financial resources at his disposal, Roberts decided to seek a partner that would not only manufacture the new home video recorder at low cost but put up the necessary capital to establish the manufacturing enterprise. I suggested two obvious candidates that had indicated a strong interest: Magnavox and Motorola. Both firms were located near Ampex facilities in the United States, which would simplify communication and foster appropriate cooperation between engineering and manufacturing. Such a joint venture would also have the expertise in display technology and consumer products that was totally lacking in Ampex. I was convinced, as I had stated in my product plan for Instavideo, that the recorder, camera, and associated displays would ultimately come together in a single package (today's camcorder). Both Motorola and Magnavox had the technology and proficiency to build displays essential to a camcorder, and both understood the consumer market. Either one would be an invaluable ally. Roberts dismissed my suggestion summarily, saying simply, "We don't need another competitor on U.S. soil." He was convinced that Japan would provide more liberal financing than an American partner and never conceived that Japan, let alone Asia, would be a significant threat to the technological dominance of Ampex or the United States.

Ampex had an existing venture with Toshiba, a major Japanese company that, under license to Ampex, was already trying to produce a reel-to-reel recorder for the closed-circuit television market. So Roberts decided to seek a partnership with Toshiba and in May 1970 accompanied me to Japan. He introduced me to the chair of Toshiba, Toshio Doko, and I was left to form a joint venture to produce the VCR.

It's important to note that in 1974 Toshio Doko would become chair of the Japan Federation of Economic Organizations (Keidanren), the private sector version of the Ministry of International Trade and Investment, and was thus very influential in Japan's business strategy and industrial policy. Therefore he not only was able to analyze the importance of this deal for Toshiba but was in a position to see the implications of Ampex technology for the entire industrial base of Japan.

After several weeks of negotiations it was agreed that Toshiba would produce the product in a joint manufacturing facility managed by Toshiba and would receive sales rights for Instavideo in Japan. Ampex would sell it everywhere else. Ampex had never made a product like this before, yet the joint venture stipulated that Ampex would provide the technical details necessary for Toshiba's manufacturing requirements and also fix any engineering problems that might limit the recorder's performance. As part of the joint venture, Ampex transferred to Toshiba every piece of data it possessed pertinent to the technology of Instavideo.

What Ampex did not possess, however, was any understanding of the engineering requirements necessary to design a product of this type for mass production. Toshiba and other Japanese companies did understand the technological and capital investment required to manufacture the precision tape decks prerequisite to the production of the VCR—they had learned this over the years from their manufacture of audio record-ing decks. Ampex had neither the level of expertise nor the resources necessary to fund the large investment in research and development needed to create that technological base. As would later become clear, Roberts had decided that someone other than Ampex would have to carry that R&D investment burden, and Toshiba, whether they knew it or not, fit that plan.

The moment negotiations were over, I was summoned by Roberts to meet him at corporate headquarters in Redwood City. When I arrived, his message was clear but puzzling. He wanted to announce immedi-ately that in approximately twelve months my division would move a key manufacturing facility from Chicago to a combined plant being built in Colorado Springs. I suggested that such an announcement made so early would alarm the Chicago employees about the stability of the orga-nization just as we were taking on a huge task in Japan, not to mention my attempt to clean up a division fraught with problems. Relocation concerns at that time would hamper the work at hand and jeopardize the introduction of Instavideo. His explanation was simple and the decision final. Because Ampex might face some financial and competitive difficulties in the coming year, it was advisable to book the relocation charges to the current fiscal year, creating a reserve now while business still looked good. Asked to estimate the cost of the move, I gave a figure of just over $2 million. The amount reported by the company in its 1970 annual report was just under $5 million. I assumed they were being prudent, but I was wrong. As it turned out, the reserve was never available to cover the costs of the move. It was used to write off excess and obsolete inventory in the current year in other divisions in an attempt to improve the appearance of that year's earnings.

Roberts returned with me to Chicago, where we announced the projected move to several hundred employees. Those whom I had hoped would be energized by the prospect of producing a great product in the new joint venture with Toshiba were told that many among them would be losing their jobs. It was one of the worst tasks I've ever had to perform. Moreover, the announcement set the stage for a morale problem I was never able to solve. Those employees knew that the heart of Ampex's executive management was not behind the success of Instavideo.

A SINKING SHIP

As we began to clean up the division's problems, an interesting situation developed. We realized that the video recorders we were manufacturing in Chicago for closed-circuit TV applications such as schools and training facilities could, if properly designed, produce pictures that would match broadcast video quality. Yet they were selling for a tenth of the cost of Ampex's broadcast video recorder. Top management warned me that this information was never to be revealed for fear it would kill the existing market for the more expensive and highly profitable broadcast line. A U.S. competitor called International Video Corporation (IVC) then began to produce a product similar to the high-end closed-circuit recorders manufactured in my division. (In an odd twist, the IVC video recorder was to be distributed by Bell and Howell.) The fact that IVC advertised their product as capable of broadcast quality put my division in a bind. I was told we could say that our products performed better than IVC's but that—by our higher standards—they were not of broadcast quality.

This strategy worked to some extent against IVC with its relatively limited market share, but it did not represent what was possible. We all knew that ultimately our lower-cost, closed-circuit video recorder could be substituted for our larger more profitable broadcast line if management were inclined to put the proper design and production effort in place. But they didn't want to introduce a simpler, smaller, lighter, less expensive product into a market where they were already doing very well. The common wisdom at that time was that this would require significant investment in a new technology that would only cannibalize existing sales. It was this kind of opportunistic strategy, coupled with a complete underestimation of Japanese ambitions, that finally cost Ampex and the United States their position in broadcast video recording.

While all this was going on, the audio-recording industry was going through a massive change. The shift by the major recording companies from vinyl records to prerecorded tape created a tremendous demand for Ampex recording expertise to provide duplication services, and the surprising profits from this service provided a much-needed cash injection and covered a multitude of sins. The demand, which was instantaneous and large, sprang from Bill Lear's design of an eight-track endless-loop cartridge that could be used in automobiles—a concept immediately adopted by Ford, GM, and Chrysler. The Japanese capitalized on this new market by producing the tape decks. Though Ampex was a logical source to satisfy the immediate need to convert records to tape, the recording companies would soon realize that they could buy Ampex equipment and do the tape duplication themselves.

Ampex saw this coming and approached the problem in several ways. One was to establish its own music company so it could own its content and distribute its own product. Ampex started an ill-fated music company that spawned a bevy of strange people wandering in and out of company headquarters—long-haired, oddly attired types who, though perfectly suited to Motown or Hollywood, seemed to an electronics engineer in the early 1970s either to have lost all hope or to be biding their time until the spaceship came to deliver them from squareness.

At one point, Ampex even backed a Broadway musical called *Purlie* in hopes that the music would become a successful part of their library. In fact, the reason several members of the management team missed the Instavideo press conference is that they were sitting in a Broadway theater watching *Purlie*. Ampex's monthly publication, *Readout,* devoted its first four pages to a sensational spread on *Purlie,* the next four to music recording, and two pages at the very end of the issue to Instavideo. (This reversed the treatment of Ampex in the media at large, 53 percent of which was on Instavideo, 22 percent on tape piracy, 17 percent on the computer business, and 7 percent on other topics.[6])

The opening of a Broadway show was exciting, and the related tape duplication business was for the moment highly profitable. In a high-risk effort to maintain the stream of cash gushing from the duplication business, Ampex entered into contract with the major recording companies, guaranteeing them high minimum royalties in return for exclusive duplication rights. It was a very big bet by a company trying to exploit a windfall of cash coming from a business it knew nothing about.

All of these tangled problems lurked beneath our triumphal announcement of Instavideo at the Americana Hotel on that September afternoon in 1970. The announcement had sparked an atmosphere of potentially explosive growth, so I was asked to make the same presentation at the stockholders' meeting following the end of the fiscal year. In the minds of investors, the future of Ampex was unlimited. But inside the company, we all knew that luck was probably not on our side. I was thrilled by the phenomenal success of the announcement. Yet as I watched the spectators reacting in awe, I felt as if I were standing on the deck of a magnificent ship that was about to sink, taking with it the lives and reputation of the crew.

FREE FALL

A few months after the initial announcement of Instavideo, I was asked to give a presentation at a conference of the National Association of Record Merchandisers, an organization vitally interested in the future of the VCR and its vast potential for prerecorded media opportunities. Representing Ampex and introducing this industry group to the possibilities of video recording in the home, I found myself on the program with Barbra Streisand, the Carpenters, and Jesse Jackson. On one hand, the presentation went well; the audience listened with rapt attention, and the response was again enthusiastic. On the other hand, I met with several executives from the recording industry who told me that they had all agreed to exclusive duplication contracts with Ampex because Ampex had made extraordinary minimum royalty offers they couldn't refuse. Their comments made it clear to me that any dip in industry sales would leave Ampex in big trouble, another reminder of just how tenuous the company's financial condition was. And yet it was obvious from the recording industry's reception of Instavideo that, properly executed, our future course was bound for the stars.

Within a year, industry sales of prerecorded audio tape turned down in the face of an economic recession. Ampex found itself immediately in serious difficulty. It somehow had to meet the minimum royalty payments it had guaranteed but lacked the resources to fund them. In the end, Ampex couldn't pay the royalties, and the future of the company was basically over. I was told later by a member of the board that they had never been informed of these generous royalty agreements. Roberts, he said, had kept it secret.

By the end of 1971, cash was disappearing, massive amounts of inventory were obviously obsolete, receivables were increasingly uncollectible largely as a result of major deficiencies in accounting, and projected profits were turning into enormous losses. The banks stepped in, refusing additional capital, and Ampex found itself on the verge of bankruptcy. Roberts had reached the end of his era. As a result of what I believe was the first class-action suit in the United States, there was a $10 million judgment against the company for misleading the public about current and future earnings. Instead of showing a projected small profit, Ampex lost well over $100 million—one-third of its annual revenues.[7] To stay alive, it was decided to reorganize the company completely and concentrate on broadcast video and professional audio recorders. Within two years the Instavideo project was dropped, and Ampex no longer participated in the market for home video systems. But the technological expertise Ampex engineers had transferred to Toshiba in the initial stages of the joint venture remained in Japan.

During this same period, U.S. corporations abandoned all other attempts at a home video system. It was becoming very difficult for them to make money at consumer electronics given the course that industry was taking in Japan. The Japanese were producing good products at such low prices that it seemed they were almost willing to give them away. So when Ampex, the dominant player in video recording, dropped the VCR, that ended it for the United States. The VCR now belonged entirely to Japan.

What Ampex had needed were options so that alternative solutions would remain possible in the face of unforeseen problems. As it was, every move was motivated not by a strategic plan but by an opportunistic reaction to an emotional crisis. They got out of manufacturing audio tape decks because they never learned how to make them reliable or in quantity. Even had they wanted to, they lacked the capital. Their competitors in Japan did learn, supplying decks not only to Ampex but to most other consumer audio companies in the United States and the rest of the world. In time, the Japanese manufacturing prowess in audio was extended not only to the VCR but to cameras and finally to all consumer electronics.

In sum, lacking resources and determined to avoid a hit to the profit-and-loss statement, Ampex declined to design and sell its lower-cost video recorders in competition with its high-end broadcast equipment. By the time it became obvious that the world wanted smaller, cheaper, simpler, more reliable broadcast systems in addition to dependable, high-quality VCRs, the Japanese had transferred the technological progress made in their development of the VCR to their own high-end broadcast equipment. Over time the United States was no longer able to compete effectively in any video-recording market, and the game was over. Japan won it all.

American industry never perceived the inevitable interconnection between information, television, and the VCR. Because of that linkage the VCR took television, displays, and the rest of consumer electronics with it the way a vacuum cleaner sucks up loose dirt. Motorola sold its television business to the Japanese, Magnavox and Philco were sold to Phillips (which later combined its display business with LG in Korea), RCA was ultimately sold to the French, and Zenith went to LG. But while the American producers disappeared, American consumers did not, and Asia's industrial base began to grow exponentially as we opened our pocketbooks and compulsively bought all those marvelous new products that now dominate our daily lives.

For want of a strategy and the infrastructure to support it, Ampex lost one of the most pivotal innovations of our time. It had owned a technology and dominated a market that was to change the world. But lack of cash and operating profits pushed Ampex toward expedient decisions at the expense of long-term planning. Thus it was constantly faced with the decision whether or not to abandon a market simply on the basis of a competitive threat that might affect short-term operating performance. Manipulating information to cloak problems, manage crises, and postpone the inevitable, the company whose superb ingenuity and creative effort had produced one of the most important building blocks of the information age delivered it relatively free of charge to the competition.

A 1985 Harvard study of Ampex and video innovation concluded: "Instavideo proceeded far enough to demonstrate Ampex's command of lead-edge technology. Subsequent events have confirmed the soundness of the project leaders' comprehension of the market opportunity. Ampex lost the chance to build on those strengths because of top management's inability to focus the firm's human and financial resources productively on the opportunity before it."[8] The legacy of Ampex is that its demise and its loss to a foreign nation of that entire technological base produced a gaping hole in the competitive infrastructure of the United States. As a result, complete industries began to flow out through that hole to the advantage of Japan and, in time, all of Asia.

I still have a snapshot of the Ampex Instavideo team celebrating the completion of our negotiations with Toshiba. It brings back the feelings I had at the time. It seemed we had achieved our objectives. But as I looked around the table at my associates who had worked so hard for that moment, my earlier suggestion to Roberts that we consider a partnership with Motorola or Magnavox came to mind. And I was struck with one overriding thought: *What have we done?* This relatively little company, with a technological base more extensive than any I had known, had completed a negotiation with a giant that knew exactly what it wanted. I was almost sure it had got what it had expected. I wasn't at all confident that we had done the same.

In 1995 I had the honor of chairing the selection committee for the National Medal of Technology. Established by Congress and presented by the president of the United States, it is the highest award given to an American making a technological contribution to the country. The recipient that year was Ray Dolby. When Ray was in his twenties, he had worked for Ampex, and as a key member of the team that invented video recording, he had made an enormous contribution to the information age—one that should have been an equally large economic gift to America. But when he received the award, it was not for video recording; it was for Dolby sound. Unfortunately for Ray and the rest of the United States, video recorders were no longer made in America.

CODA

In the early 1970s, several American firms that could have advanced video recording in the United States had the opportunity to purchase Ampex, an acquisition that would have been justified in spite of the company's problems. But by the time Ampex was finally purchased by the Signal Companies in 1980, the basic market for video recording had been lost to Japan. Not only did the Signal Companies lack sufficient knowledge of the video-recording industry and the potentials of the technology, but by the end of the 1970s the resources required to catch up to Japanese advances in both technology and product development were far beyond what the Signal Companies were willing to commit or even understood. The millions per year in licensing revenue that Ampex collected from sales of video recorders made by foreign manufacturers in the 1980s and 1990s was a pittance compared to the billions those manufacturers received from the worldwide sales of video recorders, cameras, displays, and television sets that this market generated. By the end of the '80s, the United States had virtually abandoned these and related markets, creating a situation that now threatens our entire industrial base.

Any commitment by corporate America to what remained of Ampex would have been inconsistent with the prevailing economic doctrine. The risk of taking on the Japanese in consumer electronics was shunned by American companies, who considered it a dog industry—meaning low margins, massive competition, and no clear market leadership. Companies like Kodak, who had strong positions in consumer products that would in time be overwhelmed by digital electronics, seemed totally unaware of the threat. They didn't recognize that potential interrelationships between technological disciplines could in a relatively short period of time completely change the competitive landscape and undermine the basis of their existence.

Focused on short-term profits, U.S. investors had no stomach for risky ventures into highly competitive markets that appeared to be nothing more than commodity businesses in which lower prices represented the only significant advantage. No one seemed to understand the compelling need for America to stay in the video-recording game as a part of an overall strategic plan to remain globally competitive. The widely held view was that America was the repository for entrepreneurial creativity and innovation. Lacking the imagination of U.S. entrepreneurship, the best that Asia could do was to copy, surviving on low-profit margins befitting a society that could only repetitively manufacture what others created. Nevertheless, Kodak, General Electric (RCA), Motorola (Quasar), Magnavox, Bell and Howell, Zenith, Sylvania, IBM, Polaroid, General Motors, Ford, and other U.S. companies would soon realize that the Japanese products evolving from the video-recording technology Ampex had invented would have a severe impact on their future.

What America and the world were soon to find out was that, by limiting technological investment in manufacturing, the electronics industry in the United States would lose the vision needed to conceptualize the technological advances that would ultimately drive the industry they once dominated.

Understanding the broad-based potential of video-recording technology, Japan made it a cornerstone of a national competitive strategy. Thus, while Ampex was developing a video recorder, Japan was developing a national economy that is now second only to the United States. And while Ampex and other American firms focused on short-term returns, the Japanese, who understood the global principles of economic competition, approached the same potential products in a far larger context—not a group of individual companies each attempting to satisfy the quarterly profit demands of their investors, but a concert of intra- and interdependent industries whose final focus was on a deliberate national strategy that emphasized products and markets for the long-term future of the whole. That same farsighted vision is now found in most of Asia.

CHAPTER 2

Convergence

As products, markets, and related technologies evolve, they become increasingly interrelated, interdependent, and integrated.

On the morning of July 24, 1959, in the heat of a cold war that could have easily become a nuclear holocaust, Vice President Richard M. Nixon met Soviet premier Nikita Khrushchev at his Kremlin office. Proceeding to the U.S. Trade and Cultural Fair in Sokolniki Park, the two men soon fell into a debate over whose country had the better socioeconomic system. By the time they reached the display of a model American kitchen, they were agitated and toe-to-toe. Nixon was holding his own. "There are some instances," he said, "where you may be ahead of us—in the thrust of your rockets, for example. But there may be some instances—color television, for example—where we are ahead of you."[1]

In the corner stood an Ampex engineer, capturing the debate on an Ampex videotape recorder. Standing next to him was Phil Gundy, vice president for international operations at Ampex. While Gundy instantly grasped the importance of what was being recorded on tape for posterity, it is clear from the following that both Nixon and Khrushchev, though new to video recording, also understood:

NIXON: [referring to their being videotaped] Here you can see the type of tape which will transmit this very conversation immediately, and this indicates the possibilities of increasing communication. And this increase in communication will teach us some things, and you some things, too. Because, after all, you don't know everything.

KHRUSHCHEV: If I don't know everything, then you know absolutely nothing about Communism, except for fear! But now the dispute will be on an unequal basis. The apparatus is yours, and you speak English, while I speak Russian. Your words are taped and will be shown and heard. What I say to you about science won't be translated, and so your people won't hear it. These aren't equal conditions.

NIXON: There isn't a day that goes by in the United States when we can't read everything that you say in the Soviet Union . . . and, I can assure you, never make a statement here that you think we won't read in the United States.

KHRUSHCHEV: If that's the way it is, I'm holding you to it. Give me your word. . . . I want you, the vice president, to give me your word that my speech will also be taped in English. Will it be?

NIXON: Certainly it will be. And by the same token, everything that I say will be recorded and translated and will be carried all over the Soviet Union. That's a fair bargain.[2]

Phil Gundy grabbed the tape, stuffed it in his briefcase, and took the next plane home. Videotape in hand, he headed directly for the TV networks, and overnight the "Kitchen Debate" was seen on television sets around the world. While Nixon's stature soared into the political stratosphere, the stature of Ampex was not far behind.

In 1956, the company had introduced the world's first practical video recorder, revolutionizing the television industry. For the first time, audiovisual information of broadcast quality could be reliably recorded on magnetic tape and immediately aired. It was now possible not only to produce quality television programs but to capture a moment and replay it with all the spontaneity of the original event. Viewers were enthralled. It was easy to imagine the possibilities inherent in the technology—and Ampex owned virtually all of it. Americans viewed the taped debate in a spirit of enthusiastic political freedom, proud of their modern kitchens and of the man who put Khrushchev in his place. But others, particularly industrialists in Japan, saw the larger, long-term implications of the power of convergence, visualization, and instantaneous response to momentous events—the power of audiovisual recording. Three of those gentlemen were Toshio Doko of Toshiba and Akio Morita and his partner, Masaru Ibuka, the founders of Sony.

In 1958, hoping to enter the Japanese market, Ampex had sought a partnership with a Japanese company. At that time, the Japanese government required any foreign company wishing to manufacture and distribute their products in Japan to do so in partnership with a Japanese company. Akio Morita and his mentor, Ibuka, wanted Sony to be that partner with Ampex.

DIVERGENCE

Founded in 1944, Alexander M. Poniatoff's small firm, Ampex Electric and Manufacturing Company, made high-performance motors and generators for naval radar systems. Needing a nonmilitary product after the war, Poniatoff was attracted to a magnetic tape recorder recovered by a Signal Corps officer from a German radio station. Poniatoff then developed the first American-made audiotape recorder and sold twenty machines to Bing Crosby, who later sold them to the ABC radio network. An improved model soon became the standard of the broadcast industry.

Across the Pacific, Morita was a young naval lieutenant working with a team to perfect thermal-guidance weapons and night-vision gun sights for Japan's war effort when the atomic bombs ended that hope. Like Poniatoff, Morita then pursued what seemed a promising new nonmilitary technology. In 1946, he and Ibuka, a young engineer, launched the

Tokyo Telecommunications Engineering Corporation, which Morita later renamed Sony.

Their founding prospectus was prophetic. "We must avoid problems which befall large corporations while we create and introduce technologies which large corporations cannot match," Ibuka wrote. "The reconstruction of Japan depends on the development of dynamic technologies."[3] Such ideas were enigmatic to American producers, who for years failed to see that Japan had an entrepreneurial spirit and a highly organized and strategic approach to product development.

Just as Poniatoff had learned of the audiotape recorder shortly after the war's end, Ibuka and Morita were introduced to the same technology—developed in 1936 by the German company AEG—while visiting the headquarters of occupation forces in Japan. They were impressed with the machine's superiority to wire recorders, which were the standard of the day. Convinced of the commercial viability of the product, Ibuka and Morita committed the resources of their small company to its development, and came up with what they called the G-type audio recorder. To insure its success, they focused on five goals—performance, reliability, size, cost, and manufacturability—and constantly sought convergent technologies that would achieve those strategic ends.

As Sony's audio recorder became a success and the company grew, an opportunity to obtain one of these convergent technologies came from the United States—an opportunity that would be fundamental to the growth and development of Sony and Japan for years to come. The Western Electric Company and its Bell Laboratories (a subsidiary of AT&T) offered to sell licenses for its newly invented transistor technology to qualified manufacturers. The company believed that licensing the technology would insure a large enough customer base to justify the longer term investment in manufacturing that would be required if the solid state transistor was to be a successful venture. Ibuka clearly realized the importance of this deal. "This is going to be a major revolution," he wrote. "The transistor has all the functions of a vacuum tube. It is small, but has a semi-permanent life. We must do it by all means."[4] Relentless in their effort to make Sony one of those select companies, Morita and Ibuka obtained the license agreement in 1953 for $25,000—$10,000 more than Ampex spent on the development of its first broadcast videotape recorder.

With the help of other Japanese firms and Tohoku University, and with limited information from Bell Labs, the Telecommunications Research Institute, as Sony was then called, manufactured its first transistor. Ibuka had immediately seen the value of the transistor to his company's five goals. The first significant product to result at Sony was a transistorized radio. It was much smaller, lighter, and more efficient than any other radio being produced, all of which still used vacuum tubes.

In 1955 the Bulova Watch Company asked Morita to accept an order for a hundred thousand of Sony's first transistor radios.[5] The only requirement was that they be sold under the Bulova name. Morita refused, wanting nothing to take away from the Sony brand, which he believed would one day be greater than Bulova's. Bulova's CEO was incensed at Morita's audacity, but Morita walked from the order, and Japan's first transistor radio was launched under the brand name Sony. Meanwhile, Morita and Ibuka decided to sell Sony transistors to other companies in Japan, not only to increase their company's technological reputation but also to spur further advancement in solid-state design and manufacturing. These initial customers included Matsushita (Panasonic), Sanyo, Toshiba, Victor Company of Japan (JVC), and the Standard Co. (Marantz Japan, Inc.). By 1957, Sony products had achieved worldwide attention and an expanding market share in the United States. The Sony Stereocorder and the "pocket" TR-6 transistor radio were featured that year on the cover of *Popular Science* magazine.[6]

Sony also began to manufacture magnetic tape, which was key to the recording qualities of the hardware. This was an area of expertise that it did not want to leave to chance. By the late '50s, Sony was at the leading edge of high-fidelity sound. With the development of the transistor, the "pocket" radio, magnetic tape, and the audio recorder, Sony was becoming a significant part of the convergence of technologies and products that served the audio market.

Proud of its advances in magnetic recording, Sony longed for the day when the quality of its video recording would match that of its audio. Then, in 1956, seemingly out of nowhere, came Ampex with the world's first practical video recorder. The initial reaction of Sony engineers was disdain. They felt that the Ampex machine with its vacuum tubes and extraordinary size was a monstrosity, though the picture quality was beyond anything they had seen. The Ampex approach, requiring four recording heads spinning at high speed, recording information transversely on a reel of two-inch-wide tape, seemed to them inherently unstable. If one of the four heads were to go out of alignment, the equipment would cease to perform correctly; the two-inch-wide tape also required a very large recording platform. Sony engineers were inclined to use only two recording heads that wrote information in a helical fashion, diagonally across the tape. This helical approach enabled the use of tape only a half-inch wide and seemed more reliable and less costly while allowing a far more compact design. Aware of Sony's concerns, Ampex had a similar ongoing program to design a helical rather than transverse recorder. Sony had made prior attempts to produce a video recorder of its own using a form of helical rather than transverse scanning technique, but the performance results were unsatisfactory. Despite its deficiencies, the Ampex system worked, and, relatively speaking, the pictures were spectacular.

Once again the United States presented Japan with an extraordinary opportunity to expand its technological base. When Ampex made the decision to manufacture and sell its video recorders to the broadcast industry in Japan, it knew it needed a Japanese partner. Sony offered technological expertise in audio recording, some understanding of video recording, and a significant background in solid-state transistors that could substantially improve the Ampex recorder. It was obvious to Morita and Ibuka that Sony's solid-state technology would be directly applicable to the video recorder, advancing their goals of improving performance, reliability, size, cost, and manufacturability. Morita also understood that video recorders would require electronic displays—television sets—in all configurations, a market that would become near and dear to Morita's heart. So when Ampex approached Sony, both companies knew that they had a perfect fit. With Ampex as a partner, Sony's view of the future could not have been brighter. The deal, done virtually on the back of an envelope, should have been a highly rewarding experience for both parties. Yet the partnership ended quickly, culminating in a legal dispute that would ultimately prove disastrous for Ampex.

When the Kitchen Debate made headlines the following year, the media hype only reinforced Morita's awareness that video-recording technology, then still largely in the hands of Ampex, had political and economic dimensions as well. He thus committed a major portion of Sony's resources to becoming a dominant force in the world of audiovisual recording.

The destiny of these two companies with similar beginnings would be diametrical: one soared; the other plummeted. Ironically, the invention that would drive the information age came not from the one that fate favored but from the one that would fail.

Japan was learning how to offer American manufacturers the option of outsourcing to a highly receptive and skilled Japanese company, one willing to finance the required investment in capital equipment, manufacturing know-how, and design engineering, and also to provide the finished product—all for a price that assured significant short-term profits for the U.S. firm. In time, Sony's experience in the mass production of audio recorders and radios, along with its understanding of robotics and solid-state technology, would provide the perfect infrastructure to take advantage of video recording in a burgeoning consumer electronics market. But initially, what Sony and most other Japanese firms really wanted was to insure that the research, development, and manufacturing of strategic products would reside in Japan. Magnetic recording and ancillary products like displays were considered strategic. The goal was not profit. At the end of World War II, Japan's overriding objective was to get back in the game and then leverage that position by achieving a dominant market share for Japanese companies. Ampex, like many other American companies of that era, was there to oblige.

Almost from its inception, Ampex developed a management style that was oriented toward new technological concepts. But Ampex never created the kind of engineering and manufacturing structure that would enable it to take advantage of the market potential inherent in those technological concepts. As Ampex grew during the 1950s, it never mastered the controls necessary to assess its financial position or the resources needed to advance from a small business with limited manufacturing expertise to a corporation that could meet the challenges presented by the potential of audio and video recording. Yet by 1959 a large public following was hoping to get rich from the technology that flowed so freely from Ampex engineering talent. Ampex management was prone to exaggerate claims based on unrealized potential; it lacked any understanding of how to capitalize on that potential. Its repeated overestimation of sales created a continuing mismatch between forecasted sales and actual production.

One result was a large buildup of excess and obsolete inventory and a corresponding negative cash flow. And because of its lack of controls, Ampex continually failed to honor the contractual requirements of customer orders. To offset these problems, Ampex sales and management personnel were making side deals with customers regarding payment terms. Customers were then delaying payment. The upshot was a sizeable overstatement of revenues and profits and a serious reduction in cash resources. Lacking an adequate system of accounting and control, Ampex lost its way. Yet in the high-profile years leading up to 1959, no one seemed to care that the company's financial condition was growing ever more precarious.

In 1959, there came a slowdown in the sales of broadcast video recorders, the one product in Ampex's line with sizeable profit margins. Corporate profits dropped sharply, and creative accounting methods could not hide it. As a result, the auditors gave closer scrutiny to the books and concluded that there had been an overstatement of assets and an understatement of accumulating expenses. They determined that Ampex would have to take an approximate $10 million loss on revenues approaching $60 million in sales.

Appalled by the extent of the accounting problems, the Ampex board hired the consulting firm of Aurbach Pollack to analyze the company from top to bottom and come up with a plan for reorganization. Many members of the consulting team took on temporary management roles, essentially running the business. Ampex employees, clearly apprehensive about the future of the company, faced a major morale problem. George Long was removed as CEO, and on the consultants' recommendation the board hired Bell and Howell's William Roberts to take his place.

A short time after he took over the helm, Roberts became aware of the arrangement that had been made between Ampex and Sony. Convinced that Sony was attempting to steal Ampex technology, he summarily cancelled the contract. Sony sued and won a settlement that gave them a fully paid-up license to design and produce so-called "nonbroadcast" videotape recorders. Effectively Sony was forced to concentrate on helical scan video technology, which Ampex had openly stated was not adequate for broadcast quality recording.

Ampex failed to realize that helical scan video recording, in one form or another, would in time dominate the entire industry. Sony, on the other hand, began to understand all too well the technological advantages that had been forced upon them. When Roberts split Ampex's video engineering group into two departments—one concentrating on Ampex's traditional broadcast recording technology and the other on helical scanning (then thought suitable only for closed-circuit television and potentially a home video recorder)—he not only separated the groups by thousands of miles but precipitated a total loss of communication between these organizations, making it impossible for the company to maintain a cooperative focus on total video technology and its potential application to new and evolving markets. Ampex lost valuable time and resources that it was never able to recover. Thus the groundwork for the demise of audiovisual recording in America was being laid as early as 1959, eleven years before the introduction of Instavideo.

At the same time, the resolution to Roberts's cancellation of the Sony partnership insured that Ampex's new competitor would concentrate solely on helical scan video recording. Ampex had inadvertently given Sony the impetus—and carte blanche access—to focus its resources on the technology that within twenty years would become the basis for the construction of *all* videotape recorders. Sony was virtually forced into a leadership role in video recording. The ultimate beneficiary was all of Japan.

The breakup of the partnership between Ampex and Sony, the introduction of the VCR in Japan, and the ultimate application of Sony's helical technology to broadcast video recording were the first links in the chain of events that would cost the United States not only the entire videotape recording market but most of America's consumer electronics industry. Paradoxically, these events began just when the media was making Ampex a byword in the world of video information. It was that very reputation, resting on the strength of its basic recording technology, that enabled Ampex to limp along for another two decades before losing video recording altogether.

Akio Morita clearly understood the advantage of his position once he won a fully paid-up license for design and production of "nonbroadcast" video recorders. But if there was any doubt about the power of audiovisual recording technology, Nixon and Khrushchev provided the world and Morita with a clear example. Audiovisual recording in all its forms was the technological gold of the future. To Morita, the ability to couple video information with audio recording was obvious. The power of that combination had been demonstrated by the phenomenal impact of the Kitchen Debate. Under Morita and Ibuka's guidance, Sony had already begun to lay the groundwork for video recording and the many technological innovations and products that would be built on that foundation.

Roberts's action was like manna from heaven. Sony was left to pursue its endeavors legally unfettered by obligation to Ampex, and Ampex was essentially stuck in a technological rut, its engineering split into two noncommunicative groups. In a move that suggests great foresight, at approximately the same time as Ampex and Morita reached their initial agreement on their partnership, Morita changed the name of the corporation to what until then had been only the brand name: Sony. For Morita, it was a right of passage. He wanted the name Sony to blanket the world. There was no turning back.

After jettisoning Sony, Ampex needed a new partner in Japan and chose Toshiba. Toshiba became a highly cooperative associate in a fifty-fifty joint venture called Toamco. Toshiba put up most of the manufacturing investment required to build Ampex broadcast recorders at the Toamco facility in Yokohama, and for this Toshiba got 100 percent of the sales rights for the Japanese market. But Toshiba brought much more to the party than just money and labor.

Toshiba had a long and illustrious history. When Hisashige Tanaka opened a telegraph equipment factory in Tokyo in 1875, it marked the beginning of one of the world's great electronics companies. Fifteen years later, the company manufactured Japan's first electric incandescent lamps, and in 1921, it invented the double-coil electric bulb, considered one of the major contributions to the industry. By 1924, the company was in the radio business and was entering the cathode ray tube industry, the electronic display that would help bring about television. In 1936 it became an important supplier to Nippon Hoso Kyokai (NHK), Japan's primary broadcasting company, providing it with the country's first 150-kilowatt broadcast transmitter. In 1939 the company officially became the Tokyo Shibaura Electric Company—Toshiba.

During World War II Toshiba built many products to support Japan's war effort, including the country's first radar systems. By 1952 it was heavily involved in the design and manufacture of TV broadcast transmitters and TV microwave relay systems. In the pivotal year of 1959, just before Sony and Ampex severed their relationship, Toshiba designed and manufactured Japan's first transistor television sets.

From a technological standpoint, the one major difference between Toshiba and Sony was Toshiba's experience in building a video recorder.

For all practical purposes, it had none. But in related technologies and customer relationships, Toshiba was very strong. Ampex appeared to have picked a very qualified partner. Toshiba, on the other hand, was able to use Toamco to add a fundamental building block in its quest to become a powerhouse in the communications and consumer electronics business. With the stroke of a pen, Toshiba was directly involved in the design and manufacture of video-recording equipment.

Toamco went on to build some small reel-to-reel versions of helical scan recording equipment, which, though suffering from relatively poor performance characteristics, did give Toshiba and Toamco some experience beyond manufacturing the broadcast video recorders designed by Ampex. (Thus when I was instructed years later to negotiate an agreement to manufacture Instavideo, Toshiba already had several years of experience working in partnership with Ampex in video recording.)

But perhaps the most significant relationship to come from the venture was the specific involvement of Toshiba's chair, Toshio Doko. Doko came to Toshiba as a seasoned executive, having been brought in to fix what then was considered a management crisis. It was only the second time in the company's history that an outsider was made president. Doko was previously chairman of IHI, the world's largest shipbuilding enterprise and the result of a merger he had constructed between Ishikawa-jima Heavy Industries and Harima Shipbuilding and Engineering Company in 1960. Doko remained chair of IHI even after he was made president of Toshiba. IHI and Toshiba already had major equity interests in each other, but Doko increased the equity involvement between the two companies, including board and management interrelationships and trade agreements. Toshiba's financial position was considerably strengthened as a result.

By increasing equity investments between Toshiba and IHI, Doko followed the concept of a "Keiretsu," a community of companies organized around a central bank, whose strength comes from the companies' interlocking relationships. Doko's ability to construct a Keiretsu virtually by himself made him one of Japan's leading industrialists and insured his influence over the Japanese business community as well. Like Akio Morita, he became chair of the Japan Federation of Economic Organizations. Responsible for strategic analysis, the Federation is the private sector's mirror image of the Ministry of International Trade, one of the most powerful governmental organizations in the country. Doko's name is still honored at the highest levels of Japanese society.

I was Toshio Doko's guest at Expo '70, the world trade fair being held in Osaka. The choice of Japan for the fair, which was featured on the cover of *Time* magazine, brought great prestige to the country and further honor to Toshio Doko, who had been named its chair. When my wife and I arrived—after I'd completed the Instavideo negotiations—we were shown an uncommon level of respect as Doko's guests. The breadth of his influence was made palpably clear. I left Japan with two impressions firmly embedded in my mind. First was the obvious position of power that Doko held in his country and the deferential respect shown by all who knew him. Second, I had no doubt that not just Sony and Toshiba but Japan as a whole was totally committed to video recording and the convergent technologies and products that would build what I believed would ultimately become a massive and strategic end-use market: consumer electronics.

Ampex had gotten something right. It could not have picked two more strategically savvy leaders of Japanese industry or two more powerful companies with which to cooperate. Both Doko and Morita clearly understood that over time their companies would be able to advance the state of video recording and related products. But what Ampex—and most of America—did not get right was that Doko and Morita, as concerned as they were for the future of their respective firms, were committed to a larger vision: the rebirth of Japan springing from the strength of its industrial base.

With cold determination, Japan began to build a domestic industrial complex dedicated as much to mutual cooperation (a difficult concept for many Americans) as to competition, be it internal or global. With that national strategy in place, Japan designed and manufactured what it foresaw as the taproot of the information age—a plethora of consumer products centered around the collection and distribution of audiovisual information adapted to the needs and desires of every group of people in every country in the world.

VISION IN HIGH DEFINITION

I returned to Japan many times after Expo '70, completing negotiations with Toshiba on the Instavideo joint venture, but also furthering my understanding of the state of Japanese video technology. During one of those trips in 1970, I was shown a working prototype of an initial approach to high-definition television developed by NHK, Japan's primary broadcasting company. I was amazed at the quality and realism of the video presentation. It was clearly the beginning of a great leap forward in image processing. Called Multiple SubNyquist Encoding, or MUSE, the system used a digital process to compress the analog HDTV signal for transmission purposes in order to save bandwidth. Japan was beginning to master digital technology.

The promise implied in that brief demonstration has since become reality. HDTV systems have played a major role in the development of the Japanese television industry and have had an enormous effect on the advancement of Japan's entire electronics industry. At the core of NHK's MUSE system was not only a strategic vision as to what Japan's electronics industry could become but also the seed of a major political struggle within Japan's manufacturing sector concerning the analog aspects of MUSE. Japan's television industry wanted a more digitally oriented system, while NHK, which was then broadcasting commercially using MUSE technology, wanted to stay the course. In the end, the United States would unwittingly solve this dilemma, substantially advancing Japan's industrial base in the process.

In 1970, the United States was still the global leader in computers, displays, cameras, video- and audio-recording equipment, semiconductors, and most consumer electronics. But in its desire to outsource much of its manufacturing to Asia, conserve capital, and increase profits in intensely competitive industries like consumer electronics, America was setting the stage for a massive transfer of technology to Japan. By coincidence, 1971 was the last year America would see an overall trade surplus. A dozen years later, the United States began to see a growing trade deficit with Japan in high technology products. At the same time, the value of the yen was rapidly increasing relative to the dollar. The two trends alarmed many Americans in business and government.

These events were not accidental. By 1970 Japan had developed an industrial strategy, already well along in implementation. They had a long-term plan that would be aided and abetted by America's hunger for short-term profits. At the core of that strategy was Japan's total commitment to audiovisual recording and display technology. In part because of fierce competition from Japan, these industries—devoid of satisfactory profit margins—were not held in high esteem by U.S. businesspeople and economists, many of whom referred to consumer electronics as a commodity business. The Japanese understood and exploited this American attitude, which only continued to grow. Japan remained steadfastly competitive in pricing while continuing to improve its product design and manufacturing expertise at an exponential rate. Seeing no need to compete on low-profit margins, the United States simply walked from the field. But Japan, seeing more in the future than gains in market share, had another card to play that would take years to develop. Fundamental to its strategic plan was a continuing investment in HDTV and the digital framework that made it possible. It foresaw that this area would one day bring rapid change and expansion to image processing and the information age.

In 1984, the United States initiated the Japanese Technology Evaluation Center (JTEC) in order to assess the advance of Japanese engineering and product design compared to that of America. The argument that was made in garnering the funds to establish JTEC was very simple but difficult to put across. At the end of World War II the United States led in most technologies, and this self-sufficiency fostered the complacent assumption that anything of technological substance would be developed in the United States. The one exception to this presumption was the Soviet Union's potential for innovation in weapons development. As JTEC stated in an overview of the program, "during the Cold War era, much attention was paid to the smallest bit of information coming from the Soviet Union—some real threats, some imaginary (e.g., the Alpha class submarines and poly-water, respectively). Being first into space, the Soviets potentially threatened the West with massive technological prowess to which we had little access. It was easy to convince Washington to fund Soviet technology studies, but there was little interest in learning about other foreign technologies"—little interest, that is, until our trade deficit with Japan in high technology products began to go negative. It was the realization that Japan was beginning to encroach on American leadership in technology that led to the JTEC.

In 1988, as cochair of the American Electronics Association (AEA) task force on HDTV, I put together my thoughts on the future of the technology. HDTV was getting a lot of publicity because of the extraordinary quality of its picture, something everyone could understand, and it originated in Japan, not the United States.

Why was HDTV so important? HDTV essentially provides the ability to process extraordinary amounts of information, enabling the viewer to see true-to-life pictures, still or moving, wherever or whenever desired. One can slow down a volleyball game and observe an athlete's muscle action in exquisite detail or examine with extreme clarity a small object as though it were under a microscope. The camera that records the information, the tape or semiconductor memory device that stores this information, the displays that provide the HDTV picture, and all of the processing equipment in between must be able to handle large amounts of data in a form that can be viewed on an HD television screen, computer display, cell phone, or other image-processing system. Ultimately, the sophisticated technology behind the ability to process this amount of data with great speed and clarity will substantially improve the state of the art in digital image processing for *all* electronic components and systems.

I presented my analysis to the AEA, to Semitech (a consortium established in 1988 with America's top semiconductor companies and the U.S. government to bolster the U.S. semiconductor industry), other industry groups, and ultimately the Senate Banking Committee. Beyond the pretty picture on the TV screen, I wanted to focus attention on the political and economic implications of HDTV technology for America:

> High-definition television portrays life in vivid splashes of breathtaking color and sound. But the picture may also reflect the ebbing tide of United States technological and economic leadership.
>
> When we try to assess the strategic and tactical implications of HDTV, we face a grand strategy; the domination of interrelated end-use markets against which no single technological development or expertise can be a significant threat.[7]

With digital cameras and cell phones barely on the horizon in 1988, contemporaneous examples of end-use markets—that is, markets for stand-alone products that have significant value to the individual consumer—were VCRs, 35mm cameras, TVs, and PCs. The convergence of the technologies embodied in these products was becoming evident, as was the convergence of their respective markets. With the advancement of digital circuits over analog, I could only see the ties becoming stronger. I was convinced that a competitor that dominated these products and markets could also exercise significant control over the production of electronic components important to the unique value of those products. Electronic products meant semiconductors, an industry I felt was of huge strategic value to America. By 1988, the Japanese were clearly willing to do whatever it would take to dominate both consumer electronics and the components fundamental to product design. With growing strength in this area and their complete control over the manufacture and sale of VCRs, Japan was beginning to rival the U.S. in semiconductor production. This was a principle reason for the establishment of Semitech.

In my 1988 analysis I suggested the following scenario. *"Assume that the VCR is nothing more than a storage device for moving pictures.* In time the HDTV recorder may become a plug-in module similar to a cartridge and thus a component part to the computer. The merging of technologies could give the Japanese an additional capability in their quest to dominate the world's computer market"[8] (emphasis added). Between consumer electronics and computers, I concluded, the United States could lose its position of strength in the semiconductor industry.

With the development of digital technology, advancement in semiconductor memories over the last eighteen years has indeed been phenomenal. With the invention of NAND flash memory by Toshiba, the information from a VCR can be instantly stored on a chip and available for immediate playback, giving the user the ability to transfer moving images—or any other data—between computers, cameras, VCRs, displays, and cell phones by simply removing the flash memory card from one device and inserting it in another. In large part, the design and manufacture of these end-use products and markets now resides in Asia. And with a few notable exceptions, such as Intel and Micron Technology, the semiconductor devices supporting these products are migrating to Asia as well.

In 1990, I had the privilege of being asked to chair a JTEC panel on HDTV. After visits to various Japanese companies, including Sony, Sharp, Hitachi, and Matsushita, and such government agencies as the Ministry of Trade and Industry and the Ministry of Posts and Telecommunications, I summarized the panel's findings:

"High definition" describes new products or systems whose value resides in their ability to process greatly increased amounts of audio and video information. Processing of information is fundamental to the infrastructure of electronics, telecommunication, and media markets. The panel's goal was to study technological developments in Japan pertaining to high definition systems. A brochure from Japan's Ministry of Posts and Telecommunications described high definition television as "the cornerstone of the information age," which indicated a dedication to the concept of HDTV in Japan. The purpose of this dedication seemed to be to focus the Japanese electronics industry on a problem that, when solved, might advance the state of the electronics manufacturing art in Japan a generation beyond the rest of the world.[9]

My meetings on behalf of JTEC with several leading Japanese business executives and knowledgeable government officials left me with a lasting impression: the Japanese way of doing business was far different from the American version. This was not just a process learned in Japanese schools or taught within Japanese companies. The Japanese way was ingrained in their culture. It was a concept of how the world worked that was fundamental to their daily activities, a part of the air they breathed. In the JTEC study I tried to express the substance of that concept, particularly as it applied to Japan's investment in HDTV:

To Japanese businessmen, strategy is everything. Every person, business, and industry must have a goal and a strategy by which to achieve it. Because resources are usually scarce, the successful Japanese plan includes the concept of leverage. Some markets are considered more strategic than others. By targeting strategic markets, an infrastructure can be built that ensures a solid basis for economic expansion. However, the leverage is not based simply on the importance of one market over another, but rather on the assumption that, as they develop, strategic markets will become interrelated and interdependent, with the whole becoming substantially larger than the sum of its parts. Therefore, coordination of strategy and direction is essential—a point that is fundamental to the strategy of product and market development in Japan. It is based on the concept that if the development of a product or market is pushed to its logical extreme, it becomes related to other products and markets. Thus, Japanese business strategy does not reject a product on the basis of profit potential, but rather assumes that every product becomes the basis for another, and every technology becomes the stepping-stone for the next. The resulting efficiencies of scale are enormous.

The market for high definition products and systems can help push the markets for electronics products, telecommunication services, and software (including mass media) to their logical extreme. The Japanese expressed the view that, perhaps by the year 2000, the requirements and possibilities created by improving the technology to rapidly process large amounts of audiovisual information would force a confluence of these three end-use markets into a single information systems market. They expected that the information systems market would grow to represent thirty-three percent of all capital investment, forty-four percent of all new jobs, and twenty-two percent of all economic growth.

The Japanese felt that in the future information age, any nation without a proprietary position in or reliable strategic access to each of the market segments within electronics, the media (including software and mass media), and telecommunication services would be at a significant competitive disadvantage. This concept was in part the basis for the accelerated development in Japan of high definition products and systems, and underscored the significance of high definition technology and its effect on all parts of the industrial structure of Japan.[10]

As a result of this experience I had the good fortune to develop a relationship with Akio Morita that lasted for several years until he suffered a stroke. He spent many hours with me discussing business philosophy. I don't think I have ever met a man with a greater understanding of the nuances of global competitiveness. His ideas and insight have had a profound influence on my life.

Three consistent thoughts lay at the heart of every discussion I had with this illustrious man: First, nothing good happens overnight; it takes time and significant investment not only in financial resources but in a focused commitment of individual effort. Second, this effort can succeed only by building on a foundation of past knowledge and achievement to advance the state of the art. And finally, any success that might result from a significant investment of time and effort is dependent upon a well-thought-out strategy.

A chance encounter in the wake of these discussions produced what is now an interesting vignette in the history of HDTV. In 1991 I was having dinner with my family at the Hyatt Hotel on Kauai, and, by coincidence, sitting just a few feet away were Morita and his wife. I went over to say hello and exchanged a few pleasantries. As he left the restaurant, Morita stopped by my table and introduced himself to my family. He then asked if I would be willing to come to his suite after dinner for a brief private meeting.

Later that night, over a bottle of wine in that beautiful setting overlooking the Pacific Ocean, he made a proposal:

Mr. Elkus, Sony has a problem with NHK. My feeling is that you can help Sony and we can help the United States. The MUSE system is basically analog and in our estimation will not be a competitive format for the delivery of high-definition television when you consider what can be done with an all digital system. In Japan, it is virtually impossible for Sony to try to change the mind of NHK management on this matter. When you consider the man-years of effort NHK has expended on their MUSE system—including regular broadcasts in MUSE high definition already in force to help create a market for this standard in Japan—Sony is too small to make an impact. But if the United States would be willing to establish a high-definition, all-digital standard applicable to U.S. television, I know that NHK would go along and be willing to accept the same standard in Japan. If this thought appeals to you, I would like to suggest that you call on Chairman Sikes [of the Federal Communications Commission] and Mr. Negroponte [chair of MIT's media laboratory] and tell these gentlemen that if they can help America agree on a digital standard for the delivery of high-definition television, Sony would be happy to provide appropriate manpower, technology, and money as required to aid in this accomplishment.

I asked if he cared about any of the specifications for that standard other than using digital technology to the fullest extent, and he said no. Having agreed to pass on the message, I called FCC chair Al Sikes a week later, when I was in Washington, D.C., and explained Morita's suggestion. I told him that I felt the proposal was completely genuine. But I wanted Sikes to understand what I felt was at the basis of Morita's request. Sony—and Japan—were prepared to accede to the demands of an American standard. But to them a standard was simply a technological highway for which Sony wanted to build the cars. I advised Sikes to weigh fully the consequences for America if it were not a player in the world of HD equipment.

Sikes said he understood my concerns and would consider the offer. I never found out if he took Morita up on his proposal. Under the direction of the FCC, the United States did establish a standard for the digital transmission of high-definition television. Some of the technology to achieve that end came from Zenith, the last television manufacturer in the United States, sold to LG Electronics in Korea in 1996. And Japan did subsequently adopt the American standard.

Fast-forward to the present. The theme for the celebrated 2007 consumer electronics show in Las Vegas centered on full high-definition television. The show, which attracted more than 150,000 people from all over the world, sent a clear message: Full HDTV is here. HDTV will soon be available in almost any form imaginable, and will thus affect communications technology across the board. Full HD of the future will evolve from today's most sophisticated standard for picture clarity and breathtaking sharpness: 1,080 lines of vertical resolution using progressive scanning techniques. And the future starts now.

Where does Sony stand as the world moves in unison to embrace the evolution of this new technology? Sony's revenues in 2007 approximated $70 billion with a capitalized market value of $45 billion.

(Toshiba's revenues approached $60 billion.) Having filed for bank-ruptcy, Ampex remains around $30 million. In the field spawned by the VCR, its derivative products, and related consumer electronics, there are a multitude of Asian companies in the game, including Japan's Sony, Toshiba, Matsushita, Fujitsu, Sharp, JVC, and NEC and Korea's Samsung and LG Electronics. Several of these companies have revenues in excess of $70 billion dollars and multibillion-dollar research and de-velopment budgets. These and other Asian firms supply 100 percent of HD displays—virtually all HD video cameras, recording, and produc-tion equipment, including consumer cameras and recorders; and all HD DVD and CD systems. In addition, a major portion of the semi-conductors used in this equipment are designed and manufactured in Asia. Ninety percent of memory devices—fundamental to the storage and distribution of digital media—are made in Asia. In fact, today nearly 90 percent of the advanced technology semiconductor fabrication facilities are being built in Asia. And it's worth mentioning that in 2006 the largest movie company in the world by revenues was Sony Pictures. On the technological highway, the United States got its standard; Asia is building the cars.

CONVERGENCE

Prerequisite to the advance of HDTV was the evolution of audiovisual recording. The impact of the video recorder on the electronics industry was a perfect example of the principle of convergence—the coming to-gether of two or more disparate disciplines or technologies. For example, the fax machine resulted from a convergence of telecommunications, op-tical scanning, and printing technologies. The convergence of differing technologies results in the rapid development of new advances, forming over time an infrastructure of products and markets that becomes the basis for the exponential growth of an economy. This has been Japan's strategy since World War II. With the possible exception of nations pos-sessing an abundance of natural resources available for export, economies lacking such infrastructures will experience a substantially diminished ability to compete in the global arena.

Not only was the VCR itself a product of convergent technologies—audio recording, FM signal processing, solid-state electronics, cameras, television—but it became the basis for a plethora of further innovation, the convergence of which allowed Japan to dominate the world market for consumer electronics. When the VCR hit the broad market in the years before the personal computer, it used more semiconductors than any other product and helped launch the multibillion-dollar semiconductor industry in Japan. The semiconductor and its application to digital technology became the foundation for virtually all future consumer electronic products. Video camera lenses and small motor designs for the movement of these and other parts in the VCR system advanced the state of the art for the entire Japanese camera business. The prodigious need for displays to support the consumer electronics and computer industries in Japan (and in time other Asian countries) advanced the state of the art and competitiveness of their display industry to the point that no other companies—let alone countries—wanted to compete.

The speed at which technology was advancing along with manufacturing expertise was too great for those who did not have the market drivers to keep pace with the level of investment in Japan and the rest of Asia. Image processing resulting from the development of the VCR gave those countries such an edge that there are now few—if any—electronic consumer products using image processing that are not in whole or in part manufactured in Asia. Display technology for computers and HDTV was also driven largely by the VCR. As the market for video recording grew, the demand for HDTV grew along with it, creating an ever-increasing need for improved Japanese expertise in the digital technology essential to today's state-of-the-art cameras, high-definition displays, and semiconductors.

In the decades since Ampex bequeathed its video technology to Japan, the convergence of consumer electronics in that country has grown exponentially. Video recorders, displays, and cameras merged into camcorders.

Displays became a part of calculators, personal data organizers, and cell phones. Memory evolved from tape to disks and integrated circuits, allowing the development of audiovisual record and playback media in the form of CDs, DVDs, and now flash memory. The spread of digital data storage and computing techniques to calculators and personal data organizers ultimately melded into highly complex cell phones. Soon cameras in all their complexity were combined with cell phones, launching a truly wireless world of communication. And now computers and cell phones are about to become one. Many of these products have commercial applications, providing audiovisual communication that can now link every individual, home, and business. The entertainment industry saw a sweeping transformation not only in the digital production of movies but in new markets for prerecorded media—DVDs and home theater systems—that are beginning to supersede commercial movie theaters.

I know of no other consumer product that has had such a far-reaching effect on a greater number of industries, or provided greater opportunities for convergence, than the VCR. At its height the VCR represented one-half of all Japan's consumer electronics market and two-thirds of the profits of their consumer electronics industry. The complete success of Japan and ultimately the rest of Asia in dominating the design, production, and marketing of the VCR has allowed its derivative products, including CD and DVD players, to become essentially an Asian industry. The rest of the world is at an enormous disadvantage. Image processing and its companion product, the computer, are rapidly affecting virtually every other product and market on Earth.

Capitalizing on convergent infrastructures was Sony's strategy almost from the beginning. The Walkman—the compact, easy-to-use audio-tape recorder introduced by Sony in the 1980s that became the most successful product of its kind in the world—set in motion a whole new concept of products for the consumer market that made music and other audio content available wherever and whenever one wanted it. In time this expertise in electronic circuit design spread to other Japanese companies. They became major suppliers of audiotape decks to American companies wishing to avoid the cost of mass production while taking advantage of Japan's low prices.

Sony and other Japanese companies were soon able to mass-produce tape decks that were cheap, reliable, durable, interchangeable, and made in almost any form imaginable. They determined exactly what the consumer wanted—in size, weight, price, simplicity, sound quality, serviceability, and overall appearance. Knowledge of and experience with solid-state electronics, signal processing, and the mass production of decks, along with the discerning of consumer needs, became the foundation for the subsequent development of the VCR in Japan. At its core was the development of an infrastructure—the convergence of initially disparate technologies, products, and markets—while the competition was losing theirs. In the larger context, Japanese companies had an innate ability to cooperate and compete at the same time, giving maximum leverage to the principle of convergence as the entire nation learned the business in lockstep, using its total resource base to the mutual benefit of all the participants.

As for Sony, Akio Morita recognized from the beginning that the analog signal recorded on tape in the initial VCR was destined to become digital, and that tape would progress to more convenient and adaptable forms of memory. He was convinced that television would progress to HD programs adaptable to entertainment and computers. From his first transistor radio to the Walkman and far beyond, he saw the value of small portable products. From movie theaters to home entertainment centers, from PlayStations to supercomputers that provide information and media content in any form, Morita was aware of the possibilities and the infrastructure of products and markets necessary to get there. Morita envisioned a world of information accessible in whatever form people desired, whenever they desired it. He purchased CBS Records and Columbia Pictures so that Sony's technical expertise might bring radically new forms to audio recording, moviemaking, and other program materials. Morita and Sony's goal was for their innovations to become intimate and indissoluble facets of our lives.

As America's infrastructure of consumer electronic products and markets diminished in scope and economic influence, consumer electronics and their derivatives in Japan were becoming an important part of mainstream commercial electronics. How does a personal computer as a consumer product differ from the PC used in a business? When is a cell phone a consumer item, and when is it a commercial product? The lines between consumer and commercial markets were rapidly beginning to blur. The complexity of the consumer electronics infrastructure began to permeate that of commercial electronics and affect America's competitiveness in industrial markets. Just as the loss of the VCR wiped out America's ability to participate in the design and manufacture of broadcast video-recording equipment, the loss of the design and manufacture of consumer electronic cameras in the United States virtually guaranteed the demise of its professional camera market.

In fact, as I learned in my quest to establish a U.S.-based organization for the design and manufacture of the VCR, the demands placed on an enterprise trying to develop and manufacture consumer products are far greater than the demands placed on those wanting to design a commercial version of the same thing. The consumer version, produced in vastly larger quantities than a commercial product, must be smaller, lighter, easier to operate, more reliable, attractive, durable, and substantially less costly than its commercial counterpart, yet it must approach the commercial version in performance. Volume coupled with performance and reliability can add hundreds of millions of dollars to the capital investment required to produce consumer electronic products, many times that required for a commercial version.

The Japanese investment of time and money in the technological development of consumer electronics enhanced their ability to advance the competitive state of their commercial electronics. Thus, as the United States lost its position in consumer electronics, it began to lose its competitive base in commercial electronics as well. The losses in these related infrastructures would begin to negatively affect other downstream industries, not the least of which was the automobile.

Like an ecosystem, a competitive economy is a holistic entity, far greater than the sum of its parts. Years after Sony had become the largest player in the market for VCRs, my discussions with Akio Morita made it clear that he understood this concept in depth and never wavered in his commitment to it. Sony is still the most recognized name in consumer electronics. Unlike Ampex, Sony understood that as the potentials of end-use products are developed, they become increasingly interrelated and interdependent, and the resulting infrastructure becomes an evolving wellspring of new innovation. Sony, Japan, and now the rest of Asia have a significant strategic advantage over their competitors. They are exploiting the power of convergence.

CHAPTER 3

Evolution, Part 1

Growth of products and markets is always evolutionary, never revolutionary.

On December 7, 1877, Thomas Edison arrived out of the blue at the offices of *Scientific American* and pushed a quaint-looking contrivance across the editor's desk. "Here you are," said Edison. Spying a crank, the editor instinctively turned it. "Good morning!" said the machine. "What do you think of the phonograph?"[1]

Word went through the building until people had packed themselves so tightly into the office that the editor feared the floor would collapse. Edison demonstrated the invention at the National Academy of Sciences in Washington, D.C., where the doors had to be taken off their hinges to accommodate the crush of the curious. Congressmen assembled in the Capitol to hear the talking machine, and President Rutherford Hayes detained Edison at the White House until 3:30 A.M.

Crude tinfoil phonographs were soon being demonstrated all over the country, and public interest assumed the proportions of a national fad. Some accused Edison of ventriloquism, and a Methodist bishop came to Edison's lab to test the machine by uttering a long string of abstruse biblical names. In each case, of course, skepticism gave way to amazement. Journalists hailed Edison as the nation's greatest inventor. On April 1,

1878, the New York *Daily Graphic* went so far as to print an April Fool's bannerline: "Edison Invents a Machine that Will Feed the Human Race— Manufacturing Biscuits, Meat, Vegetables and Wine out of Air, Water, and Common Earth." Other papers around the country picked up the story and ran it straight. No feat seemed beyond the reach of a wizard who could make a machine that talked. If someone today were to announce the invention of a machine that could record the details of a person's thoughts, we would probably be less astounded than those who jammed into entertainment halls to hear Edison's tinfoil talking machine.[2]

The long-term result was that the phonograph, along with Edison's later invention of the motion picture, launched an audiovisual transformation that affected nearly every aspect of the twentieth century. The phonograph appeared on the eve of two great transformations in the history of technology: the shift from steam to electric power and the convergence of technology and science, particularly chemistry and physics. In the steam age, the machine was a superbeast of burden requiring the physical degradation of men for its operation; the tasks machines accomplished were mainly those that could have been achieved by a sufficient quantity of human power; most were but an extension of the larger muscles. Early in the electrical age, however, the image of the machine as a benevolent force that increased leisure and physical comfort became more compelling and more explicit. Machines began to do things that no quantity of people could do, becoming extensions not only of the finer muscles but of the eyes, ears, and even the brain itself. The phonograph was the first machine to awaken the mass mind to the potential of the new age.

But was it in fact a revolution? How "revolutionary" was the phonograph? Use of the word often confuses cause and effect—inventions that send shockwaves through the culture may, in and of themselves, represent merely the next small ripple in a long chain of innovations. Though it seemed radical at the time, the phonograph did not represent a sudden discontinuous leap comparable to extraterrestrials landing with news of some ultimate reality underlying the illusion of space and time. Rather, a revolution—social or technical—is simply the next incremental step in an unceasing *evolution*. Restructuring our collective experience, it is radical only in effect.

At the simplest level, this distinction between cause and effect is illustrated by boiling water. When an accelerating increase in temperature reaches exactly 212 degrees, there occurs what in chaos and complexity theory is called a "phase transition." The water restructures itself and suddenly enters a different state. The *cause,* however, is an evolving temperature; the "revolution," though striking in effect, simply reflects the last incremental change from 211 to 212 degrees.

This distinction between cause and effect can be seen in the evolution of the phonograph and Edison's other inventions. In the public eye, Edison was a "wizard," the father of the new electrical age. Not only was his phonograph the precursor of all modern forms of mechanical memory, and his light bulb and "Edison effect" the forerunners of the vacuum tube (the seed of electronics), but his dynamo and system of power distribution took the machine from the exclusive hands of the producer and put it in the home of the everyday consumer. The machines with which Edison usually worked were not mammoth mechanical brutes like the locomotive, the essence of which did not extend much beyond the valves, pistons, tubing, and vapors visible to the eye. Rather, his reputation rested on small and delicate contrivances with obscure "magical" powers, such as the ability to duplicate a human voice, capture living motion on a two-dimensional surface, or dispel darkness at a finger's touch.

A child of the steam age and chief engineer of the electrical age, Edison was a living illustration of how developments in transportation fathered those in communications. He and his dynamo stand as transitional symbols between the brute snort of the locomotive and the soft dissonance of the first computers.

There is little coincidence, of course, in the fact that America and its greatest inventor grew up together. Born in the 1840s, during what has been called the "take-off period" in our economic history, Edison grew along with the West, the cities, the railroads, and the productive power of America. At twelve years old, Edison supplemented the family income by

selling newspapers and candy aboard the Grand Trunk Railroad, which
had reached his hometown of Port Huron, Michigan, in 1859. He soon
began spending spare hours in a section of the smoker car, experimenting
with some chemicals brought from his cellar laboratory at home. After
giving part of his earnings to his parents, he spent the rest on books and
chemicals. The Grand Trunk Railroad was part of the Michigan Central
system, which had been the first to install a telegraph line along its routes
in order to prevent collisions (the early railroads having built only single
tracks, with side tracks for passing). At every station, therefore, was a
telegraph, which fascinated boys in the mid-nineteenth century just as
planes, radios, and rockets did in the twentieth. At fifteen, Edison learned
telegraphy from a grateful stationmaster whose small son he had earlier
plucked from the path of a rolling boxcar.

He worked nights in railway stations as a telegraph operator, and by
day experimented with electrical gadgets and various modifications of
the telegraph itself. To practice receiving messages more rapidly, he took
the strips of paper on which dots and dashes were imprinted by the old
Morse embossers and created a "repeater," which converted these strips
back into electrical signals at any speed desired. Then he developed a
telegraphic printer that translated signals into Roman characters, all the
while tinkering tirelessly with the idea of duplex telegraphy (sending
two messages simultaneously over one wire). Frequently fired for experimental mishaps and personality clashes, Edison drifted about the country in the 1860s, riding or walking the rails, working in telegraph offices.
Eventually his wanderings brought him to Boston, then the center of
American scientific and electrical research. His work on the telegraph
printer led to his involvement with the stock ticker (a specialized
printer), first in Boston and then in New York City, where he developed
an improved ticker of his own. With the money and backing he received
from his stock ticker patents, he was able to set up his first "invention
factory" at Newark, New Jersey, later moved to Menlo Park.

The succession of Edison's inventions followed as naturally as the events
in his life. He continued his work on the telegraph, eventually developing

the quadruplex system. His interest in automatic telegraphy—eliminating the hand-powered telegraph key with faster encoding and decoding devices—led him to intensify his studies of chemistry and chemically treated paper, and hence to the invention of the mimeograph. His crucial improvements on Bell's telephone (which was called a "speaking telegraph transmitter") involved refinements in the quality of voice reproduction. The final product, the carbon-button telephone transmitter, was derived from Edison's discovery, during automatic telegraph experiments, that the conductivity of carbon varied according to the pressure it was under.

Also during his experiments with automatic telegraphy, which involved a stylus (contact point) and chemically treated paper, Edison discovered that if he wrapped the paper around a cylinder and connected both a stylus and the rotating cylinder to a battery, the friction of the stylus against the paper increased or decreased according to the strength of the current. He called this apparatus an "electromotograph" and attempted to find uses for its principle in a number of areas in which he had been working simultaneously: the mimeograph, autographic telegraphy (transmitting handwriting or drawings), a telephone speaker, and a means of somehow electrically encoding voice messages from the telephone onto paper so that Western Union might convert them without prohibitive longhand transcription. "We picture inventors as heroes with the genius to recognize and solve society's problems," writes Jared Diamond. "In reality, the greatest inventors have been tinkerers who loved tinkering for its own sake and who then had to figure out what, if anything, their devices might be good for."[3]

Edison had been at Menlo Park little more than a year when these lines of experimentation converged in an aura of serendipity. Although his electromotographic telephone speaker had failed to transmit his shouts when tested, the slight impressions they had made on the paraffined paper vibrated the speaker diaphragm as he continued to turn the cylinder. The musical hum haunted him for days. What would happen if he simply ran a strip of paraffined paper under the stylus? He tried it, shouting "Halloo!" into the diaphragm, and then ran the strip back through. There was a distinct sound, Edison later related, "which strong imagination might have translated into the original Halloo!" It was at that instant, on a hot July afternoon in 1877, that both the phonograph and the electrical age were conceived.

In the following year, Edison applied the principle of the carbon button telephone to a heat-sensing device (called a tasimeter); this led him to the idea that a heat sensor might solve the main problem then confronting those tinkering in incandescent lighting—namely, an overheating filament. Although his eventual solution was different, this idea set him to work on the lightbulb. With the exception of his contributions to the motion-picture camera and projector—the result of his attempts to synchronize the phonograph with a zoetropic device (pictures on a rapidly rotating wheel reflected in a mirror)—all of his subsequent major inventions were outgrowths of his work on the lightbulb. His initial search for platinum as a filament substance led to his development of magnetic ore-separating machinery, a technology later applied to iron mining. His plans for the installation of lighting systems demanded that he create a greatly improved generator, along with all the aspects of the power distribution system. The generator was in turn converted into an electric motor to drive machinery, which then led him to designs for electric locomotives and cars, and to his final major invention, a storage battery to power them.[4]

The point of rehearsing this chronology is that virtually all technical innovation requires an *infrastructure* of knowledge and prior innovation. This infrastructure is more than just a base of past endeavors—all history can be summed up that way—but involves more specifically a chain of technological antecedents. The advent of the phonograph required, among many other things, discoveries in electricity and the invention of the battery and the telegraph. An inventor of the Edison type is not a wizard but a patient plodder who tries all possible combinations and permutations, aiming for that logical but infinitesimal step that follows from the fund of previous knowledge.

This process, primarily a trial-and-error search for materials and the struggle for practicability, is what Edison had in mind when he said that "genius is 1 percent inspiration and 99 percent perspiration." It also helps explain why the same innovation is often introduced nearly simultaneously by separate individuals. The derivation of calculus, the discovery of the planet Neptune, the introduction of the decimal point, and the Charles Darwin and Alfred Wallace theories of natural selection are among many examples. Inventor biographies are replete with countless court cases disputing their patent claims. The lawsuits against Edison were so numerous that his famous quip could just as well have been, "Invention is 1 percent inspiration and 99 percent litigation." Notable among these challenges were Joseph Swan's work on the electric lightbulb, Charles Cros's phonograph, Frank Sprague's electric railway, and W. K. L. Dickson's development of the movie camera. Contrary to Thomas Carlyle's "Great Man" theory of historical causation, innovators do not stand apart from history; rather they are a significant part of the converging infrastructure they help to create. They are not outside of history; they *are* history.

WHO INVENTED THE TELEPHONE?

One of the best examples of the evolutionary nature of phase transformations is the invention of the telephone. It is often noted that Alexander Graham Bell's application for a patent on the telephone in 1876 was given precedence over Elisha Gray's because it was submitted a mere two hours earlier. But the contesting claims for the telephone are more tangled than even that story suggests and, in the case of Antonio Meucci, equally incredible.

Meucci, an Italian emigrant who had made his home in Cuba, invented the telephone in 1849. But instead of filing a patent, he spent years improving his device. He eventually moved to New York's Staten Island, where his poor English skills had him associating almost exclusively with other Italians. When he organized a demonstration of his telephone, the story was published only in one of New York's Italian newspapers. A potential Italian backer took the clipping and a model of the phone back to Italy, but nothing came of it. Unable to afford the cost of a patent, Meucci sold the rights to his other inventions in order to make ends meet. While he lay in a hospital, severely burned from an explosion, his wife sold his working models along with the telephone prototype to a secondhand dealer for six dollars. Meucci tried to buy them back but to no avail—whoever bought them from the dealer remains unknown to this day. He worked day and night to reconstruct his invention and in 1871, still lacking the $250 for a patent, filed a caveat, or notice of intent.

He took his model to the president of Western Union hoping the company would test it, only to be told after many follow-up inquiries that it had been "lost." When Bell filed his own patent for the telephone in 1876, Meucci protested to the Patent Office, only to learn that the documents filed in his caveat had also been "lost." Later investigation produced evidence of illegal relationships linking certain employees of the Patent Office to officials at Bell's company. "In the court case of 1886," writes Meucci's biographer,

> although Bell's lawyers tried to turn aside Meucci's suit against their client, he was able to explain every detail of his invention so clearly as to leave little doubt of his veracity, although he did not win the case against the superior and vastly richer forces fielded by Bell. Despite a public statement by the then Secretary of State that "there exists sufficient proof to give priority to Meucci in the invention of the telephone," and despite the fact that the United States initiated prosecution for fraud against Bell's patent, the trial was postponed from year to year until, at the death of Meucci in 1896, the case was dropped.[5]

The story doesn't end there. A man named Innocenzo Manzetti invented a "speaking telegraph" in 1864 but never patented the device. A German, Philipp Reis, also began work on the telephone in 1860, taking his essential idea from an 1854 paper by a Frenchman named Charles Bourseul. Reis's phones were demonstrated all over Europe, including Scotland, while Bell was there visiting his father. Bell could hardly have been unaware of Reis's work.

There's more. Neither Bell nor the two-hours-late Gray had actually *built* a working telephone when they filed their patents. Though Bell's device used a multi-reed transmitter, three days after filing his patent he experimented with a water transmitter, the principle used in Gray's device. The famous sentence—"Mr. Watson, come here; I want you"—was spoken into a liquid transmitter. One had to shout into Bell's crude phone to be heard even over short distances. It was not until Edison improved it with the carbon button that it became practical for long distances.[6]

So who invented the telephone? The answer, as with most great inventions, is many people, each of whose work is rooted in the achievements of myriad others. In the case of the telephone, these would include Volta's battery, Oersted's electromagnetism, and Faraday's generator, to name just a few links in the chain. Great inventions are the product of ever-evolving, expanding, and convergent infrastructures—both broadly historical and industry-specific—without which no single advance could ever occur.

The broader the familiarity with existing infrastructure, the better the chances of success. Bell's success owed much to the fact that he understood both electricity and acoustics (the latter rooted in his concern over his mother's deafness). Those who were less successful knew electricity but little of acoustics. The logical end of the need to base innovation on a broad grasp of existing infrastructure are the industrial research laboratories such as Bell Labs, established in 1925, the descendent of the Bell Telephone Company, which Bell cofounded in 1877. The concept of the research laboratory actually dates from Edison, the scope of whose achievements rests largely on the fact that he invented the profession of inventing. Edison initiated the kind of team research, involving machinists, technical men, and trained scientists, that served as a pilot model for the huge industrial research laboratories, the very first of which was established by General Electric, a company formed from Edison's power companies in 1889. In 1900, GE's chief consulting engineer, Charles Steinmetz, convinced CEO Charles Coffin that they would need a research lab if the company were to maintain its edge in lighting and electricity and find new areas in which to grow. And so the first research laboratory in America was born in a carriage barn in Steinmetz's backyard.

"THE INDUSTRIAL MIRACLE OF THE AGE"

Not all innovations, of course, trigger phase transitions. Those that do—those that seem "revolutionary" to the untrained, unsuspecting eye—rest on the two conditions underlying all the principles discussed in the remaining pages: the *evolutionary* nature of the *convergent infrastructures*. The automobile is one such innovation. The automobile not only ushered in radical advances to industrial production but it transformed the American way of life, creating a national highway system, allowing the growth of suburbia, and granting the individual—notably youth—new dimensions of freedom and autonomy.

When Henry Ford formed the Ford Motor Company in 1903, the automobile was a plaything for the rich, usually requiring a chauffer to drive and maintain it. Ford's goal was to build a simple, reliable car that the average American worker could afford. Constantly experimenting, improving on existing methods, incorporating ideas from other industries, and inaugurating business practices that looked beyond immediate profit, he converted the automobile from a luxury to a necessity.

In the winter of 1906, Ford secretly blocked off a twelve-by-fifteen experimental room on the third floor of his Detroit plant, and two years later the Model T was born. But that room was not some mysterious black box; the Model T and the innovative methods that mass-produced it arose from a convergent knowledge of existing materials and methods. The central breakthrough, in fact, was in the realm of materials and occurred literally by accident. Since early automobile promotion took place largely on racetracks, Ford was attending an auto race in Florida when he had the opportunity to examine the wreckage of a French car and notice that the steel was much lighter than that being used in American cars. The steel was a vanadium alloy with nearly three times the tensile strength of plain steel, and yet in spite of such strength it could be machined more easily. No one in America knew how to make vanadium steel, so Ford imported a metallurgist and built a steel mill.

George Eastman had tried the assembly line in his work on photo-processing, and Eli Whitney had experimented with standardized parts in gun manufacturing, but it took Ransom Olds to incorporate these major innovations in the production of automobiles. The result was the 1901 Oldsmobile. Ford, however, took these methods to new levels. In 1910 he built a new facility for the production of the Model T at Highland Park, New Jersey. Designed by Albert Kahn, the facility was unparalleled in scale, sprawling over sixty-two acres; John D. Rockefeller called it "the industrial miracle of the age." There Ford experimented with factory automation every day for the next seventeen years, trying work slides, rollways, conveyor belts, and countless other ideas. His major innovation—the continuous moving assembly line—was suggested by an employee who had visited a Chicago slaughterhouse and seen how animals were butchered as the carcasses moved along an overhead trolley. Ford was impressed by the efficiency of one person removing the same piece over and over in this "disassembly line" and reversed the process. At first workers simply put the frame on skids, hitched it to a towrope, and pulled it along with a capstan. But as the process evolved and became increasingly automated, with subassembly lines feeding into the main line, the interval between Model T chassis coming off the line dropped from twelve hours, twenty minutes, to twenty-four seconds.

In the early 1920s Ford completed the world's largest and most efficient automobile factory at River Rouge, near Detroit, Michigan. Covering two thousand acres with ninety miles of railroad track and seventy-five thousand employees, the Rouge plant was vertically integrated, with its own power plant, fabricating facilities, steel mill, and glass factory. Iron and coal were brought in by rail and Great Lakes steamers. Foundries converted the iron into engine blocks and cylinder heads, while rolling mills, forges, and assembly shops transformed the steel into springs, axles, and car bodies. By 1927, every step, from the refinement of raw materials to the final assembly of the automobile, was handled in the vast Rouge plant. The plant—another Albert Kahn design—was one of the first to use rebar in its concrete structure (not coincidentally, an invention of Kahn's brother Julius), which enabled a building of enormous size to withstand the vibration that came with the mass production of automobiles.

Ford also raised production and profits through innovative business practices. In 1914 he astonished the world by cutting the workday from nine hours to eight and by raising wages to five dollars a day—more than double the going rate. The best mechanics soon flocked to Ford, avoiding the high turnover of unskilled workers and lowering training costs. He also created a massive publicity machine and inaugurated the franchise system, putting a dealership in every city in North America.

The River Rouge plant was intended to produce a car from scratch without relying on foreign trade. Ford's philosophy was one of American economic independence, and both supporters and critics viewed "Fordism" as the epitome of American capitalist development. His notorious prejudices and eccentricities aside, it is probable that no other individual in his century so completely transformed the nation's way of life.[7]

GENEALOGY: THE TRANSISTOR

According to legend, when the chief of the British Postal Service was told about Alexander Bell's invention of the telephone, he was basically unimpressed. "Americans," he said, "have need of the telephone, but we do not. We have plenty of messenger boys." The mayor of a large American city, on the other hand, was wildly enthusiastic about the telephone. "I can see a time," he said, "when *every city* will have one."

Transported to the present, the mayor would have been less astonished at the phone's ubiquity than at the world it had set in motion. For it was the telephone, a half century later, that sparked the exponential rise of the information age. Bell Telephone was renamed American Telephone and Telegraph in 1885. An agreement with Western Electric made that division the sole manufacturer of phone equipment. With control of both service and manufacturing, AT&T enjoyed a solid monopoly. By the end of the century, however, competition began to arise as Bell's patents expired, and AT&T started seeking new technologies to maintain its leadership.

The first transcontinental phone service was thus completed in 1914. AT&T bought Lee De Forest's patent on the triode vacuum tube, a means of amplifying signals as they were transferred across the country from one switch box to another. Vacuum tubes, however, were extremely unreliable. In the 1930s Mervin Kelly, director of Bell Labs—AT&T's research arm established in 1925—realized that something better than the vacuum tube was needed if the telephone business was to continue to grow. The solution, he felt, might lie in a mysterious class of materials called semiconductors. In 1945 Kelly put together a team to develop a solid-state semiconductor switch using some of the wartime advances in semiconductor research that had made radar possible. AT&T's solution would be the transistor.[8]

The evolutionary nature of convergent infrastructures requisite to major innovations is underscored even more dramatically in the story of the transistor. Like Edison's phonograph, Bell's telephone, or Marconi's radio, Shockley's transistor was revolutionary in effect while evolutionary in fact. Kelly's team, headed by William Shockley, unveiled the transistor in 1948. The team had simply taken the next incremental step on the leading edge of an infrastructure produced by a century of convergent innovation in electricity and electronics.

Like so much of the twentieth century, that infrastructure owed much to Edison. While working on the lightbulb he had noticed that the current would jump from the hot filament across the vacuum to a metal plate at the bottom. Called the "Edison effect," it had no useful application until John Fleming invented the diode vacuum tube in 1904. Forcing current in the tube to travel in only one direction, the tube was a great improvement over the weak and quirky diode crystals used in Marconi's first radios. By putting a metal grid in the middle of the tube and using a small input current to change the voltage on the grid, Lee

De Forest developed the triode in 1906; this added the ability to turn weak current into strong current. The amplifying tube became the basis for everything from hearing aids to radio and television.

The paths leading to De Forest's triode were far more numerous and complex than any summary paragraph can suggest. Among these were Michael Faraday's electromagnetic theories in the early nineteenth century, James Maxwell's prediction of radio waves (1864), David Hughes's microphone (1880), Heinrich Hertz's first artificially created radio waves (1885), Oliver Lodge's radio wave detector (1894), Marconi's first transmissions (1895), and J. J. Thompson's discovery of the electron (1897). Again, few such innovations turn out to be clear milestones. The so-called "Edison effect" was actually observed a few years earlier by Frederick Guthrie. Hughes's microphone was an improvement on Edison's carbon telephone transmitter. Walter Kaufmann stumbled on the electron the same year as J. J. Thompson but doubted what he had found. And Marconi, who based much of his work on the lectures of Augusto Righi, must share credit for radio transmission with the Russian Alexander Popov.[9]

The evolution of the transistor includes not only the history of the vacuum tube it replaced but also the course of crystal diodes, first used as rectifiers in early radios. Russell Ohl, a Bell Labs engineer, persisted in studying crystals long after the vacuum tube replaced them. In the process of removing the impurities from silicon crystals, which greatly improved their performance as rectifiers, Ohl encountered one that remained as quirky as any used in the first radios. It had a crack in the middle, with different levels of purity on either side. Ohl found that shining a light on it created an electric current. An excess of electrons on one side were stimulated to move to the side with a deficit, creating a thin barrier of excess charges at the crack. The result was a current that could only travel in one direction. Ohl's crystal was the precursor to solar energy converters. But it also gave Mervin Kelly and Bell Labs the idea that something like that crystal might replace vacuum tubes. Ohl had accidentally discovered what would later be called the silicon P-N junction, the basis of the transistor.[10]

When Bell Labs assigned Shockley the task of creating a solid-state amplifier, his first attempt, a "field-effect" transistor, failed. Two members of his team, John Bardeen and Walter Brattain, then built a germanium "point-contact" device, the first working transistor. Determined to receive credit for the invention, Shockley spent four intense weeks in a Chicago hotel room designing a substantially better "junction" (or sandwich) transistor, the one finally unveiled by Bell Labs in 1948. In 1960 Bell scientist John Atalla developed a new design based on Shockley's original field-effect theories. Today most transistors are field-effect transistors. Most of us use millions of them every day.

In 1951 Western Electric had decided to license the transistor to qualified companies in order to expand its potential customer base. Among those licensed were Sony and Texas Instruments. Sony's license became the basis for many of their future products, including the pocket radio. Yet it was Texas Instruments, in joint venture with the Regency Division of Industrial Development Engineering Associates, that introduced the first transistor radio in October 1954. Though the Regency sold everything the joint venture could manufacture, the product stayed on the market for only a short time. Texas Instruments wanted the public to gain an insight into the possibilities of this new technology. Once they felt that had been accomplished, the project was cancelled, and Texas Instruments went on to other ventures they felt were in line with their core business.

The invention of the transistor got little attention at the time, but Shockley saw its potential and left Bell in 1956 to form a company in Palo Alto, California, called Shockley Semiconductor, the seed of Silicon Valley. Shockley's paranoid, micromanaging personality, which caused him to leave Bell and kept his company from producing any viable commercial product, also drove out eight of his best engineers and physicists. The so-called "traitorous eight" founded Fairchild Semiconductor in 1957. All the original Silicon Valley companies can trace back through two or three degrees of separation to the mother ship of Fairchild Semiconductor.

Fairchild developed the first commercial silicon transistor, pioneering the use of photolithography and a new form of mass production that allowed multiple transistors on a single wafer. It then developed the "planar" process that protected the circuits from contamination and produced an ultrareliable transistor. It was the planar process that enabled Fairchild to develop the first reliable, mass-produced integrated circuit. And the rest, as they say, is history.[11]

Descending from pioneers like Morse, Bell, and Edison, a separate but closely related infrastructure of electronic and electromechanical products set the stage for today's electronics and telecommunications industries, from television and the digital world to wireless communication and the internet. This realm of advanced technology in turn not only further improved the manufacturing of materials, automobiles, and aircraft but ultimately affected the advancement of every other product in the world.

Most important, not all the discoveries were planned, let alone thought possible. They simply occurred as the infrastructure of electronic components and related products and markets evolved over time, converging to create product concepts and industries in which the unexpected could be expected. Commercial products like broadcast recorders morphed into the VCR, which in turn spawned digital cameras and related industries such as prerecorded tape. In time, far beyond the hopes of AT&T management, the development of the semiconductor advanced telecommunications to levels never previously imagined, ultimately building the infrastructure that supported the development of the internet. In retrospect, it is apparent that without appropriate infrastructure good ideas are more science fiction than science fact, and their conversion to product would never happen.

PAX AMERICANA

On July 16, 1945, the first atomic bomb was detonated on a hundred-foot tower in the New Mexico desert. Those present described an enormous flash of light that filled the whole sky—the brightest light anyone had ever seen—and a blinding heat in the cold desert morning. Watching in awe, project leader Robert Oppenheimer recalled a line from the Bhagavad Gita: "Now I am become Death, the destroyer of worlds." In the wake of the Manhattan Project came a new sense of the power of science, which became a Janus-faced tool of government.

The atomic bomb was the crowning example of the strategic collaboration between government, industry, and science that won the war, ended the Great Depression, and left America the most powerful nation on Earth. The extraordinary and uncompromising drive to victory had developed the greatest industrial infrastructure in human history, dominating virtually every technology, product, and market of importance on the planet. The one additional piece of infrastructure required to secure America's position was the bomb, and it was developed for a single reason: in the hands of the enemy it would alter the outcome of the war. The United States got it first, and in the glow of the postwar 1940s, America had it all.

In the wake of World War II, America stood like a Colossus astride the Earth. In the four years of war, its national income, wealth, and industrial production had more than doubled, while every other industrial nation was left poorer and weaker than before. The United States had by far the best infrastructure of technology, products, and markets in history and was able to choose which of those it would dominate almost without limitation. Producing more than two-thirds of the world's goods and services, the nation had an abundance of land, food, power, raw materials, industrial plants, monetary reserves, scientific talent, and trained workers, and for a brief moment, America alone had the Bomb.

Most viewed the atomic bomb as a technological miracle. Yet the bomb was no more a sudden leap than the phonograph, telephone, radio, or transistor. The intertwining paths that led to the bomb included the discovery of uranium (1789), X-rays (1895), and radium (1898); Einstein's Special Theory of Relativity (1905); early-twentieth-century progress in understanding radioactivity; the discovery of the neutron (1932); the bombardment of atoms with accelerated protons and neutrons (1935); and the demonstration of atomic fission (1939). With the coming of World War II, many laboratories turned their efforts toward producing a nuclear bomb, forming the new isotopes neptunium and plutonium, and developing the concept of the critical mass needed to produce a self-sustaining release of energy. But the final proof that a bomb was possible was the work a man who had fled Germany in 1933.

As a boy in Budapest, reading H. G. Wells's novel about a nuclear war that destroys most of Europe's cities, Leo Szilard concluded that the world should be governed by a group of gifted scientists. He envisioned the development of atomic energy as both a limitless power source and a weapon that might force nations into peace. Devoting his life to that end—living in hotels, doing his thinking in bathtubs—he hit on the idea of an atomic chain reaction and filed the patent in 1934. In 1939, faced with the possibility that Hitler might develop an atomic bomb, Szilard convinced Einstein to send a letter to Roosevelt advising the president that a nuclear bomb might be possible. In a room beneath the stadium stands at the University of Chicago, Szilard built a reactor and achieved a controlled chain reaction, proving that a bomb was feasible. He called it "a black day in the history of mankind." Shunned by the military as a suspect foreigner, he had Einstein sign a second letter to Roosevelt threatening to publish his results unless the project was funded. Ironically, Roosevelt approved the Manhattan Project the day before the attack on Pearl Harbor.[12]

But America's supremely secure position as the only country with the bomb did not outlast the late 1940s. On September 21, 1949, Air Force Chief of Staff Hoyt Vandenburg sent a memorandum to Louis Johnson, then secretary of defense, headed "Long Range Detection of Atomic Explosions": "I believe that an atomic bomb has been detonated over the Asiatic land mass during the period 26 August 1949 to 29 August 1949. I base this on positive information that has been obtained from the system established by the U.S. Air Force for the long range detection of foreign atomic energy activities."[13] The Russians had the bomb. The future of America's long-evolving infrastructure, built by the Edisons, Bells, Fords, Shockleys, and Szilards, emerging triumphant through the wartime sacrifices of a whole people, seemed suddenly less certain.

CHAPTER 4

Evolution, Part 2

*For the fortunate amongst us, the danger, my friends, is com-
fort, the temptation to follow the easy and familiar paths of
personal ambition and financial success so grandly spread before those who have the privilege of an education. But that is
not the road history has marked out for us. There is a Chinese
curse which says, "May he live in interesting times." Like it or
not we live in interesting times. They are times of danger and
uncertainty; but they are also the most creative of any time in
the history of mankind.*

—Robert Kennedy, June 6, 1966

I t had been a dark and bitter year. The war languished in Vietnam,
students rioted around the globe, the Soviets invaded Czechoslova-
kia, North Korea seized the USS *Pueblo,* a B-52 crashed carrying four
hydrogen bombs, Chicago police battered demonstrators at the Demo-
cratic convention, Robert Kennedy was assassinated in Los Angeles, and
Martin Luther King was shot down in Memphis. Discontent was epi-
demic and disillusion profound as American families sat down to dinner
on Christmas Eve, 1968.

Yet for many people the most indelible memory of that evening is
the hush of kitchen clatter as their gatherings were drawn to the

TV—children, grandparents, cousins, in-laws, aunts and uncles—to gaze through a spacecraft window at the mountains and craters of the moon, a phosphorescent world creeping across the screen, curving away to the black of space. And a metallic voice across a quarter million miles from those first men to circle the moon: "Merry Christmas, and God bless all of you—all of you on the good Earth." And once again the Earth seemed good. *Time* magazine scrapped plans to feature "the Dissenter" as Men of the Year, substituting the three astronauts.[1]

Like the editors of *Time,* Americans in the 1960s found it hard to reconcile the extremes of what was, in essence, a phase transition in American history. Emerging from the more placid 1950s—though that decade sowed the seeds of the '60s—the world seemed suddenly polarized between heaven and hell. On one hand, the Cuban missile crisis of 1962 brought the world within minutes of a nuclear holocaust; then came Kennedy's assassination, waves of racial violence, two more assassinations, and Johnson's escalation of the war in Vietnam with massive bombing in the North and a fiftyfold increase in troops sent overseas, intensifying violent protests at home. On the other hand, a nation whose prosperity was unprecedented in human history enacted Johnson's "Great Society," and with it Medicare, Medicaid, aid to education, the "war on poverty," and extensive legislation to protect and extend civil rights. All of this occurred amid an explosion of creative and fractious departures in lifestyle and the arts. Meanwhile, what had begun with Russia's launch of *Sputnik* and the resulting fear of a "missile gap" ended with the planting of the American flag on the moon. And for the first time, in that dawning of the information age, all the turmoil and triumphs could be witnessed nightly, from the comfort of one's living room.

In the 1960s, a long tradition of strenuous self-confidence, of Yankee enterprise and know-how, crowned by success in the war, seemed suddenly uncertain. The primary question was no longer how to solve the problems but whether or not they *could* be solved.

STARS, CASH COWS, AND DOGS

Amid the ferment and confusion of that decade is a less publicized story, one that poses yet another set of polar alternatives—in this case, choices that would heavily influence the future competitiveness of the United States in global markets. In the mid-'60s, two men who would become highly influential around the world offered precepts that would significantly influence economic development. Both dictums were conceived largely through empirical analysis of the same industry. One formulated a profitable business strategy; the other simply explained a fundamental pattern that would define the future of an industry and alter the course of global economics. The first was articulated by Bruce Henderson, founder of the Boston Consulting Group, the second by Gordon Moore, cofounder of Intel Corporation.

A graduate of the Harvard Business School, Bruce Henderson worked at Westinghouse Corporation and Arthur D. Little's management services operation before starting a consulting business for the Boston Safe Deposit and Trust Company. It was from this base of experience that Henderson founded the Boston Consulting Group in 1963. In his book *The Hero's Farewell,* Jeffery Sonnenfeld, a professor at the Yale School of Management, comments that "Bruce Henderson has often been called one of the founding architects of modern strategic planning."[2] The impact of Henderson's ideas about strategy changed the direction and focus of a major segment of the U.S. business and educational community. In an October 2007 article in the *New Yorker,* Ryan Lizza related a conversation he had with Christopher McKenna, author of *The World's Newest Profession,* who said that "BCG . . . helped reinvent the way its clients did business."[3] The effects of the original BCG concepts remain a significant force behind the strategic thinking of America's industrial enterprise to this day.

In a historical overview of the company, BCG notes that one of their "first breakthrough concepts grew out of work for a leading semiconductor manufacturer."[4] The company that Henderson studied was Texas Instruments, and the breakthrough concept, which came out of extensive empirical analysis, was what Henderson called "the experience curve." It was a very simple idea: "unit costs characteristically go down over time as 'experience' increases." The strategy that resulted from this concept became BCG's basic operational strategy and had an immediate and profound appeal to American business. It became known in the hallways and boardrooms of industry and in the classrooms of the most prestigious American business schools as "stars, cash cows, and dogs."

At the foundation of the experience curve was what BCG identified as a critical observation. Understanding the implications of the experience curve made it possible to deliberately acquire and manage competitive advantage. According to Henderson and his associates, costs will decline 10 to 15 percent because of learning, plus an additional 10 to 15 percent because of experience that comes from specialization. This potential 20 to 30 percent cost reduction depends upon volume. Doubling market share over the competition should provide 20 percent or more in margin, which might add 5 to 25 percent or more in after-tax profits. The remaining question was what strategy would allow a business to maximize its use of available resources. The key was market share. Henderson concluded that it was necessary to insure that both the market for a company's products and its market share were large enough to generate the volume necessary to take advantage of the experience curve and thus ensure the success of the business.

Bruce Henderson told BCG's clients that gaining market share over the competition was the road to financial success. Appropriate exploitation of the experience curve would bring better margins, lower costs, and ultimately significant cash generation. For Henderson, the one true test of a successful venture was the generation of cash. "Many businesses require far more cash input than they can ever generate," he said. "A few businesses generate far more cash than they can profitably reinvest. A few businesses are self-sufficient in cash flow. Over time they will become much larger and also large net generators of cash. Most businesses, however, generate very little cash even though they use little. The reported earnings must be reinvested and probably always will. These businesses are 'cash traps.'"5

How important was market share to Henderson? From his standpoint, you had better be in the number-one position if you wanted to be sure of success—if you wanted to be a star. Though the market leader would produce great profits, in the end it was really cash that counted. Profit was a promise. Cash was king. But it was essential that the star of the portfolio maintain its number-one position in market share if it was to continue to shine.

To translate the experience curve into action, Henderson introduced what BCG termed the "growth share matrix." This represented a strategy that was the direct outgrowth of the experience curve. Henderson referred to the matrix as "stars, cash cows, and pets." But pets were quickly translated in the vernacular as dogs.

"Stars, cash cows, and dogs" was powerful in its logic and simplicity, providing a relatively simple decision matrix that could be applied to any product, market, or company. It seemed to explain what was necessary to optimize the use of available resources and. in the American tradition, make money. Money, according to the Boston Consulting Group, resulted from a highly selective decision process. You want to invest in those products and markets that will be stars, which represent areas where the business will experience high market share and high growth. Cash cows are those products—usually former stars—that have high market share and low growth; they throw off lots of cash. Dogs are those products and markets that represent low market share and slow growth for the company; they are a drag on success and are for all practical purposes worthless except in "liquidation." And then there are the "question marks," products and markets that demand significant investment of resources. They usually represent low market share in what appears to be a high-growth environment. In such cases, it is essential that the business make a clear, thoughtful decision relatively quickly. Is further investment worth turning the question mark into a star, or should it be deemed a dog within the context of the business and shut down? Lingering in a state of ambivalence, the question mark will become a large liability and potentially damage the rest of the enterprise.

The United States bought into the logic of the growth share matrix hook, line, and sinker. It is still taught in various forms in American business schools. In one form or another it is still a major factor in planning product, market, and general business strategy in corporate America. It is a prime mover when investment advice is given to an individual or an investment fund in search of immediate profit. Concepts implicit in the growth share matrix lie at the heart of America's short-term thinking—the predominant desire to achieve positive quarterly, if not monthly, results. Above all, the logic of the growth share matrix is implicit in the decision to make or buy. You search for the stars, milk the cows, and dump the dogs.

But in this seemingly logical, fail-safe matrix remains a question that is not so easy to answer: How do you pick the star? An old joke aptly describes the dilemma. Two men are arguing about which product represents the greatest invention of all time. One of them suggests the thermos. "How," asks the other, "could the simple thermos be the greatest invention of all time?" "Well, think about it," says his friend. "If you put hot water in the thermos it keeps it hot. And if you put cold water in it, it keeps it cold." "So what?" says the other. "Well," his friend responds, "the thermos has a decision to make: Does it keep it hot or cold? As far as I know, it has never made a mistake, and yet it's just a glass container. How does it know?" There's the rub. Is it possible that events can conspire to confuse management to the point where it really cannot tell what's hot and what's not? Can one really differentiate that easily between a star, a cash cow, and a dog? Is it possible that stars can become dogs, or dogs become cash cows, or cash cows become stars? And if this were to happen— that is, if management guessed wrong—when would it know that it had made a mistake, and what, if anything, could it do about it?

There's also the question of why one would pursue a dog simply on the chance that it might become a star. Why would a company want to

compete in a market knowing it may never be the principle competitor—
especially when a mistake recognized too late might leave it without re-
course? Even if management decided that certain products and markets
were strategic, regardless of any near-term benefit, investors would be
reticent to support an apparent collection of dogs in lieu of existing stars.
The fundamental issue is whether the growth share matrix based on the
experience curve represents how the world really works. Is the concept
behind the growth share matrix sound, or does it simply support an opportunistic strategy popularized for its promise of short-term profits?

Part of the answer to this question lies in a concept based, like Henderson's, on empirical analysis derived from observations directly related to
the semiconductor industry. In 1965, Gordon Moore, cofounder of Intel,
penned a brief description of what he observed about the design and development of the transistor and the industry that would be built around it.
Carver Meade, one of America's most prestigious computer scientists and
the Gordon and Betty Moore Professor Emeritus at the California Institute of Technology, termed these predictions "Moore's Law."

MOORE'S LAW

The year 1956 was seminal for William Shockley and electronics. Shockley and his former associates, John Bardeen and Walter Brattain, were
awarded the Nobel Prize for inventing the transistor. That same year
Shockley left Bell Labs and established Shockley Semiconductor Laboratory as a new division of Beckman Instruments. Located in the Stanford Industrial Park, the division was set up to develop a "four-layer
diode" that would increase the speed and usage of current transistors.
Also that same year, only a few miles away, Ampex introduced the first
practical video recorder. The destiny of the two events is one of history's
ironies. An outgrowth of the Ampex recorder, the VCR used more semiconductors at the time than any other product. Yet the VCR, which
should have been a major factor in the growth of semiconductor manufacturing in the United States, was defaulted to Japan. Thus the seeds of

Silicon Valley and of Japan's subsequent dominance in consumer electronics were sown in the same year, a stone's throw apart.

Shockley's concept of technological advancement in the arena of semiconductor development would soon change the competitive landscape across the globe. But this shifting landscape resulted less from Shockley's vision for the new enterprise than from his ability to hire a remarkable group of technical and managerial talent. The initial roster at Shockley Semiconductor included Julius Blank, Victor Grinich, Jean Hoerni, Eugene Kleiner, Jay Last, Gordon Moore, Robert Noyce, and Sheldon Roberts. But this "traitorous eight," as Shockley later called them, tired within a year of his difficult personality and left to form Fairchild Semiconductor, a division of Fairchild Camera and Instrument Corporation. These eight men, along with other executives from Fairchild Semiconductor, including Wilf Corrigan, Jerry Sanders, and Charlie Sporck, would go on to found most of the key companies in the part of Santa Clara Valley that journalist Dan Hoefler in 1971 christened "Silicon Valley."

With the perfection of the silicon transistor and the development of the integrated circuit, the "traitorous eight" provided the foundation for what we now call the information age. Julius Blank went on to cofound Xicor. Victor Grinich became a professor at Stanford and the University of California, Berkeley. Jean Hoerni, along with Jay Last and Sheldon Roberts, formed Amelco Semiconductor, which became Teledyne Semiconductor. Hoerni later founded Union Carbide Electronics and Intersil. Eugene Kleiner launched Kleiner Perkins, one of the preeminent American venture capital firms and a principal investor in such companies as Amazon.com, AOL, Electronic Arts, Genentech, Google, Sun Microsystems, and LSI Logic. In 1968, Robert Noyce and Gordon Moore, coming respectively from the positions of CEO and director of research and development at Fairchild, founded Intel. Wilf Corrigan, Fairchild CEO after Noyce, went on to cofound LSI Logic, Charlie Sporck to launch National Semiconductor, and Jerry Sanders to form Advanced Micro Devices, which competed with Intel as the number-two supplier of microprocessors.

These incredibly creative and motivated individuals and those attracted to them launched the information age as we know it, spawning the digital revolution, the internet, and what may in retrospect be a turning point in human evolution. What they initiated—an explosion of technological innovation of unimaginable proportions—was anticipated in a brief article by Gordon Moore, "Cramming More Components onto Integrated Circuits," in the April 1965 issue of *Electronics* magazine. It was this article that introduced what the world now refers to as "Moore's Law."

> Reduced cost is one of the big attractions of integrated electronics, and the cost advantage continues to increase as the technology evolves toward the production of larger and larger circuit functions on a single semiconductor substrate. For simple circuits, the cost per component is nearly inversely proportional to the number of components, the result of the equivalent piece of semiconductor in the equivalent package containing more components. But as components are added, decreased yields more than compensate for the increased complexity, tending to raise the cost per component. Thus there is a minimum cost at any given time in the evolution of the technology. At present it is reached when 50 components are used per circuit. . . . The complexity for minimum component costs has increased at a rate of roughly a factor of two per year. . . . That means by 1975, the number of components per integrated circuit for minimum cost will be 65,000. I believe that such a large circuit can be built on a single wafer.[6]

What Moore's Law implied was a doubling of computing power per given area of silicon every year at basically the same cost; that is, the number of transistors that could be placed inexpensively on an integrated circuit would continue to increase exponentially. Moore modified his projection in 1975, suggesting that the number of transistors on a chip would double every two years, a prediction that has proven incredibly accurate.

LIKE STEPPING IN FRONT OF
AN EXPRESS TRAIN

Some may feel that Moore's projection fails to consider the complex variables that affect the manufacturing of semiconductors. Yet the impact of his road map for the semiconductor industry has changed the competitive advantage of not just companies but nations. Moore's Law has called into question commonly accepted business strategy in America and has undeniably affected major investment decisions on an international scale. In unexpected ways, Moore's Law is beginning to alter the course of political relationships between nations no less than military might did in the past.

Many companies and nations that participate in the semiconductor industry have aligned their economic pursuits with the success of that industry. It has become strategic to their long-term interests. It is evident to them that what Gordon Moore predicted over forty years ago has proceeded just about as he projected, with no clear end in sight. Most participants in the industry now feel that to assume things will be different in the future is like stepping in front of an express train. It might stop in time, but who wants to take the risk?

A 2003 publication from the Anderson School at UCLA quotes an "industry observer" as saying that "Moore's Law is important because it is the only stable ruler we have today. It's a sort of technological barometer. It very clearly tells you that if you take the information processing power you have today and multiply by two, that will be what your competition will be doing 18 months from now. And that is where you too will have to be."[7] It is unlikely that a prediction made by one person near the inception of an industry has ever resulted in greater capital or technological investment. Moore's Law has become a part of any consideration regarding future investment in the manufacturing of semiconductors worldwide.

Some have suggested that Moore's Law could be the ruination of the industry by spurring runaway investment beyond anyone's ability to fund the projected growth in cost and need for capital. Others have criticized the simplicity of the concept by noting—in great detail—that segments of the industry grow at substantially different rates. Some suggest that the rate of growth Moore projected will by definition overpower the size of the market necessary to absorb the production. For years the semiconductor industry has experienced major cyclical periods of over- and undersupply caused by fluctuations in the economy and massive changes in technological development. These periods have brought great pain and concern to those who feel that they must continue to make what often amount to multibillion-dollar bets in the face of an unclear future and little near-term return on investment. Transistor demand has increased at a compound rate of 50 percent per year since the 1970s, while semiconductor devices have fallen in price at an average compound rate of 29 percent. All the while, producers have tried to maintain or increase market share in spite of any short-term drop or surge in market demand. All of this investment and attendant risk have been assumed by the participants with full knowledge that semiconductor prices have dropped and will continue to drop, often precipitously.

So why have so many committed so much based on the fulfillment of one man's prediction? Look at it this way: If you start with one penny and double the amount every day, in thirty-one days you will have over $21 million. Another week and you would approach $3 billion. Such is the power of exponential growth. In 1964, one year before Gordon Moore wrote his prophetic article, semiconductor sales reached $1 billion. Today sales are in excess of $260 billion. It is projected that in a dozen years the number may reach $1 trillion. And this growth in revenues has occurred while prices have dropped at an average compound rate of 29 percent annually. But that is really chump change when you realize that $260 billion of silicon makes possible a $2 trillion electronic systems industry today.[8] Moreover, that industry has paralleled chip growth since 1995. So it is possible to imagine an electronic systems market approaching $4 to $5 trillion in the next twelve to fifteen years—an amount equal to the current GDP of Japan, today the second-largest national economy behind the United States. But beyond this is an essential fact: electronic systems remain fundamental to the success of every other product and market in the world.

RUNNING WITH THE RED QUEEN

One of the more prominent spokespersons on the potential impact of Moore's Law is Ray Kurzweil, who invented, among many other things, the first practical flatbed scanner, launching a multibillion-dollar industry. Granted the National Medal of Technology, named Inventor of the Year by MIT and the Boston Museum of Science, inducted into the U.S. Patent Office's National Inventors Hall of Fame, honored by three U.S. presidents, and recipient of eleven honorary degrees and numerous other awards, Kurzweil has become one of the most recognized inventors in America. An eminent prophet of technology, Kurzweil contends that the curve of exponentially increasing technology rises smoothly, as though on rails. He sees it as a force of nature—a voyage of tiny advances that is unstoppable. Though software has not advanced as fast as hardware, he estimates that its value doubles every six years, noting that his company's voice-recognition software, which cost $5,000 for a thousand-word vocabulary in 1985, cost $50 for a hundred thousand words by the turn of the century. "An analysis of the history of technology shows that technological change is exponential, contrary to the common-sense 'intuitive linear' view," wrote Kurzweil in 2001.[9]

> So we won't experience 100 years of progress in the 21st century—it will be more like 20,000 years of progress (at today's rate). The 'returns,' such as chip speed and cost-effectiveness, also increase exponentially. There's even exponential growth in the rate of exponential growth. Within a few decades, machine intelligence will surpass human intelligence, leading to the Singularity—technological change so rapid and profound it represents a rupture in the fabric of human history. The implications include the merger of biological and nonbio-

logical intelligence, immortal software-based humans, and ultra-high levels of intelligence that expand outward in the universe at the speed of light.

This might sound like science fiction were it not rooted in such realities as those reported in a 2005 address by Chang-Gyu Hwang, president and CEO of Samsung Electronics' semiconductor business: "The business focus is shifted as technologies and standards evolve. Samsung has redefined accepted memory growth standards. Where Moore's Law represents semiconductor density and advancement doubling every 18 months, Samsung has now doubled memory density every year for six consecutive years since . . . 1999, developing the industry approved New Memory Growth Model—an entirely new industry standard."[10] Hwang went on to suggest that by 2010 all digital devices would be in an integrated format without boundaries, a form soon to be known as "fusion technology," a convergence of information technology, biotechnology, and nanotechnology that will supplant PC-centered devices with those of the mobile and digital era. Hwang also predicted that by 2030 semiconductor technology will match the vast, hundred-terabyte memory capacity of the human brain.

The April 12, 2007, issue of *EE Times* reported that Toshiba expects the bit growth for NAND flash memory to expand ten times by 2009 while anticipating a drop in the average selling price of 50 percent per year.[11] To participate in the achievement of these results, Toshiba expects to invest heavily in new design and manufacturing technology and plant expansion. This is counter to the whole concept of stars, cash cows, and dogs. Why would the company make these investments, which will amount to billions of dollars, when it does not have a commanding market share in the NAND flash business? First, Toshiba and others will learn how to make money at these ever-decreasing prices. Second, the manufacturing of low-cost solid-state memory that requires no moving parts and provides exponential growth in storage capacity will enable new and increasingly integrated end-use designs for cell phones, digital cameras, notebooks, and television displays, with features and computing power unimaginable today. And third, if Toshiba does not continue to invest, it will likely find it impossible to stay in the game as the competition continues to improve its design expertise and manufacturing know-how. Toshiba considers these advances in technological capability fundamental not only to the long-term success of the corporation but to the evolving infrastructure of Japan. Like most Japanese companies, Toshiba has learned over the years that the success of the corporation and the country are interdependent.

Moore's Law fosters a condition similar to that of the Red Queen in Lewis Carroll's *Through the Looking Glass*, who must run as fast as she can just to stay in the same place. There is an ever-increasing need for additional investment to capture exponential growth and the endless rewards of technological advance. But constant demand for advances in the state of the art is offset by the unsettling knowledge that if you stop for a moment to catch your breath, your competition will pass you by, and you will never catch up. At that level of risk, one can see the lure of Henderson's growth share matrix: Be opportunistic, look for products that provide overwhelming market share, and, above all, generate a lot of cash in a relatively short time. When the star burns out and the cash dries up, get out. Leave the dogs to someone else.

But company decisions based on Henderson's growth share matrix may simply deal with short-term phenomena rather than long-term investments in a growth business. Do these opportunistic decisions exploit and increase existing infrastructure in related technologies, products, and markets? While there is nothing wrong with exploring every avenue that enhances short-term profitability and cash flow, the real question is whether or not the company is staying on the technological road that will continue to support future success.

A decision to stay the course requires not only insight into the business but considerable courage. Though the anticipated payoff may be very large, the cost of sticking with it can become extremely expensive. Henderson had an answer for such a paradox. He suggested that on the growth share matrix this type of situation might be denoted by a question mark, representing a business opportunity that could become a sink hole for available resources without gaining adequate market share advantage. It might turn into a dog business, not the star one hoped for. Henderson suggested that in this situation management would have to choose what to pursue. If the deal didn't look right, the company should get out and find another.

Contrary to Henderson's matrix of stars, cash cows, and dogs, faced with the relentless growth of interrelated technologies, products, and markets in the world of Moore's Law, you ultimately have no choice. You are in, or you are out. And if you decide you want out, know that you may never get back in. Such was the dilemma that Eastman Kodak faced in 1975.

"YOU PRESS THE BUTTON; WE DO THE REST"

It was George Eastman's invention of roll film in 1884, replacing fragile glass plates with a photo-emulsion coating on paper, and his patent on the roll film camera in 1888 that made Eastman Kodak a household name and put the United States at the forefront of image processing on film. For more than a hundred years Kodak dominated this market. Eastman understood the need for a quality product and effective marketing and delivered on both fronts. While the quality of his film and camera was excellent, his concept of marketing was exceptional. Not only was the Kodak camera easy to operate and very inexpensive, but the real money lay in a marketing policy that tied the sale of the camera to selling and processing the film and printing the pictures on Kodak paper. By the mid-1970s, largely as a result of extraordinary profits from the sale and development of film, Kodak had achieved a 90 percent share of the U.S. film market and an 85 percent share of cameras sold in America. In spite of its successful camera business, the expertise developed in ensuring the quality of its film led Kodak to consider itself primarily a film company.

In the world of information, communication rests predominantly on image processing technology. From 1921 to 1963, Kodak spent $120 million perfecting the ability to record color on film.[12] That Kodak became the principal supplier of image processing equipment and materials to a broad-based consumer and professional photography market owed much to its production of marvelous color images. Its photofinishing process was considered the standard of the industry and was for years a major barrier to competition. Aware that manufacturing competence lay at the heart of Kodak's ability to provide the world's best color film, its top management remained immersed in the design and manufacturing technology developed at the company's huge fabrication facility in Rochester, New York.

But film for the consumer camera market, the largest segment of Kodak's business, was not the company's only source of income. Back in the early 1880s, French physiologist Etienne-Jules Marey had devised a camera that could record a sequence of images on a glass plate and later on strips of film. Working under Edison in 1891, William K. L. Dickson produced the first true motion-picture camera, a convergence of Marey's work and Eastman's roll film. Dickson's key contribution was a sprocket mechanism linked to the camera's shutter, which momentarily stopped the perforated film roll for each exposure. From Dickson's Kinetograph (camera) and Kinetoscope (projector) and later improvements by the Lumière brothers in France came the motion-picture industry. Kodak film became fundamental to that industry.

Even the dawn of television was initially another boon for Kodak. Four years before Eastman founded the company, both Edison and Bell had mused about the possibility of telephone devices that would transmit images as well as sound. They were undoubtedly familiar with the earlier work of Giovanna Caselli, the first person to transmit an image over wire, and Willoughby Smith, who discovered the photoconductivity of selenium in 1873, suggesting the possibility of converting images into electronic signals. But the development of modern television awaited the input of many inventors, notably Paul Nipkow's scanning disc (1884), A.

A. Campbell-Swinton's electronic scanner (1908), the electro mechanical systems of John Baird and Charles Jenkins (1920s), Vladimir Zworykin's TV camera tube based on Campbell-Swinton's ideas, and the first complete electronic television system developed by Philo T. Farnsworth in 1927. Farnsworth held his first demonstration in 1928; the first image transmitted was a dollar sign. After a long legal battle, the U.S. Patent Office awarded Farnsworth priority over Zworykin for the invention of television. Zworykin had been working with RCA, which finally paid $1 million for Farnsworth's patents in 1939 and began producing television receivers.[13] In 1940 Peter Goldmark of CBS invented a color television system with 343 lines of resolution.

By 1950, when the FCC released its first color television standard and the number of TV sets in the United States had increased tenfold in two years, movie studios began to realize that their theaters were about to encounter an ominous form of competition. But the fact that TV shows were done live or recorded on film only meant there were now even more uses for Kodak products. Anyone watching a film, whether on TV or in a theater, was more than likely to be viewing information stored on material produced by Kodak.

Kodak seemed to have it all. The production of film for both movies and personal use—a virtual monopoly for Kodak—was not only a star business but a magnificent cash cow. As the world's preeminent producer of cameras and film, Kodak reached $1 billion in revenues by 1962. By 1981, its sales reached $10 billion. The film business provided Kodak with strong profits and growth until the mid-1990s. The year 1996 marked the company's peak, with sales cresting at $16 billion and operating profits just over $2.2 billion. But it was also the turning point for Kodak. The next ten years undid what Kodak had built in the previous one hundred. For more than a century, prosperity at Kodak was a given. Today the world is awash in vivid images so current, available, and ubiquitous that the effect on the politics and economics of nations is rapid and profound. But in this world, founded largely by the company who coined the phrase "you press the button; we do the rest," Kodak is becoming an afterthought.

The warning signs of a brewing storm had been everywhere for the last half century. In 1956, two events occurred in northern California that should have caused a major stir in every form of film business—the invention of the practical video recorder and the development of the transistor as a commercial product. With the advent of these two products, electronic imaging on a grand scale was born. If the potential impact had been assessed correctly in real time, there would have been plenty of opportunity for strategies that might have produced a different outcome. No such assessment was made, certainly not from a national perspective. Yet the arrival of these inventions did not go unnoticed; when Ampex introduced its broadcast video recorder, everyone connected to the industry knew it would affect the future of multimedia. Hollywood knew, and Kodak knew. The entire television industry knew, especially the broadcasting companies. Some onlookers expressed fear that the industry based on film as a storage medium was in jeopardy. On the other hand, very few people in the multimedia industry understood that what was happening in video would somehow be inexorably tied to the launch of the semiconductor industry.

Ibuka and Morita of Sony clearly did grasp the importance of the situation. They had been learning about the semiconductor while working on consumer and commercial audio products since 1953. Just as Sony saw the need to take advantage of a license agreement with Bell Laboratories for rights to further develop the transistor, Matsushita sold 35 percent of the company to Phillips in 1952 in return for Phillips's cooperation in transferring much of its technological understanding and intellectual property pertaining to consumer electronics. Sony and Matsushita were both aware that magnetic recording would someday be applicable to video imaging. It was only a matter of time before both companies would capitalize on one of the great technological developments of the century.

Broadcast video recording, developed initially by Ampex but oriented toward the consumer market, required the integration of many technologies and products, including the ability to manufacture millions of reliable items at a reasonable cost. All of these component parts were under development in Japan, where consumer products were considered a strategic industry. The electronically operated camera was being perfected in Japan, as was the mass production of tape decks with the precision required for interchangeable tapes. Several Japanese companies were developing the display technology that converted electronic signals into television pictures. The convergence of these technologies and products had become the mantra of Sony and Matsushita. It was therefore only a matter of time before they both introduced one of the most important and economically powerful consumer products of the age, producing the first commercially viable VCRs, Beta and VHS, in 1975 and 1976.

As was true of so many seminal advances, both video recording and the transistor had been invented in the United States. Yet the reaction of American industry to the implications of these new, highly convergent electronic technologies and products was sporadic, opportunistic, and limited in scope. Japan understood exactly what was happening and took advantage of America's lack of a national strategy. Japan wanted to build not just a business but a nation.

By 1970 a significant portion of the United States business and investment community had bought into Henderson's growth share matrix. In America, opportunism had trumped strategy. Asia, however, bought into Moore's Law.

"LET'S TALK AGAIN IN FIFTY YEARS"

Beginning in 1956, major changes in the multimedia industry took place rapidly. On the surface it appeared to be business as usual. It wasn't. Beneath the surface of revenue and profits much was happening that would not only bring great harm to Kodak but would severely damage America's image processing industry.

In 1956, shortly after the first sale of a broadcast video recorder, CBS videotaped *Douglas Edwards and the News*, and for the first time electronic images were recorded and replayed for the television audience. Ampex and Sony signed their joint agreement in 1958. Sony had already licensed transistor technology from Bell Labs and had developed a level of expertise in electronic packaging based on that technology, which it also shared with Ampex. Ampex broke the agreement in 1960 and signed a joint venture agreement with Toshiba. Sony then got a fully paid-up license to produce video recorders, and Toshiba was brought into the game.

In 1959 the integrated circuit was designed by two Americans, Jack Kilby and Bob Noyce, and growth in the semiconductor industry began to accelerate. Nikon entered the home movie market in 1960 with a camera that included the first cadmium sulfide sensor to determine the intensity of available light. And in 1963 Bell and Howell introduced a "dial" camera designed and manufactured by Canon that offered a half-frame format in a very compact design. Shutter speeds were set manually. The aperture could be set manually or automatically using a cadmium sulfide sensor. By 1964, NASA was transmitting television pictures from the moon using a television camera based on cathode ray technology.

Yashika Electro of Japan introduced an all-electronic stepless shutter in the mid-'60s. Japan was beginning to increase the sophistication of the camera using sensors and small motors that were at first applied only to film but in time would apply to all cameras whether they used film or electronic imaging.

In 1969 Willard Boyle and George Smith completed the first design of a charge-coupled device. The CCD is a light-sensitive integrated circuit used in a wide variety of applications, primarily imaging. From this work, Bell Laboratories built the first solid-state video camera using a CCD device to collect the image.

In September 1970, Ampex introduced its Instavideo product line, based on Ampex video-recording patents and using a helical scan recording method. This was the world's first attempt at a totally automatic, compact, lightweight video recorder and camera for the home and commercial markets. Under license to Ampex Corporation, several Japanese companies, including Sony, Matsushita, Japan Victor, and Toshiba, began to work in earnest on a home video recorder. That same year, I watched a demonstration of HDTV in Japan sponsored by NHK, Japan's broadcast network. The prototype equipment I was shown included a combination of analog and digital technology. Behind the life-like picture on the screen, HDTV required the ability to process large amounts of data, a requirement that years later would spur development of high-definition displays, computer systems, and very sophisticated semiconductor components.

In 1971, Intel introduced the world's first microprocessor, catapulting the computer industry into futures unimagined. The computer became a principal component in the storage, editing, and distribution of digital images. In that same year the Department of Defense contracted the firm of Bolt Beranek and Newman to build the ARPANET, the precursor to the internet.

In 1975, Sony introduced its "beta" format VCR, which it called Betamax. Matsushita, Japan Victor, and other Japanese companies followed with the VHS format within a year. The largest single user of semiconductors of any product then in existence, the VCR became the most successful electronic consumer product to date and the primary factor in the growth of Japan's consumer electronics industry.

Kodak was not entirely asleep at the switch. In the same year that the VCR was about to take off, Steve Sasson, a Kodak engineer, constructed the first still-image digital camera. Using the Fairchild CCD sensor, it was able to record a single digital image onto a digital cassette tape in about twenty-three seconds. Kodak was now fully aware that there was going to be a future in filmless digital cameras. The question was what would it do with this information.

In 1976 Canon introduced the first 35mm camera with a built-in microprocessor; and Konica, another Japanese camera company, brought out the first compact point-and-shoot auto-focus camera. In 1979, Pentax, also Japanese, produced the first single-lens reflex camera using through-the-lens auto focus. And in 1981 Sony introduced its Mavica electronic camera. This "Magnetic Video Camera" recorded images on a floppy disk and played them back through a standard television set. A single-lens reflex camera with interchangeable lenses, its resolution was specified to equal that of a standard TV monitor.

Now a fully commercialized electronic camera had been introduced. All that was needed was improvement in performance. There was constant pressure to that end within Japanese industry. With the growing demand for HDTV, already a decade in development, their need for exponential improvement in image processing, computing power, and memory storage increased almost in lockstep with the need to improve the quality of photographic images. The confluence of semiconductor technology, electronically controlled motors, auto-focus systems, and light sources came together in a full array of consumer products that were themselves advancing the state of magnetic recording and display technology. In turn, magnetic recording—first audio and then video—would enhance analog and then digital electronics. The result was the creation of a massive infrastructure that would totally reorder the world of photography and shift the balance of power from chemical processing to electronic imaging.

As this highly sophisticated infrastructure developed, it became apparent to Japanese industry that one technology—the ability to process digital information—was imperative for improving electronic image processing and at the same time insuring that all parts of this ecosystem could be interconnected seamlessly. Digital technology had significant advantages over analog. Analog signals used an inordinate amount of bandwidth, complicated the transfer of information from one product to another, and were subject to signal degradation. The solution lay in the advancement of semiconductor technology. Semiconductors are specifically adaptable to digital signal processing and provide exponential increases in data management speed, functionality, and memory capacity.

Japanese electronics companies clearly understood that digital electronics was needed to insure the promise of high-definition television.

This was at the heart of my discussions with Akio Morita. The payoff of going digital was at the core of every Japanese and ultimately every Asian consumer electronics company. Going digital would exponentially accelerate the convergence of Japanese consumer electronic products and markets, building a massive infrastructure that would become the basis for future technological advances. Japanese industry was already visualizing the combination of a camera, cell phone, and computer as a single unit. So when I discussed stars, cash cows, and dogs with businessmen in Asia in the 1970s, '80s, and early '90s, their response was always the same: "Who knows what will become a star, a cash cow, or a dog? This is a short-term mind-set. Let's talk again in fifty years."

A "CRAPPY BUSINESS"

Kodak knew that electronic image processing could become a problem. But in spite of its development of a digital camera prototype, and Sony's introduction of its all-electronic camera, the Mavica, Kodak's management, including CEO Colby Chandler, felt that the public preferred pictures taken with Kodak cameras, using Kodak film, and printed on Kodak paper. Without question, the resolution of film in the 1980s was substantially better than that of electronic imaging. A standard 35mm film negative contains, according to some estimates, the equivalent of about twenty megapixels, nearly a hundred times what would have been available in 1981. In addition, Kodak cameras were very cheap and easy to operate. If there was to be a problem, Kodak's management felt it would probably take a long time to materialize, and Kodak had the time and resources to win. Yet some within the company were very concerned. A Harvard Business School paper, "Kodak and the Digital Revolution," quoted one manager as saying, "'It [the prospect of electronic image processing] sent fear through the company.' The reaction was, 'My goodness, photography is dead.'"[14]

But probably the biggest surprise to Kodak was the rise of Fujifilm, which in 1981 represented the dominant share of the film market in

Japan. Competing in the U.S. market since 1965, it was the first film company to produce 400 ASA color film. Selling its products at prices 20 percent below Kodak's, it began to take market share. Moreover, customers were very pleased with Fuji's quality. Then in 1981, while Kodak was wondering about electronic imaging, Fuji became the official sponsor of film at the 1984 Olympics. (Kodak didn't want to foot the bill.) This turned out to be a marketing coup for Fuji, whose share of the U.S. and world film market began a steady ascent. By 1990, Kodak's share of the worldwide film market was approximately 60 percent. Fuji had 15 percent. From that point, the drop in Kodak's share and the rise of Fujifilm followed a linear path. A decade later, the two companies had split the market worldwide. Thereafter, Fujifilm sales exceeded Kodak's.

Though Kodak had always seen itself as a film company, it wasn't long before it began to understand that electronic imaging could threaten the very core of the business—just as it realized it was in the fight of its life simply trying to maintain market share in film. The problem for Kodak was that until 1980 it had a virtual monopoly on film and cameras in the United States (a market large enough by itself to sustain Kodak's ambitions) and was thus isolated from any evolving infrastructure of related technologies that might have propelled it into the digital world.

In Japan, where consumer electronics was becoming a strategic industry, many companies were approaching photography from a multiplicity of technological disciplines, including film and electronics. Japanese companies saw success in consumer electronics as an imperative. They understood that over time it might be difficult to tell a consumer product from a commercial product; thus the potential markets for consumer products were probably much larger than one might expect. While Japan's industrial base embraced Moore's Law from any number of angles, the United States considered consumer electronics a dog business. Japanese corporate managers felt that the exponential growth predicted by Moore would more than likely affect related technologies, products, and markets in a similar fashion. The power of convergence and evolving infrastructure would also give their country a major competitive advantage in markets beyond consumer electronics. What the CEO of Kodak faced in 1981 in Rochester, New York, the CEO of General Motors was facing in Detroit, Michigan. What was happening to photography was happening to automobiles. Aided by the cohesive relationships inherent in the Keiretsu, Japan had determined that a national strategy encompassing convergence and infrastructure would provide a significant competitive advantage in a world of global competition.

Losing market share in film, Kodak began to understand what was coming. There was a growing fear that digital image processing might spell the end of film as a growth business, perhaps even the total marginalization of film photography. But Kodak had experienced market dominance and high profits for fifty years. Anything less made Kodak management uncomfortable and investors more so. As one senior vice president and director of Kodak research commented, "We're moving into an information-based company, [but] it's very hard to find anything [with profit margins] like color photography that is legal."[15]

Kodak tried everything in the book. In an attempt to jump-start a digital research program, it first tried to solve its technological problems internally. As the Harvard Business School analysis noted in interviews with the head of Kodak's digital research group, "Kodak wanted to do it in their own way, from Rochester and largely with their own people. That meant it wasn't going to work. The difference between their traditional business and digital is so great. The tempo is different. The kind of skills you need are different. [Kay Whitmore, company president] and [Colby Chandler] would tell you they wanted change, but they didn't want to force the pain on the organization."

Kodak also attempted to ward off declining film and camera sales by purchasing several medical companies including the bioscience and lab research firms Clinical Diagnostics and Sterling Drug, for which they paid $5 billion.

In the early 1990s, Kodak attempted to combine film photography with digital images ultimately stored on CD-ROM. None of these programs really worked. Then, in 1993, the company hired George Fisher, former CEO of Motorola. Fisher decided that Kodak's business was really based on imaging, not film, and he began to sell off all those divisions not directly related to Kodak's imaging business, using the proceeds to pay down debt. He also attempted to reenergize Kodak's traditional camera and film business by concentrating on China. In an effort to give Kodak a local manufacturing and distribution presence, the company purchased three Chinese companies, forming Kodak China. The effort was a success and became Kodak's second-largest market for cameras and film. But a major problem wouldn't go away: digital imaging was becoming a reality.

Fisher then attempted to combine Kodak's digital research activities in an effort to design state-of-the-art digital cameras. But the competition from Japan was too severe for Kodak to do it on its own. So in 1997 he turned to relationships with companies that offered Kodak the opportunity to outsource most digital photographic equipment—again, companies principally in Japan.

By the late 1990s, Kodak digital cameras began to penetrate the U.S. market. Another American competitor, Hewlett Packard, entered the fray with a line of digital cameras. In both cases the cameras were largely outsourced. According to a survey published in January 2007 by ChangeWave Alliance, 15 percent of consumers owned Kodak digital cameras, and 4 percent owned Hewlett Packard digital cameras; only 3 percent planned to buy a Kodak digital camera and 1 percent, a Hewlett Packard camera.[16] The remaining 96 percent planned to buy a Japanese digital camera. That same month a Lyra Research Industry report indicated that worldwide digital camera shipments will exceed 130 million units by 2010, approximately 30 million units more than were shipped in 2006.[17] The same research organization predicted that "by late 2008 or early 2009, the cumulative number of camera phones shipped would surpass the cumulative number of both conventional and digital cameras shipped in the entire history of photography, and camera phones have been on the market for less than a decade." Asia—principally Japan,

South Korea, Taiwan, and China—is by far the largest manufacturer of cell phones, let alone those with cameras built in. Virtually none are manufactured in the United States.

For a brief period in 2005 Kodak actually led digital camera sales in the United States. Its digital sales surged 40 percent while its film-based business fell 18 percent. But the moment was short-lived. According to *Business Week,* in that same year Antonio Perez, Kodak's CEO, called digital cameras a "crappy business."[18] Why? Simple: no margin and no profits. So Perez announced, as many had before him, that Kodak would pursue a different strategy.

FROM CONVERGENCE TO CRITICAL MASS

A lot of articles have been written about Kodak's troubles since the early '80s. Many discussions have been held in business schools and elsewhere in an attempt to learn from Kodak's mistakes. But like General Motors in automobiles, Kodak had little chance to compete as a digital camera company, let alone succeed as a film business in the manner to which it had become accustomed. American business decided many years ago that consumer electronics was a dog business. As a result, the low margins, high capital investment, and intense competition in an industry that after 1965 began to track Moore's Law became anathema to investors in U.S. companies who had gotten used to a far more favorable financial model of risk and reward. At first slowly, and then with a passion, America abandoned the industry—especially its manufacturing base. Over time the convergence of the infrastructure developing in Japan and the rest of Asia began to establish a confluence of integrated manufacturing and design technologies. Based significantly on the semiconductor industry, that infrastructure began to replicate Moore's Law. And as everyone who understands Moore's Law knows, if you don't keep abreast of the competition, the exponential advance of the technology and the cost of its development will eat you alive. Once you lose your position, it's a very difficult road back.

For one hundred years in the American film and camera business, there was essentially only Kodak. Film fit all the parameters of a star that generated lots of cash. For years, Kodak had been a poster child for proponents of Henderson's growth share matrix. Yet the film business, like all related technologies, was subject to the principles underlying convergence and infrastructure. Though it took years, these principles would change everything as they moved exponentially across the spectrum of technological development. The concept of the growth share matrix, however cash efficient in the short term, became Kodak's nemesis.

When Japanese companies like Sony, steeped in the precepts of Moore's Law, decided to enter the business, they had a different approach. With a more global concept of technological development, they understood at their point of entry that camera and imaging technology would become part of a larger infrastructure of products and markets. The general market that would provide the parameters for the development of cameras and imaging technology was consumer electronics. In that context, cameras, audio and video recording, semiconductors, and television were all connected. The Japanese realized that the economic rewards of success in consumer electronics were of national significance, deserving a major commitment of resources. For Japan, infrastructure was synonymous with critical mass. Kodak was soon staring down the barrel of a huge competitive force that included Canon, Casio, Contax, Epson, Fujifilm, JVC, Konica, Minolta, Kyocera, Nikon, Olympus, Panasonic, Pentax, Ricoh, Sony, and Toshiba. And then came Korea, Taiwan, and China.

CHAPTER 5

Chasing the Rainbow:
The Cost of Infrastructure

As the cost of building an infrastructure rises exponentially, the price of reentry to those who have lost that infrastructure becomes overwhelming.

In 1878, Almon B. Strowger, a Kansas City undertaker, invented a switch that could connect one phone line to many others. It was the precursor to the rotary phone. In 1896, one of Strowger's associates replaced the switch with a rotary dial. More than a hundred years later, rotary phones operating on a pulse rather than a tone are still for sale—a fortunate fact for callers who feign using a rotary phone to break through the menu maze and capture a live person.

Within the housing of the rotary phone, which remained for years the main method of remote voice communication, is a simple electromechanical product with few functions. It displays neither the number you call nor who is calling; it provides no date, time, or tally of minutes spoken. It is not wireless and has no memory, computational functions, video games, music, calendar, phone directory, or spreadsheet. It doesn't dial numbers for you, remember calls, automatically determine which phone system is used in what country, or hand off from one cell site to another. It can take no photographs or videoclips, let alone send them instantaneously to another phone, computer, or television set. It simply recognizes and transmits a signal resulting from the clicks of a dial so that another phone somewhere at the end of a wire will recognize the call and connect. But it has done that with utmost reliability for well over one hundred years. Now, almost overnight, overwhelmed by Moore's Law, it is a collectors' item. Yet the evolution of the simple rotary phone provides a major lesson in competitiveness, demonstrating in graphic terms why the world is not flat.

Every one of those classic black phones was the property of AT&T, which became the world's largest corporation and most powerful communications company. It owned every part of its immense operation. It was *the* telephone company, "Ma Bell." It had built a massive infrastructure, wiring the nation to transmit telephone calls to central offices in every community, and from there to the home. This highly complex communications grid required multibillion-dollar investments year after year with the ever-growing need for more switches, over- and underground lines, and millions of new phones. AT&T reached every family and business in the country. Like the Great Lakes or the Grand Canyon, AT&T was an American fixture.

In 1907, AT&T president Theodore Vail coined a slogan that served as the company guideline for decades: "One system, one policy, universal service."[1] That policy was reinforced in 1913, when AT&T settled an antitrust case with the government. In return for divesting its control over Western Union and allowing for noncompetitive local phone companies to interconnect with AT&T's long-distance network, the company was granted monopolistic powers. You didn't buy a phone from AT&T; you leased it. You leased everything and bought nothing. The customer could choose which products he or she wanted, but they remained the property of AT&T. The phones and all of the component switches and transmission equipment for the Bell system were manufactured and serviced by Western Electric, a subsidiary of AT&T.

Bell Laboratories, a division of Western Electric, was perhaps the finest research laboratory in the United States, and certainly one of the best in the world, boasting seven Nobel Laureates. Its research was fundamental to the development of data networking, the invention of the transistor, the initial proposal for a cellular network, the first practical device to generate electric power from the sun's energy, the invention of the laser, the development of the touch-tone telephone, and the introduction of the digital signal processor that enabled multimedia devices in the digital world.

But for the average American, AT&T was best known through its local Bell operating company. By 1963, the world's largest telephone company had installed eighty-one million phones in the United States, more than half the phones on the planet.[2] And in part because of its appeal to the ordinary consumer, AT&T had more stockholders than any corporation in the world. Ma Bell was an international telecommunications superpower with significant influence over every other company in the business.

In its prime, AT&T stood unassailable, providing research fundamental to America's technological preeminence not only in telecommunications but in almost every field. In spite of the billions invested in its basic infrastructure, the value of AT&T would ultimately pale in comparison to the investment in technologies that both enabled its functions and relied on its existence. At the same time that the United States was losing its position in a significant portion of those technologies—computers, phones, cameras, television, and the semiconductors that allowed the system to function—AT&T was being dismembered by legislative decree. If there was some strategic connection between the timing of AT&T's breakup and a net improvement in U.S. competitiveness, it seemed lost in translation. Perhaps the missing link was a national perspective on what was needed to insure America's technological and productive future, one that looked beyond domestic competition to America's role in a global economy. This is glaringly obvious when one looks at the global implications of the interrelationship between segments of American industry and the exponential increase in the cost of replacement when strategic parts are lost.

In the past the various means of communication were separate and distinct. Mail always went by post. Television and radio were broadcast to local antennas; cameras were mechanical; sound was reproduced by a mechanical pickup connected to a paper cone. Security was a uniformed guard. Those days are gone. In the digital world, these forms of communication have converged. What we once knew as the "Phone Company" evolved beyond itself, supplanted by a massive system, wired and wireless, that provided a continuous exchange of information—voice, video, and data—connecting all of America and tying the nation to the rest of the world. Yet by 1968 AT&T fell victim to an industrial policy that would significantly reduce its benefit as a strategic American enterprise.

LEGISLATING COMPETITION

In the 1940s, Tom Carter, a Texas businessman, introduced a device that enabled one to acoustically transmit a two-way radio conversation over AT&T's phone network. This was particularly useful to oilmen operating from remote oil rigs who wanted to communicate with the home office. The words of the oilman were sent over the radio and forwarded into the phone using a speaker-like device. The so-called "Carterfone" was quite popular. Though the Carterfone was only acoustically attached to the telephone, when AT&T found out what was going on, they tried to shut the business down. Carter countered with an antitrust suit in 1965. The battle to survive nearly cost Carter his life savings, but in 1968 the FCC decided in his favor and issued the Carterfone decision, which allowed Carter to sell his product without interference from the "Phone Company."

The decision, however, went further, allowing *other* telephone products—not simply the Carterfone—to be connected to AT&T as long as they did not cause damage to its system. Though there was an ongoing dispute regarding how this decision would be implemented, by 1978 the entrepreneurial gates were opened to those who wished to follow in Tom Carter's footsteps. In honor of his efforts, he was inducted into the wireless telecommunication industry's Wireless Hall of Fame in May 2001.

Further marketplace upheavals were under way. In the 1970s AT&T introduced the telephone jack, which made it much easier to change phones that until then had been permanently attached to a wired system in the home or office. To install a piece of equipment other than that supplied by Ma Bell, one needed permission from the "Phone Company"—permission invariably denied. With the phone jack, AT&T saw the potential for introducing stylized phones that could be ordered and easily installed at higher monthly rates. Their rotary Princess and push-button Trimline phones became extremely popular. Other companies, of course, wanted a piece of the action. The question wasn't how, only when.

With the Carterfone decision on the one hand and the phone jack on the other—making the system more open and adaptable to a variety of alternative products—there came a groundswell of complaints that AT&T was holding up progress in telecommunications, one of America's most important industries. In 1974 the Department of Justice filed an antitrust suit against AT&T. The fight to break up this huge behemoth had begun. The communications system of the United States was headed for a perfect storm.

The implications for AT&T and the nation were enormous. Before the initial breakup occurred in the early 1980s, the phone company held accumulated assets approximating $150 billion.[3] In 1982, AT&T agreed to a consent decree with the Department of Justice, and its breakup began in earnest. The consent decree split up AT&T and the Bell operating companies and opened the door for them and their customers to purchase phones and basic capital equipment manufactured by both foreign and domestic competition.

Later, the Telecommunications Act of 1996, directed at the entire system of companies created from the initial consent decree, effectively put the bulk of AT&T's assets in play. It allowed new competitors (called Competitive Local Exchange Carriers, or CLECs) to use the AT&T and Regional Bell Operating Company networks—the telecommunications infrastructure originally created by Ma Bell—at bargain-basement prices (i.e., at a significant discount to the actual investment required to build and maintain the infrastructure of wire and switches). As expected, this new piece of legislation added an additional surge of competitive fervor at the expense of AT&T and its former operating companies. The executives of the Bell System had to sort out what the courts had decided while operating in what became an inordinately competitive environment as myriad companies both foreign and domestic entered the marketplace for the first time.

What remained of AT&T, after compliance with the initial consent decree that forced divestiture of the Regional Bell Operating Companies along with Western Electric and its billion-dollar-a-year research facility, Bell Laboratories, was an asset base of only $34 billion, 23 percent of the total before the breakup. After divestiture, AT&T was basically a highway for communications. Over the next few years, the major investment and real growth in the system were in the hardware and software attached to AT&T's network. Ultimately, a significant portion of that investment in communication products would be made outside the United States.

The change was wrenching. It was hard to find a cool head. A sign found in many Bell facilities at the time read:

There are two giant entities at work in our country, and they both have an amazing influence on our daily lives: one has given us radar, sonar, teletype, the transistor, hearing aids, artificial larynxes, talking movies, and the telephone. The other has given us the Civil War, the Spanish American War, the First World War, the Second World War, the Korean War, the Vietnam War, double-digit inflation, double digit unemployment, the Great Depression, the gasoline crisis and the Watergate fiasco. Guess which one is now trying to tell the other one how to run its business.[4]

Without question, AT&T had abused many of its privileges as a monopoly, but the cure seemed worse than the disease. In effect, the dismemberment of the telecommunications infrastructure took but a moment to enact. The infrastructure that had given the U.S. the benefits noted on the sign had taken more than a hundred years to build.

Today, after years of trial and error, AT&T is returning to something like its original form through mergers and acquisitions within the former structure of Ma Bell's companies. But much of that infrastructure, including Western Electric's product and manufacturing base and the research prowess of Bell Laboratories, has been substantially if not permanently diminished. Western Electric and its research division, Bell Laboratories, were renamed Lucent Technologies. Suffering losses in market share over the years, Lucent ultimately merged with Alcatel, its French competitor. Corporate headquarters are in Paris. Moreover, the ability to coordinate strategy and action across the original AT&T system may be very difficult to recover. As a result of the consent degree and the Telecommunications Act of 1996, competition increased as intended, but long-term value of that competition to America's global competitiveness is more difficult to determine. What was destroyed by the divestiture of AT&T's operating companies was the ability to bring to bear the full weight of AT&T's original asset base as a force for America's leadership in telecommunications.

In retrospect, the timing of the final stage of divestiture in 1996 could not have been worse. The Telecommunications Act occurred at almost the same moment that the internet became a commercial reality in America and wireless communication was taking off. It is likely that no one connected with that legislation had any notion of the radical changes in telecommunications that the internet would bring, let alone the strategic decisions affecting communications infrastructure soon to be made by other nations as the effects of the internet and wireless communications spread over the globe. The Telecommunications Act in fact rendered any significant coordinated U.S. telecommunications strategy associated with the birth of the worldwide internet and expansion of cellular infrastructure virtually impossible. The question remains: Apart from the desire to increase domestic competition, did those who initiated the act, or those on the Federal Communications Commission who administered it, consider the implications of their actions for America's ability to compete in the converging infrastructure of a digital world?

THE WORLD IS NOT FLAT

The development of the internet and wireless communications was crucial to the evolution of a technological infrastructure that would bear heavily on the global economics of telecommunications. That infrastructure was a direct outgrowth of the digital revolution.

In February 2001, the Information Theory Society (part of the IEEE, one of the world's leading professional associations for the advancement of technology) ran a short but significant obituary:

> Dr. Claude Elwood Shannon, the American mathematician and computer scientist whose theories laid the groundwork for the electronic communications networks that now lace the earth, died on Saturday. . . . He was 84. Understanding, before almost anyone, the power that springs from encoding information in a simple language of ones and zeros, Dr. Shannon as a young man wrote two papers that remain monuments in the fields of computer science and information theory. "Shannon was the person who saw that the binary digit was the fundamental element in all of communication," said Dr. Robert G. Gallager, a professor of electrical engineering who worked with Dr. Shannon at the Massachusetts Institute of Technology. "That was really his discovery, and from it the whole communications revolution has sprung."[5]

Shannon was working at Bell Labs in 1948 when he published a paper titled "A Mathematical Theory of Communication," promoting the concept of communicating in binary code. That same year, also at Bell Labs, Shockley, Bardeen, and Brattain unveiled the transistor, which was initially developed at the behest of AT&T as a substitute for the vacuum tube. AT&T had one principal goal at the time: to build a reliable telecommunications infrastructure that would sustain its powerful communications empire long after the original Bell patents ran out. The telecommunications system AT&T was trying to protect was analog, not digital. But the transistor could handle either signal, and it was smaller, cheaper, and far more reliable than a vacuum tube, using much less power and generating substantially less heat.

What no one realized then was that the concept proposed by Dr. Shannon at one end of Bell Labs would create a digitally driven world when applied to the transistor and the semiconductor industry, then in embryo with Shockley's group at the other end of AT&T's remarkable research facility.

The harbinger came in 1976—just two years after the Justice Department filed suit against AT&T—when Apple Computer sold its first system. In 1981 IBM introduced the PC. The operating system was contracted to a small start-up, headed by Bill Gates and supported by Paul Allen, soon to become Microsoft. Intel supplied the microprocessor. The world was about to go digital. In 1982, the year the consent decree began the breakup of AT&T, the FCC approved independent licenses for start-up companies wishing to enter the digital cellular market.

The ability to adapt electronic products and networks to the digital world resulted largely from advancements in the semiconductor industry. Semiconductors provided computing power, digital signal processing, and memory for markets that demanded small, highly reliable, and powerful but inexpensive products. The availability of semiconductor devices brought an explosion of new product applications in the telecommunications industry, including cell phones, digital displays of data and images, highly automated successors to the analog rotary phone, and above all, the ability to transfer data and images from one communications system to another anywhere in the world. Digital communications, along with the telephone jack and the consent decree of 1982, presented a major opportunity for competitive telephone manufacturers, many of which were based in Asia, to enter what had been AT&T's proprietary space. These alternative manufacturers provided products that would become the essence of modularity in function, design, and use. With the breakup of Ma Bell occurring at the same time, it was not only the industry that was about to become modular in the extreme, but AT&T as well.

In sum, with the consent decree of 1982 and the Telecommunications Act of 1996, there was no longer a single giant dominating the American telecommunications industry. The "Phone Company" became many individual companies not only competing with each other for survival but joined in an intense struggle with a multiplicity of new organizations, foreign and domestic, all of which vied for what seemed an unlimited market of opportunity. The impact of this legislation—along with the digital technology that brought the internet, the burgeoning cell phone market, and the convergence of almost every aspect of telecommunications technology—created a competitive environment beyond anyone's expectation. The initial result was an economic boom in the U.S. telecommunications industry that seemed without end.

An outstanding example was the origin of Cisco Systems. In 1984, Leonard Bosack, Sandy Lerner, and several others decided to commercialize a router, the so-called "blue box" that had been developed at Stanford to connect small computer networks using the Ethernet. The blue box had become popular at Stanford and other college campuses. After a rocky but successful emergence from under the Stanford umbrella, Cisco went public in 1990 with revenues of $69 million.[6] Spurred on by mergers and acquisitions and the advent of the Worldwide Web, Cisco quickly became the number-one provider of networking equipment for the internet, with sales increasing thirtyfold by 1995 and reaching $22 billion by 2001. Cisco's stock peaked at over $80 a share in 2000, making it the highest-valued public company in the world. For a moment, its market capitalization was greater than Microsoft or General Electric.

But largely as a result of legislated competition and the now rapid, almost uncontrolled growth of the internet and cellular communications, the boom in American telecommunications soon became a competitive nightmare. In the tumultuous years from 1996 to 2000, the industry went through a massive cycle of boom and bust. During this period the Regional Bell Operating Companies and AT&T were inclined to underinvest in critical infrastructure now legislated to serve their competition (CLECs) at a discount from real operating costs. This may well have reduced investment in fiber optic cable to the home. Though expensive to install—some estimated $200 billion to provide fiber to the nation's homes in the mid-1990s—fiber offers virtually unlimited bandwidth compared to other forms of electronic communication.

At the same time, these same regional companies that were formerly under the umbrella of Ma Bell, along with a group of new competitors, chose different cellular communication systems that used different communication architecture as they vied with one another for market share in the Web and wireless communications. Three different wireless digital standards evolved almost simultaneously: Time Division Multiple Access (TDMA), initially adopted by AT&T wireless, BellSouth, and Southwestern Bell; Code Division Multiple Access (CDMA), adopted by Air Touch, Bell Atlantic/Nynex, GTE, and Sprint; and Global System for Mobile Communications (GSM), adopted by Omnipoint, Pacific Bell, BellSouth, Sprint Spectrum, Microcell, Western Wireless, Powertel, and Aerial. What might have been a coordinated approach to a national wireless communications system under the aegis of a unified AT&T was becoming a highly fragmented and very expensive America-centric competitive struggle. Following legislative decrees, the U.S. telecommunications system ended up competing with itself. At about the same time as AT&T was being disassembled per the Telecommunications Act, the European telecommunications markets were experiencing a liberalization in government control. Nevertheless, although during the 1990s significant privatization of the various European national telecommunications companies occurred, there was an understanding within the European community that its communications infrastructure was strategic. This understanding was rooted in the belief that, properly handled, European telecom companies could be a major competitive advantage to the region.

An excerpt from a case study of the establishment of the international GSM system characterizes the mood of the day:

> Prior to the market liberalization of the 1990s, European telecom markets were firmly controlled by national governments and their respective PTT monopolists. Over the past decade, European telecommunications policy has been characterized by principles of market liberalization, harmonization of conditions of the regulatory framework, and the promotion of the European telecommunications industry. "GSM momentum" has been born of this environment, and is by far the biggest 2G system, with pan-European coverage and systems also installed in Asia, Australia, North America and more recently in South America.
>
> The deployment of GSM is most aptly characterized by the commitment of twenty-six European national phone companies to standardize a system, and the working process responsible for this accomplishment has been deemed a great success worthy of replication. Essentially, those countries and firms involved realized the advantages of a cross-border standard and the amount of money and energy that can be wasted when competing for mobile technology "world domination." Generally speaking, the story of the establishment of GSM is of interest to anybody studying the growth and trajectory of digital technology and its commercial applications. After all, as some have argued, the nature of digital economies implies that control over network evolution translates into control over the architecture of the digital marketplace. The GSM case has proven that a hold over national networks has global economic ramifications.
>
> Among the factors that helped to precipitate the creation of GSM was the realization that localized solutions to the development of mobile communications would not be able to generate the economies of scale—from the R&D, production as well as distribution standpoints—necessary to attain very significant market penetration. With strides in the development of the realm of R&D came also the realization that

only international market penetration goals could justify such extensive programs of investment. Long-term economic goals would be subjugated to the constraints of an unstandardized mobile communications sector, unless action could be taken to create some sort of consensus.[7]

The result of the FCC's efforts to increase competition within the United States in order to benefit the American consumer by offering lower prices and a multiplicity of product choices created a highly fragmented American communications system that ultimately lagged behind foreign competition. The results of the European communications establishment were quite different. GSM became a de facto standard that has increased the power of its governing body to maintain an orderly future for its telecommunications infrastructure. In no small part as a result of the development of the GSM standard, Finland's Nokia has become the most significant mobile phone company in the world.

The situation AT&T and the Regional Bell Operating Companies faced in 1996 was similar in many respects to that of Kodak. Consumer electronic companies in Japan and the rest of Asia had been preparing for years to compete with AT&T products, developing and producing advanced phones, both wired and wireless, that leveraged Asian technology in displays, semiconductors, and consumer electronics, industries that were rapidly disappearing from America's manufacturing base.

For a time after the Carterfone decision, U.S. telecommunication markets appeared to offer gold at the end of every new rainbow. For better or worse the "Phone Company"—having survived six thousand competitors after the original Bell patents ran out—was gone, legislated out of existence. In its place for years to come was the free-for-all of companies seeking their own fortunes. Coupled with antitrust measures and advances in semiconductor technology, the coming of wireless technology and the internet meant that AT&T as Americans knew it would no longer be the familiar fixture in their homes. In its new, highly fragmented state, the creator of the largest and most powerful telecommunications system in the world was out of control.

Propelled by the explosive growth of the internet and the cell phone, the seeming prosperity of this new period of legislated competition was short-lived. Based on poor business fundamentals, the telecommunications market began to disintegrate. The CLECs didn't find the customer base they needed to compete with the well-established Regional Bell Operating Companies. And when they finally had to pay the going rate for infrastructure, virtually all of them failed. Equipment suppliers and component manufacturers ended up with inventory they couldn't sell. Financially overextended in their quest for the gold at the end of the rainbow, individuals and companies were forced out of business.

Shocked by these reversals of fortune, the stock market collapsed. By 2000, those chasing the rainbow found that much of the gold was gone. The dot-com boom, set in motion largely by the Telecommunications Act, was over. What remained was the investment in technology and manufacturing know-how, fostered by the rapid advance of telecommunications gear built to support the unrealistic demand of this period. A major portion of that investment was used to increase Asia's technological and manufacturing infrastructure of telecommunications and related products, including cell phones, semiconductors, and displays.

The convergence of the internet and wireless communications centered on a highly functional mobile communications device. In line with Moore's Law, subsequent generations of phones would be a lot smarter. As a result of the convergent infrastructures that evolved with digitization and rapid advances in the development of semiconductors, displays, and consumer electronics, the successors to the historic black rotary phone would not only show the date, time, number called, and number calling but could function wirelessly, take and send pictures or videoclips, and in many cases replicate a computer, transmitting and receiving both data and voice communications. The technological advance of these telephone devices and supporting systems grew exponentially as their computing power kept doubling. The phone went from a simple device carrying a conversation between two parties to a totally integrated, feature-rich audiovisual communications system with vast computational powers.

But just as consumer electronics, riding on the technological advances of the VCR, had long before migrated to Japan, the infrastructure that nurtured the evolution of telecommunications equipment began moving markedly to Asia, where development and manufacturing know-how was now well established. Yet descendants of the rotary phone were not evolving in an environment characterized simply by low-cost labor. As the complexity of the telephone's features and design increased, along with the pressing need to reduce unit cost, the investment required to manufacture the related displays, semiconductors, and consumer electronics was rising exponentially. In time the investment needed to design and manufacture the rotary phone's progeny would ultimately require tens of billions of dollars more than was needed to produce the parent. The problem was that a major portion of that investment had been and would be made outside the United States.

For more than two decades the United States had been transferring to Asia much of its basic expertise in the design and production of component products directly applicable to the manufacturing of phones and other communication devices. This occurred as America abandoned or substantially reduced its investment in consumer electronics, displays, and semiconductors. By the time America realized what had been transferred to Asia in terms of technology and productive capacity, the cost of retrieval was becoming overwhelming. Semiconductor fabrication facilities that had been lost were costing several billion dollars apiece to build and equip. Display manufacturing plants were about to cost the same. Highly automated plants that produced cell phones and related consumer communication products were costing hundreds of millions of dollars. But most important, the expertise to develop the technology and design the products had gone as well. Whether what was lost was a star or a dog made no difference. The industrial base was not going to come back any time soon. The effect of Moore's Law on the investment required to overtake the explosion of product functions evolving from that simple black phone had created a technological and monetary mountain between current producers and those who might want to take up or get back in the game. The world, had it ever been so, was no longer flat.

THE FLY ON THE REBAR:
WHEN LESS COSTS MORE

The semiconductor as an integrated circuit is the foundation for all digital telecommunications networks. The production of the semiconductor relies on the precision output of the fabrication, test, and measurement equipment produced by the semiconductor capital equipment industry. There are four facets to that industry: equipment necessary to fabricate silicon wafers that have the designs of individual semiconductor devices imprinted on them, equipment necessary to insure that those wafers are defect-free and meet the precise dimensional characteristics of the design engineer's specifications, equipment that separates the devices from the wafer and assembles them into individual packages, and equipment that tests the finished chip.

KLA-Tencor is perhaps the preeminent company in the world today providing defect inspection and measurement equipment for the semiconductor industry. It was the amalgamation of three companies: KLA, Tencor, and Prometrix. KLA was founded in 1976 by Ken Levy and Bob Anderson. Tencor, launched in 1977, was the dream of Karel Urbanek. Prometrix, which started operations in 1983, represented the combined efforts of Dave Perloff, Talat Hasan, Chet Mallory, and me. The coming together of these three companies was certainly one of the most successful set of mergers in the history of the semiconductor equipment business. In 1994 the combined revenues of the three firms amounted to $376 million. By 2007 the revenues exceeded $2.7 billion with a market capitalization approximating $10 billion. The company is now part of the S&P 500 index.

To achieve the characteristics of size, speed, power usage, and capacity of a semiconductor device today, the industry talks in terms of nanometers. A nanometer is one-billionth of a meter. How small is that?

As a member of the board of directors of KLA-Tencor in 2003, I remember hearing Executive Vice President (and now CEO) Rick Wallace put it this way: if a fly were to land on the end of a half-inch-thick piece of steel rebar, protruding one foot from the concrete it reinforced, the deflection of the bar from the weight of the fly would amount to one nanometer. Only a few years earlier microns were the concern. A micron is one-millionth of a meter, one thousand times larger than a nanometer. The ability to measure a nanometer was then only a dream. But in the world of Moore's Law such dreams soon become reality.

It is the purpose of equipment manufactured by KLA-Tencor to measure and look for defects in these tiny devices, whether the size is measured in microns or nanometers. The task is a critical one. Semiconductor fabrication, measurement, and inspection equipment are what give the engineer and the manufacturer confidence in the design of the chip and the process that produces it.

The semiconductor has become the engine that powers today's world of information, including the information systems in automobiles, aircraft, telecommunication, television, displays, computers, and all other consumer and military electronics. The semiconductor industry, which launched Moore's Law, may now be the most strategic industry on Earth.

In the years since Prometrix was founded, the changes that have occurred in semiconductor manufacturing equipment, fabrication facilities, and devices have been as extraordinary as the now familiar improvements in the phones, computers, televisions, and other products that depend on them. For example: Prometrix was founded in 1983 on an investment of $300,000. Though additional capital was raised, it was never needed. Generating cash in its first quarter of operation, Prometrix was profitable from day 1. Prometrix sold its products to semiconductor fabrication facilities that cost approximately $50 million to build, including plant and equipment. The first metrology (or measurement) product that Prometrix offered was sold for $35,000. The size of the critical dimension in a transistor designed in 1983 was approximately 1.5 microns—1.5 millionths of a meter.

At the time, we at Prometrix thought that was a remarkably small piece of real estate. Yet it was so large that most Japanese companies felt they could build their devices with perhaps one initial inspection of the process, which they felt was so stable that further analysis was unnecessary. Thus, in the beginning, Prometrix's market in Japan was very limited. But it wasn't long before Moore's Law kicked in, and 1.5 microns went to 1 micron on its way to nanometers. Almost overnight it became obvious that equipment designed to insure the precision of the semiconductor manufacturing process was essential.

As the dimensional characteristics of the semiconductor got smaller and smaller, the cost of manufacture went up exponentially. Today it could easily cost hundreds of times what it took to launch Prometrix just to design and develop a state-of-the-art defect inspection system at KLA-Tencor. The amount of money to design a single piece of semiconductor fabrication equipment today might be several times larger than the cost of an entire manufacturing facility in 1983. This is a lot of money to spend in advance of any immediate chance for profitability, knowing that the first investment will be but a down payment on the future. This is especially true when one considers just how cyclical the equipment industry can be. For example, in the aftermath of the dot-com bust and 9/11, orders for semiconductor capital equipment for some companies in the sector fell in excess of 60 percent in sixty days. That's enough to send a chill through even the most stalwart investor. But as Moore's Law implies, if you don't invest and stay on the development curve of your customer, let alone that of your competition, you might as well pack up your bags. The game is probably over.

As one might expect, the cost to build a facility to manufacture semiconductors has risen dramatically over the years. A $50 million fabrication facility built in 1983 can cost in excess of $3 billion today. Toshiba recently announced that it plans to build a $6.6 billion fabrication facility for the production of NAND flash memories.[8] This is $1 billion more than Toshiba's recent purchase of Westinghouse Electric to expand its capability in nuclear energy and just under what the private equity firm Cerberus paid to buy Chrysler Corporation from Daimler-Benz.

But the sixtyfold to one-hundred-thirty-fold rise in the cost of the semi-conductor manufacturing facility is only part of the story. To build a fabrication plant at the leading edge of technology today, one must be steeped in both chip design *and* the science of the production process. This is no mean feat. From 2000 to 2007, Intel will spend $80 billion on plant and equipment and related R&D in its attempt to stay ahead of the game.[9] The investment is more than just designing a product that will offer Intel customers the maximum in functional capability. The technology is becoming so advanced, and the process so difficult to implement, that the ability to manufacture the product within specifications—with reasonable yield to meet cost and performance objectives—is becoming as proprietary as the design of the chip itself. Even more important, perhaps, is the research necessary to develop a manufacturing process at the leading edge of technology—technology that will in turn provide an understanding of how to proceed to the next level, where the dimensions are even smaller and the functions ever more complex.

To grasp the implications of Moore's Law for the semiconductor industry is to understand how large the investment may become before one has any idea whether or not one has invested in a star, cash cow, or dog. It's possible one will never know because the game is always changing. But there is one fundamental truth for anyone involved in semiconductor design and manufacturing: technological advancements and new products are basic to the success of that industry's customer base and in most cases the economy of the countries hosting the industry. Thus the competition is fierce and unrelenting. To back off—that is, to underinvest—is to back out.

Of the top semiconductor manufacturing companies in the world in 2007, sixteen spent more than $1 billion on capital equipment. Only four of the sixteen are U.S. companies. Two of them, AMD and SanDisk, will make the bulk of their investment outside the United States. With assistance from the German government, AMD will be investing a significant

portion of its funds in its Dresden factory as well as outsourcing some of
its microprocessor manufacturing activities to TSMC, a Taiwan semiconductor foundry. SanDisk will co-invest most of its funds in a Toshiba
manufacturing facility in Japan and in Hynix in Korea. Of these sixteen
firms, Samsung outspent Intel in capital expenditures for semiconductor
manufacturing in both 2006 and 2007. Samsung planned an outlay of
funds for capital investment in semiconductor plant and equipment approximating $13.6 billion for this period against an expected total invest-
ment by Intel of $11.3 billion. Hynix is in third place, anticipating $10
billion. Of the sixteen largest spenders, Asia supports ten, the United
States four, and Europe two.[10]

THE GENESIS OF A FABRICATION PROCESS:
THE STORY OF THE STEPPER

In 1973, I was offered the job of executive vice president of Geometrics,
a small geophysical instrumentation company in Silicon Valley. It had
two divisions: one manufactured spectrometers and magnetometers used
to locate mineral and oil deposits, and the other provided geophysical
mapping services to companies and countries interested in locating key
natural resource reserves. Geometrics was sold in 1977 to EG&G, a New
York Stock Exchange company headquartered in Boston.

The year before, EG&G, along with San Francisco venture capital
firm Continental Capital, made the initial investment in KLA, the company that was later to partner with Tencor Instruments and Prometrix.
KLA's first product was a very successful photomask inspection system
applicable to the advancing state of mask making and photolithography,
both of which are essential to the imprinting of chip designs on the silicon wafer and thus fundamental to the semiconductor industry.

A photographic process is used to create the image of a substantially
reduced chip design on the surface of a wafer. This is accomplished by
passing a laser beam through patterns on a mask that replicates the desired image on the surface of the wafer. To manufacture that mask, the

pattern of a chip design is formed by a laser or electron beam on a pure quartz glass plate covered by a film of chromium and photoresist material. An integrated circuit may require sixteen to twenty-four or more layers on the chip to form the circuits. If the layers are not exactly the same, each layer requires another mask. The result is a very expensive plate or reticle representing one mask through which a laser can pattern the surface of the wafer. Fabrication of a finished set of reticles can cost $1 million or more. The mask or reticle inspection systems of KLA have therefore become an integral part of the fabrication process.

A short distance from EG&G, the Geophysical Corporation of America was also offering mapping technology to the geophysical industry. GCA ultimately applied its technological expertise to the development of mask making. The result of its initial efforts was the photo repeater, a product developed by David Mann that allowed semiconductor manufacturers to reduce the image from the mask used to imprint the chip design on the wafer.

In the world of technology the concept of convergence is fundamental. In time, convergence evolves into infrastructure that often forms the backbone of an industry. In 1941, Cecil Green, J. Erick Jonsson, Eugene McDermott, and Patrick Haggerty bought Geophysical Service Incorporated, which provided seismic exploration services to the oil industry. They expanded its product line into the instrumentation field, and in 1951, the company changed its name to Texas Instruments. Like GCA, TI also gravitated from geophysics to semiconductors. In 1953, it purchased a license from Western Electric to develop the transistor along with Sony, Fairchild Semiconductor, and other companies. Then in 1958, Bob Noyce, CEO of Fairchild and later cofounder (with Gordon Moore) of Intel, and Jack Kilby of Texas Instruments invented the integrated circuit. In a few years TI became the world's largest supplier of digital-signal-processing integrated circuits.

The integrated circuit as we know it today would not exist if it were not for one piece of capital equipment: the stepper. In 1978, GCA introduced the DSW 4800 wafer stepper. Using the technology of photolithography, this was the first successful product enabling a semiconductor manufacturer such as TI to imprint multiple images of a specific chip design on the surface of the wafer with reasonable precision and reduced defects. The stepper, which got its name from the mechanical step-and-repeat system fundamental to its operation, became essential to the growth of the semiconductor industry. With the technology of the stepper, it became possible to satisfy the semiconductor industry's insatiable desire to shrink the dimensional characteristics of chip designs while improving the economics of the manufacturing process.

Prior to the GCA stepper, the most popular competitive product of the day was a projection printer invented by the PerkinElmer Company in 1973. With an initial selling price of just under $100,000, PerkinElmer's Micralign system established it as the largest equipment company in the industry. Then came GCA's stepper, selling for $450,000. The improvements it brought to the number of good chips per given lot, especially as the functions of the chip grew increasingly complex, made the higher-priced lithography system well worth it. Thus GCA garnered a majority of the world market for photolithographic imprinting systems. But because the stepper became such a fundamental part of the production process, GCA began to feel the heat of competition almost immediately, as equipment suppliers, particularly in Japan, attempted to fill the highly strategic need for new and improved stepper systems.

In Japan, Nikon and Canon began development of their own stepper-related programs with specific help and guidance from a highly motivated Ministry of International Trade and Industry (MITI). The stepper was crucial to Japan's semiconductor industry. The growth of its consumer electronics business was dependent above all on the expanding market for VCRs, which became the largest single user of integrated circuits of any product in the world at that time. And by the 1980s, Japan was by far the leading supplier of VCRs.

In 1980 Nikon, which manufactured its own lenses in support of its well-known line of cameras, introduced Japan's first commercial stepper. GCA purchased its lenses from the German company Zeiss. Because of some internal management problems and vendor supply issues relating to its relationship with Zeiss, GCA was late with its newest competitive product. In 1982, GCA purchased Tropel, a small lens manufacturing company, to help alleviate the critical problems of lens manufacturing. But GCA's efforts to maintain its market position were to no avail. By 1984 Nikon was shipping more steppers than GCA at substantially higher prices. The Nikon stepper was selling for more than $1.2 million. With a better light source, the Nikon stepper created fewer defects and offered higher productivity. GCA was no longer competitive.

But GCA had more than Nikon to contend with. In 1970 Canon had begun building mask aligners, a basic tool used to insure the alignment of the image to be imprinted on the wafer. By 1976, with help from a contract by MITI, Canon was attempting to develop a projection alignment system designed to copy the PerkinElmer Micralign system. This first system ran into trouble with PerkinElmer patents in the U.S. but was finally shipped to Texas Instruments in 1983 after concluding intellectual property licenses with PerkinElmer. Canon shipped its first stepper in 1984. By 1990 it was shipping a substantially more advanced stepper. The United States lithography manufacturers, including GCA and PerkinElmer, were not only aware of their Japanese competition; they knew they were in serious trouble.

When Prometrix began operations in 1983, one of its first customers was GCA. The Prometrix metrology system provided fundamental information that assured the successful operation of the GCA stepper. The fact that GCA was a key customer not only helped Prometrix get its start but allowed the company to become close to GCA's organization and marketing plans. Through GCA, Prometrix was introduced to Sumitomo Corporation, the joint venture partner of GCA in Japan. In a relatively short time Sumitomo became the Japanese distributor of Prometrix products. The relationship between Sumitomo and Prometrix was solid and beneficial to both for many years.

Because of the size and importance of Sumitomo as a major Japanese Keiretsu and its relationship with other Japanese companies in the semiconductor capital equipment field, Prometrix was able to gain insight into the GCA stepper's mounting competition from Nikon and Canon. As we, the founders of Prometrix, watched the efforts of those two large, integrated, and financially secure Japanese manufacturers, we were most impressed by the close and highly involved relationship they had established with their customers. It seemed clear that behind those relationships, along with a significant level of interchange with the Ministry of International Trade, was a deep sense of commitment, both philosophical and financial, to the success of Japan as a nation in the production of steppers in particular and the semiconductor equipment market in general. On the list of priorities, profit was at the bottom. The obvious sentiment in Japan was that the semiconductor equipment industry was strategically essential to the economic and political success of the country.

Competition from Nikon and Canon was like nothing GCA had ever experienced. Nikon and Canon were both expert in the art of manufacturing large numbers of complex products requiring precision automation, the result of years of experience in the consumer electronics and optical instrumentation markets. Nikon was born in 1917, Canon in 1933. A conglomeration of three Japanese optical companies, Nikon went on to develop microscopes, cameras, binoculars, optical instrumentation, and ultimately the complete line of digital cameras integrating all the convergent components so well known today. (By 1998 Nikon's revenues approximated $3 billion.)[11]

Canon was in many ways a very similar company. A significant manufacturer of cameras prior to World War II, the Precision Optical Company was disbanded in 1945 only to regain full operation in 1947, manufacturing cameras under the name Canon. Working with NHK (the national Japanese broadcasting company), Canon developed a television camera in 1954 for the birth of television broadcasting in Japan. From that point on, Canon branched into various product areas, including copiers, calculators, optical fiber development, and computers. By 1997, Canon was a $22 billion company.

By comparison, GCA was a small company with revenues of a few hundred million dollars at its peak. Some of its manufacturing techniques would have been considered antiquated by Japanese standards of the day. In its field, GCA was basically a stand-alone company with a limited history in the optical lithography business and a substantial lack of other resources related to the overall task it faced as an integrated manufacturer of steppers (i.e., one producing the components as well as the end product). This was in sharp contrast to Nikon and Canon, with their broad manufacturing experience, integrated production of lenses, and vast financial resources, including a continued strategic interest on the part of the Japanese government. The competition must have seemed overwhelming.

Moreover, Nikon and Canon, along with the industrial base of Japan, were well aware of the implications of Moore's Law. As leaders in the production of cameras and related consumer and industrial electronics, all dependent on semiconductors, both companies would benefit from their success in semiconductor capital equipment beyond the immediate financial rewards from the sale of steppers.

Yet a third player of consequence appeared on the horizon in 1984, when stepper technology developed within Philips Corporation of the Netherlands was spun out to Advanced Semiconductor Materials International (ASMI), also of the Netherlands. In 1986, ASMI introduced what turned out to be a semipopular stepper. By 1991, ASMI felt it was no longer able to maintain the losses incurred by this product line, and a new company, ASML, was established to take over the stepper business, 60 percent owned by Philips and 40 percent by two Dutch banks. ASML went public in 1995. Aside from its strong connection with Philips (also a producer of VCRs and a complete line of consumer electronics at the time), ASML established an important strategic relationship with the German lens manufacturer Zeiss. In time ASML became quite successful in its advanced product designs, passing Nikon in 2002 to become the number-one lithography tool supplier in the world.

THE PERILS OF INNOVATION
WITHOUT INFRASTRUCTURE

But long before ASML became a factor in the fortunes of GCA, the
script was pretty well written for the future of the American stepper.
GCA had its own financial and management problems, but its primary
problem was that it had been established as a venture, rather than a
strategic entity fundamental to an industry that was vital to a strategic
set of markets. So GCA had to function in an environment where the
concern focused on the company as a financial entity rather than as a key
part of America's economic infrastructure. Between 1985 and 1986,
GCA lost approximately $100 million.[12] In 1988, the company was sold
to General Signal, a U.S. conglomerate, for $76 million.

During this period the U.S. government became concerned that the
semiconductor equipment industry might well be lost to Japan, potentially imperiling the future of the American semiconductor industry.
In 1988, an organization called Sematech was established that included
several of the top American semiconductor manufacturers. Sematech
was funded with an annual contribution of $150 million from the
semiconductor industry and $100 million from the government.[13] In
turn, Sematech invested between $60 and $75 million in GCA to develop the next generation of steppers. But General Signal was not
really in the semiconductor business; it was in the business of buying
and building profitable companies and selling the dogs, and GCA
showed little prospect of becoming a financial success. By 1993, General Signal had had enough. It was not able to find a buyer for GCA,
so it shut it down. Tropel was spun off as a management buyout and finally sold to Corning in 2001 for $190 million. The remaining assets of
GCA were also subject to a management buyout and then acquired by
Ultratech Stepper.[14]

In 1989, PerkinElmer announced that it would withdraw from the
semiconductor equipment business. No longer facing the losses incurred
in that industry, its stock on the public market spiked up almost imme-

diately. Its photolithography business was purchased by the Silicon Valley Group for $20 million. IBM also made an investment with SVG for a minority interest. From 1990 through 1993, Sematech invested an additional $30 million to help develop SVG's Micrascan stepper based on intellectual property from PerkinElmer. The tool was introduced in 1992. In 2001, ASML acquired the Silicon Valley Group for $1.6 billion and shortly thereafter discontinued the Micrascan product line. Intel, which had contributed to the success of SVG as both a customer and a source of funding, remained a customer of ASML.[15]

Many feared that these events were a serious blow to the future success of the U.S. semiconductor industry. In 1980, American suppliers of lithography tools represented 90 percent of the market. By 1990, the U.S. market share had dropped to 10 percent, a loss so large that the ability to recover seemed virtually impossible, let alone profitable. Since the stepper was fundamental to the manufacture of semiconductors, this should have been a warning to the American semiconductor industry that control of this critical product in the wrong hands could threaten its future. But the rise of ASML offset the potential impact of an industry controlled by Nikon or Canon.

In addition, just when competition from Japan's industrial base seemed poised to truncate the success of America's economy, Japan was hit suddenly by what many thought to be a knockout blow. In the wake of Japan's astounding economic ascendancy in the 1970s and '80s, its real estate market, supported by domestic interest rates that were the lowest in the world, reached unheard-of levels. One analyst calculated that in 1990 "the aggregate value of all land in Japan was fifty percent greater than the value of all land in the rest of the world."[16] There were some buildings in Tokyo selling at prices equivalent to $139,000 a square foot. The value of Japan's stock market reached similar proportions. When NTT, Japan's equivalent of AT&T, went public in the late '80s, its initial value was greater than all the stocks on the West German stock exchange. The bubble was unsustainable and came to a crashing end in 1990. The Nikkei stock index, like NASDAQ in 2000, dropped by 80 percent.

For many, the collapse of the real estate market in Japan negated any unease about the competitive nature of the Japanese economy. Significant concerns in the United States about Japan's domination of photolithography were ameliorated. Common wisdom assumed that they would be happy to sell their steppers to anyone, especially U.S. companies, which most assumed would now dominate the semiconductor industry for the foreseeable future. But consider this:

- Nikon and Canon, which today represent approximately 30 percent of the revenues and 40 percent of the units of the stepper industry, are not going to go away. Though Canon is billions larger than Nikon, Nikon is a part of the Mitsubishi Keiretsu, which includes the Bank of Tokyo-Mitsubishi, Mitsubishi Electric Corporation, Mitsubishi Motors, Mitsubishi Research Institute, Nippon Oil Corporation, and countless others.

- The United States now has virtually no position in photolithography pertaining to the stepper business.

- The majority of new customers (i.e., new investment) in semiconductor equipment that make up the market for advanced photolithography are principally in Asia. More important, the majority of those customers are not Western but Asian manufacturers building plants in Asia. They will decide who ultimately wins or loses in the race for advanced steppers.

- The majority of end-use products that create the market for advanced photolithography equipment are produced in Asia.

- In time, the largest markets for the end-use products already produced in Asia will also be in Asia.

- Though Japan's real estate market collapsed and never returned to the values experienced in the 1980s, its strategic desire to maintain its manufacturing prowess remained intact. The rest of Asia followed suit. What seemed to the United States in the 1990s as a competitive win by default turned out to be short-lived. The extraordinary cost of maintaining a world-class high-tech electronics manufacturing base is no longer an American phenomenon. Asia is becoming the investor of choice.

In 2002, Sematech produced a chart that plotted the increase in the cost of steppers and scanners from 1978 through 2000. The conclusion it reached was that the tool price in this category of equipment had doubled approximately every 4.4 years. The original PerkinElmer Micralign system that sold for approximately $100,000 in 1974 was ultimately replaced by a stepper that cost $10 million in 2000 and offered dramatic improvements in specifications and functions.[17] Today an immersion stepper as a part of a lithography system necessary to meet the needs of a design specification at thirty-two nanometers may well cost in excess of $50 million per tool. If extreme ultraviolet light (EUV) steppers become a requirement as the dimensional characteristics become even smaller, the price could rise another 50 percent. With that background, ASML, whose principal product is its line of steppers, has a current market capitalization in excess of $13 billion, a significant increase over that of GCA, which owned the market twenty-five years ago.

Another way of looking at these facts and figures is to realize that the total sales price of GCA Corporation in 1988, including all of its intellectual property, was little more than the anticipated cost of a single EUV stepper and approximately one-third more than the cost of an immersion stepper today. A single stepper sold today could equal the cost of an entire manufacturing facility in 1983. When U.S. companies decided it was no longer in the best interest of their investors to remain competitive in these markets, they made a business decision that will be difficult to reverse. As a result, while America may have avoided the cost of a dog business, it also significantly reduced its ability to re-create strategic infrastructure fundamental to America's future.

The power that decides who wins or loses in the competitive race for economic supremacy in any market usually lies with the producers who control the strategic elements that influence not only technological innovation but the ability to implement that innovation—to manufacture the product. The two are inexorably tied together. So the evolution of the classic black phone, from its rudimentary inception to the functional equivalent of a full-fledged wireless computer in your pocket, began with a telecommunications infrastructure that cost billions to build and a component essential to its operational growth, the transistor. The evolution of the transistor into an integrated circuit that would eventually utilize the computing power of billions of transistors on a single chip made possible the telecommunications system that we now take for granted. The design and manufacture of the amazingly complex circuits embedded in today's semiconductors would not have been possible without the development and manufacture of the capital equipment fundamental to their production. It is from the semiconductor capital equipment industry, one of the most technologically intensive businesses in the world, that the stepper was born.

The corporate leaders of these strategic industries understand all too well the importance of the technological linkages between them. They also understand the extraordinary cost associated with the success of each link in the chain. Because of the nearly limitless growth potential in end-use markets for products like the offspring of the original black phone, the level of competition between companies and nations in the business of consumer electronics is remarkable. Even more striking is the level of competition between these same companies and nations to secure a strong relationship with each of the links in the technological chain that makes the end-use product possible. (These links involve many other areas of expertise including chemistry, materials, optics, robotics, and software.)

In a world governed by the acceleration of convergence, infrastructure, and investment, it is difficult to do everything. The cost and complexity become too great. This dilemma is solved by strategic relationships. If a key relationship in the design and manufacturing chain is lost, success in the end-use market may be in jeopardy. To survive in this kind of environment, it is essential for a nation to understand what technologies and products must be developed and manufactured domestically in order to maintain its competitive infrastructure. It is equally important for the nation to know what relationships can be developed that insure access to those technologies and products that, though relatively important, would most likely be outsourced because of resource constraints.

The semiconductor industry is strategic, and so is the equipment industry that supports it. Displays are essential. The real rewards, however, are in the multiplicity of end-use products that result from the technological and capital investments in supporting industries. The revenues from the sale of cell phones, computers, television sets, cameras, recorders, medical instrumentation, automobiles, and airplanes create the multibillion-dollar end-use markets that make it all worthwhile. But without a satisfactory component manufacturing base, American industry will find it far more difficult to maintain a proprietary position in those end-use markets that represent the gold at the end of the rainbow.

THE WORLD IS NEITHER FLAT NOR FAIR

New concepts, new technologies, and new manufacturing techniques will continue to evolve into something no one could have foreseen even in the recent past. In this kind of environment, the chances for opportunistic profits are high. Those who are determined to remain in the game, and who understand the difference between "stars, cash cows, and dogs" and Moore's Law, are often willing to bid what appear to be high prices for the assets of those who have decided to withdraw, even though the cost of staying in the game is rising exponentially. Why? Because they are able to build infrastructure relatively quickly and thus exploit the advantages of Moore's Law.

Using its initial infrastructure as a base of operations, Cisco Systems successfully acquired a multiplicity of companies that allowed it to build rapidly on that infrastructure of technologies, products, and markets faster than it could have developed them from scratch. The result was an acceleration in the momentum of the entire corporation, which had developed the skill of integrating newly purchased enterprises, producing an innovative company more dynamic than the sum of its parts.

On the other hand, opportunistic sale or withdrawal from markets can improve near-term corporate profitability and cash flow while enabling management to abandon what they perceive as dog businesses. It was for this reason that America began to withdraw from the display industry in the 1970s.

For some, the accumulation or sale of business enterprises can become the purpose of the game, as management and investors begin to concentrate on profit created simply by turning over assets. If those assets are treated as economic entities with little consideration for the infrastructure that they represent, the individual company as well as related infrastructure may suffer the consequences. This was the situation that confronted the lithography industry in the United States. GCA was first bought by General Signal as a cheap and thus possibly rewarding financial venture. When it no longer appeared to provide significant value as a financial entity or receive adequate support from remaining infrastructure, the desire to invest disappeared, and it was shut down. These circumstances contributed significantly to the demise of the stepper industry in America.

This is not to suggest that there is no value in the purchase and sale of companies. This activity can be fundamental to the development of a nation's infrastructure and contribute significantly to the effective management of a corporation. It's a matter of degree. But at some level there must be an assessment of mergers and acquisitions beyond the financial considerations of the deal in order to determine the transaction's effect on the nation's competitive strategy.

Far more than a large distraction for Ma Bell, the consent decree and the Telecommunications Act of 1996 brought a major challenge to the various industrial components of the U.S. communications industry as it rushed to take advantage of opportunities left in AT&T's wake. But by 1982, Japan's increasingly active pursuit of consumer electronic products had put it in a unique position to compete with growing success in these new markets. By the 1990s, Asia's investment in plant and equipment, let alone technological infrastructure, was in the billions of dollars in the display industry alone, an area in which American investment was to become relatively insignificant. Similar imbalances existed in consumer electronics. All of this was spilling over into the semiconductor industry.

Some of the concerns of Roger Smith, CEO of General Motors in the 1980s, as he saw a trend in Japan away from the pure mechanics of an automobile engine and toward electronics and related manufacturing technology, were beginning to become evident in ways that few would have expected. Communication systems were about to become an integral part of the automobile. Kodak would face the same fate as electronic image processing eliminated much of the value of film.

Prior to the consent decree and the Telecommunications Act, AT&T represented the world's most powerful communications system. When the world went wireless and digital, one might have expected that the "Phone Company" would have become a wellspring for advancement in the design and manufacturing of telecommunications equipment, computers, television, semiconductors, and electronics in general as a key part of America's industrial base. Certainly the ubiquity of the information that coursed through its electronic and photonic veins provided a foundation for innovation beyond anything ever imagined as the company's substantial and enormously expensive infrastructure was being built. But with some notable exceptions, this situation did not benefit the American economy to the extent that one might have expected. Japan and the rest of Asia invested billions in technologies and products highly convergent with the demands of the newly opened U.S. telecommunication markets, formerly the purview of AT&T. Asia was already there, ahead of the pack. When it came to the American demand, created by the explosive growth of the telecommunications system, for displays, cell phones, television sets, cameras, recorders, semiconductors, and other consumer electronics, Asia was the most significant beneficiary. The world is neither flat nor fair.

So the question remains: To what extent is the United States willing to invest in the design and manufacture of technological components and end-use products desirable not only to the American consumer but to other markets around the world? When it costs and yet counts, is America willing to stay in the game? One thing is certain: in Bell Laboratories, at the heart of AT&T, Dr. Claude Shannon and the team headed by William Shockley altered the course of history. The technological base they developed forever changed the global competitiveness of nations.

CHAPTER 6

Education and Competitiveness: The Vicious and Virtuous Circle

The nation's political and economic strategy is primary in establishing its educational agenda. The educational agenda seldom establishes the nation's political and economic strategy.

America is worried about its education system. Many people feel that the schools would go far toward remedying the nation's competitive deficiencies if they would only get their act together. The education system is not a leading indicator of national competitiveness but a lagging indicator. It reflects rather than anticipates the national vision. It will not succeed any better than the economic and political system it is designed to support, and it will not meet our expectations if we continue to abandon technologies and products strategic to global competitiveness.

In September 2003, speaking for a subcommittee of the President's Council of Advisors on Science and Technology, Robert Herbold, then executive vice president of Microsoft, noted a massive exodus of technology jobs to places like India and China, where salaries were substantially below those of the United States. He added that 39 percent of Chinese students receiving bachelor of science or bachelor of arts degrees were studying engineering, compared to only 5 percent of American students.[1] Some of the statistics he cites are found in Table 1.

	B.S./B.A. Degrees	B.S. Engineering	% Degrees in Engineering
United States	12,530,000	595,000	5
China	5,679,000	2,196,000	39
South Korea	2,097,000	565,000	27
Taiwan	1,174,000	266,000	23
Japan	5,423,000	1,045,000	19

Source: "Leisure Class," VC Confidential (http://www.vcconfidential.com), quoting analyst Marc Faber, April 2006.

Between 1987 and 2001, the number of U.S. citizens receiving Ph.D.s in physical science or engineering dropped 6.4 percent, while the number of Asian citizens getting Ph.D.s in these fields increased 345 percent.[2] The United States presumes to lead the world in information technology and boasts the best university system in the world. But if America continues on its present track, that system will ultimately be unable to attract and graduate enough homegrown engineers to maintain the competitiveness of the nation's technological base.

Today, nearly 60 percent of those earning doctorates in engineering are from other countries.[3] Meanwhile, America increasingly sheds its design, development, and manufacturing expertise in strategic technologies by outsourcing to other nations. This outsourcing might suggest that the nation's need for graduates in science and technology can decline and still leave no meaningful shortage in technical talent. But this strategy eventually begins to feed on itself. Who wants to prepare for a career in a field that the nation may eventually abandon? The best and the brightest, both foreign and domestic, are starting to look into other fields and other countries. As a result, the supply of graduates available for the U.S. job market may drop too fast for outsourcing to compensate. There is thus an ever-increasing need for the United States to look outside its borders for engineering and manufacturing resources. If America were to decide it was strategically important to reverse its position on out-sourcing, it might find itself facing a sudden shortage of technical talent that would take years to correct.

This situation is compounded by the fact that foreign students—who in the past came for American universities and stayed for the jobs—are no longer staying. In "Where the Engineers Are," a 2007 article for *Issues in Science and Technology,* Vivek Wadhwa and colleagues at the Pratt School of Engineering at Duke University concluded that "the United States lacks enough native students completing masters and Ph.D. degrees. The nation cannot continue to depend on India and China to supply such graduates. As their economies improve, it will be increasingly lucrative for students to return home." They added that "30 percent of all Chinese students studying abroad returned home after their education . . . [and] this number is steadily increasing."[4]

As graduate engineers become less available, the need to outsource will become ever more essential as America awakens to its crucial loss of both talent and industry. If the nation then decides to reverse its out-sourcing strategy, it will discover that both that outsourcing and the momentum of exponentially accelerating convergence, infrastructure, and investment will have enabled competing nations to build a massive technological lead and the momentum to maintain it. To reverse course becomes a staggering problem. With strategic components of its industrial base outsourced, America's dependence on others will become not a choice but a requirement.

The nation's competitive position will ultimately be reflected in its system of education. One continually hears complaints about education in America. Many feel that the nation's education system lacks the motivation, direction, and effectiveness necessary to maintain U.S. competitiveness in global markets. Suggestions for improvements include more and better-trained teachers, smaller classes, and more relevant course materials. Requests for additional funding are constant. But these problems beg the much larger question of what kind of education we need and why we need it. The answer is not to be found in the buildings of our state departments of education but in our nation's politics, economy, and culture. It all comes back to strategy.

Students, faculty, and everyone else with a vested interest in a nation's education system must first understand that the overall health of the system depends on the nation being globally competitive in those markets deemed essential to its well-being. This requires a national strategy understood by all sectors and segments of the economy, one that considers the necessity of participating in those technologies, products, and markets that are crucial to the nation's industrial base.

If the nation's political and economic leadership has agreed on a competitive strategy, the education system can begin to lay the groundwork necessary to implement those goals. As the nation begins to reflect its strategic priorities, education will follow suit. Key participants in the education system can suggest to business and political leaders that they consider various alternatives; for example, the educational community constantly comments on the need for more emphasis on math and science. In the long run, however, the direction of the nation's technology, products, and markets will not be set by the education system but by the political, economic, and business leaders of the country.

Like any organization, the education system responds to the quality of its leadership. If the nation's strategic goals are clear and their relevance is understood, the incentive to develop the curriculum, students, and faculty necessary to provide an educational basis for competitiveness is a given. The belief that the nation as a whole can be competitive, and that the education system and those involved in it can participate in the consequent rewards, is inherently motivating. And the victory is both individual and collective.

Being globally competitive rests heavily on the ability to create and commercialize technology. This ability determines who dominates in computers, communications, entertainment, automobiles, medicine, aircraft, military preparedness, and more. If America's leaders lack a vision of national technological competitiveness and do not understand the level of commitment required of the education system to do its job, the education system alone will not be able to provide the motivation and resources to alter its plight. The rapid advance of convergent technology in an expanding infrastructure, coupled with the exponential increase in time and money required just to stay even, will ultimately marginalize the educational resources needed to stay in the game. In time technological expertise will wither away. The complex technological demands of the market will be underestimated or misunderstood, leaving the education system inadequate and incomplete.

It is crucial that Americans understand how the education system pertains to the world it supports. It goes much farther than the specifics of a given technology. To function as an effective system that attracts those who want to learn, those who want to teach, and those who want to invest in it, America's educational program not only has to keep in lockstep with the strategic needs of the nation but must commit enough resources to significantly advance those ends. Otherwise, the relevance of the education system will decline to such a degree that those who would invest their time and money lose interest. Like every other organization, the education system has limited resources and must set priorities, and those priorities must in large part reflect a national strategy for competitiveness.

When education and strategic industries combine, however, they can create a virtuous, mutually reinforcing circle. Fred Terman, dean of Stanford's school of engineering from 1946 to 1965 and later provost of the university, wanted more of Stanford's engineering graduates to remain in the area rather than build their careers in other parts of the country. He thus encouraged two engineers, Bill Hewlett and Dave Packard, to form a company and provided them with customer lists for their first product, an audio oscillator. His efforts stimulated Stanford's ongoing collaboration with Hewlett Packard and many other companies that grew out of an original association with the university.

The success of these companies—often in technologies, products, and markets highly strategic to the nation—provided clear motivation and direction for the educational institutions in the vicinity of what is now known as Silicon Valley. HP, Cisco, Google, Sun Microsystems, and many others owe much to the educational endowment they received from Stanford. At the same time, the monetary and technological collaboration of successful companies with Stanford and similar institutions has contributed to the brilliant history of those schools and boded a successful future for the Valley's educational base. The future of education in Silicon Valley, however, requires that these companies and others like them remain solid competitors in the global arena and retain a significant portion of their engineering and manufacturing in the United States.

The competitive strength of a nation does not occur by accident. Even if a country is blessed with a natural resource like oil, things can change. The resource can be depleted, or the convergence of related infrastructure may lead international competition to find a substitute. Oil may be supplanted by solar energy, synthetic fuels, and nuclear power. It is therefore necessary for every nation to try to anticipate the future so that its strategic plans do not degenerate to the merely tactical—to opportunism and reaction to current events. As a nation's reliance on any given resource for its competitive edge is changed or challenged, the education system is challenged accordingly. Because education must stay ahead of the game in a world where the complexity of the technology database is accelerating at an ever-increasing rate, the job of educating the country must be an essential part of the nation's competitive strategy.

EDUCATION AS THE PRODUCT
AND BASIS OF COMPETITIVENESS

In the early 1990s, I had the opportunity to listen to a well-known economist opine on America's problems with the Japanese and South Korean semiconductor industries. Accusations had been made and legal action taken by America's semiconductor industry and the federal government to halt the alleged dumping of Asian-manufactured dynamic random access memory chips, or DRAMs, in the U.S. market. The pricing of those chips, coupled with limited access to Asian markets, was putting American manufacturers out of business. The economist suggested that American businesses should be smart enough to buy those chips while they were being sold below cost and use the savings to leapfrog the competition.

I remember feeling at the time that this man did not fully understand the implications of his remarks. The DRAM was originally patented in 1968 by Robert Dennard, a staff engineer in the research division of IBM. For this and other inventions he was awarded the National Medal of Technology in 1988. As a result of his original work, several American companies became major suppliers of these memory chips, including IBM, Intel, Texas Instruments, Motorola, National Semiconductor, Fairchild Semiconductor, and Micron Technology. But by the late 1990s, every U.S. company but one, Micron Technology, had gotten out of the DRAM business because they could no longer make an acceptable profit. If Micron had abandoned it as well, America would have only limited participation in the memory chip market today. The memory chip is one of the primary semiconductor devices that stores the information processed in most electronic systems. The total loss of DRAM manufacturing could have dealt a devastating blow to the American semiconductor industry. More important, the DRAM became for years a driving force in advancing semiconductor manufacturing technology.

The success of Japan and South Korea in gaining market share in DRAM manufacturing motivated Asia to build an educational capability that would support the advancement of semiconductor design and manufacturing technology. Coupled with integrated circuit demand from the Asian consumer electronics and computer industry, dominance in the design and manufacturing of memories contributed significantly to what may be an inexorable shift in semiconductor production from the United States and Europe to Asia.

Meanwhile, consistent with Moore's Law, Japanese and South Korean memory manufacturers learned how to make money at even lower prices than those that had prompted the early 1990s dumping charges. The production of DRAMs became one of the biggest money machines the semiconductor industry had ever seen. Given the multibillion-dollar investment required to replicate—let alone leapfrog—an entrenched competitor in this industry, it is, at best, highly unlikely that some remarkable R&D advance would give advantage to a U.S. company not already actively involved in a significant ongoing DRAM manufacturing effort.

Few in the education world were in a position to suggest that this economist's view might fly in the face of reality. MIT's *Made in America* study attempted to warn the public about the dangers of losing manufacturing, but its comments fell largely on deaf ears. The United States nearly lost its entire position in the memory market, and very few seemed to care.

Moore's Law has broad implications for a nation's education system. A competitive society must be an educated society that understands the interrelationship between exponentially accelerating convergence, infrastructure, and investment. The popular concept of stars, cash cows, and dogs could become a major problem for America's education system in a world where global competition pursues the implications of Moore's Law. Why? Because if you lose to the competition without understanding why, wrongly assuming that you had the bad luck of picking a dog business or that your competition was willing to "give it away," you may lose more than the knowledge base to compete. You may lose the motivation to maintain an education system designed to provide the skills and technological advances essential to stay in the business.

Simply put, students study and teachers teach subjects related to where the jobs are. If there is no demand for a particular expertise, there is little incentive for either students or teachers to invest their time in it. (And thinking they will invest regardless is naïve at best.) Without an industrial base demanding ever-higher levels of technological skill to meet global competition, there is no compelling reason to graduate additional professionals. There will be nothing for them to do. When lack of demand for talent goes on too long, and the talent well dries up for loss of career opportunity, withdrawal from the market is often rationalized as leaving the dirty work to the competition.

In 1991, when electronics consultant Lawrence Tannas agreed to join my Japanese Technology Evaluation Center study on HDTV as an expert in display technology, he helped me understand the inextricable interrelationships that existed between electronic cameras, television systems, and VCRs. It was clear that the technological base Japan had established in consumer electronics and displays was causing a mass migration of this intellectual property from the United States to Japan. Along with this technological transfer, Japan had made major inroads into the semiconductor industry.

As a lecturer on the subject of flat panel displays not only in the West but in Japan, Korea, and China, Tannas was asked to head a study in 1992 specifically on display technologies in Japan. His study concluded that Japan was expanding its lead in product development, dominating investment and manufacturing implementation, and competitive in basic research. If things didn't change, he suggested, America was on its way to losing the entire display business. By 1996, it was essentially gone.

Larry Tannas's dedication to his country, and his specific concern that little technological expertise remained in the United States, led to his endowment of the Carol and Lawrence E. Tannas Jr. Chair in the Engineering Department of UCLA with explicit instructions that it focus on advanced display technology. Though one could dismiss this effort as symbolic, it represented his concern that the loss of an educational base in the display industry should be of great strategic concern to the United States.

As the proponents of Moore's Law have learned from experience, when you get off the train, it is very difficult to get back on. When a nation's politics and economics fall out of step with its education system, the cost of reengagement is extraordinarily high. Therefore any attempt to explain the plight of education in America must look first at the country's current political and economic attitudes. They are directly linked.

For example, America often assumes it has the luxury of ignoring a competitive environment in which other nations strive to take up the "burden" of manufacturing products or component parts, despite the fact that in time these products may have strategic significance for the United States. Their motives and methods unexamined, these foreign competitors are simply deprecated, often by comparing their lower returns on investment to that of an American company that has given up its manufacturing. This is a deceptive comparison, since the lack of investment that results from outsourcing can generate higher margins and lots of cash for several years. Concerns about losing position in a particular technology, product, or market are overridden by short-term profits, and for a time the decision looks masterful.

But eventually the supplier may decide to integrate its manufacturing expertise with its knowledge of the product and become a competitor, or the outsourced activity may become more strategic than the end-use product it supports, and the supplier begins to take control. A loss of business under these circumstances is near impossible to turn around. Eventually, because of the exponential acceleration in convergence, infrastructure, and investment, there's a cascading effect, and the loss of one industry begins to threaten the stability of others. These events are noticed by the educational community, which must provide a measure of career guidance for its student population and thus looks to political, economic, and business leaders for answers.

Consider this: For the United States to maintain a competitive position in consumer electronics, displays, and semiconductors—which have become a major part of the convergent technological infrastructure of most other industries—it must attract the best and the brightest engineering talent graduating from America's university system, a system still regarded as the world's best. Yet in today's environment, unless the graduating engineer hopes to establish his or her own business, it is often more profitable, even more intellectually challenging, to pursue a career in finance and investment banking. Again, in the *Issues in Science and Technology* article, Wadhwa and his coauthors pointed out that engineering salaries in the United States "are not competitive with those of other highly trained professionals," and they concluded that "it makes more financial sense for a top engineering student to become an investment banker than an engineer." On the other hand, in China, "researchers who publish their work in international journals are accorded status as national heroes."

As manufacturing for high-tech industries has moved offshore, much of the R&D associated with these industries has gone as well, a depletion clearly visible to any engineer seeking a technical career in the United States. In the world of high technology, exciting opportunities for engineers and scientists are declining in America. For those graduating with technical degrees, it is becoming more attractive to engineer a deal than a new product.

Loss of U.S. infrastructure in key industries is becoming endemic. A *Wall Street Journal* headline on July 30, 2007, should have alarmed anyone considering a career in the U.S. automobile industry: "More Parts Producers Give Up on Auto Industry." The article reported that "exposure to the domestic automotive business, battered by global competition that has already forced many auto-component-only producers such as Tower Automotive Inc. and Delphi Corporation into bankruptcy proceedings, has become too worrisome for these producers, while other parts of their businesses are more promising."[5] Among the companies cited in the article were Motorola (which sold its automotive sensor and control business to Continental AG of Germany) and PPG Industries. Parts for automobiles will still be made in America, but much of the manufacturing expertise and R&D that had been shared with other parts of the auto business may be lost to American manufacturers, which no longer want the risks and low profit margins. It's hard for the education system to promote the importance of a career in an industry where even the participating businesses decline to take the risk.

THE CARROT CIRCLE: K–12, COLLEGE, AND THE COMPETITIVE NATION

The current state of America's education system seems paradoxical—or at least strangely bifurcated. The nation boasts the greatest collection of higher learning institutions in the world, while many of its primary and secondary schools languish as if in a torpor. Though the educational pipeline is intended to feed our university system, or at least prepare students for an entry-level career, it fails to do so for a large number of them. A significant part of the problem lies in the motivation of the students and the system to compete in a global economy.

At the university level, competition is a motivating factor for both students and faculty. Many factors drive the university system to remain at the top of its game. Most basic is the need to gain popularity and expertise in those areas that will attract the most students—and hence stay in business. Students are customers. If too few of them choose any particular school, that school may find itself in financial trouble. Thus the customer-student has a tremendous influence on the curriculum. If expertise in language and liberal arts is what is in demand, then the college or university must offer the best education for the money in those fields. If science is not on most students' agenda, then only those institutions that offer renowned science programs for the right price can adequately maintain that curriculum.

On the other hand, the university system in the United States can be regarded as a successful export industry. American universities have always appealed to foreign students as premier enterprises of higher learning, and this international exposure has helped fill the ranks of U.S. colleges and universities when the supply of homegrown talent has been lacking. One might say that American universities produce surplus teaching capacity that they "export" by training foreign students. In this sense, they outcompete the rest of the world. But of utmost importance to the competitiveness of America's university system is its final product, the graduate. If he or she is recognized and accepted by companies and institutions everywhere in the world, the hiring institution benefits, the student benefits, the respective economy benefits, and the reputation of the university or college remains secure.

Research provides yet another level of competition. Valuable research programs that stimulate interest and provide students with potentially lucrative careers abound. Competition for these research funds is fierce and drives faculty and students to advance the state of learning. In addition, countless students have formed businesses based on their college experience, often with their professors' participation. The ideas and research brought to fruition within the university structure have created economic enterprises of startling value. Patent departments within universities are becoming increasingly important, as those institutions expand their licensing programs and otherwise further public interest in their intellectual property. In addition to businesses like Google, Cisco, and Hewlett Packard, fostered by Stanford University, examples include students from the University of California founding Qualcomm and Broadcom. Harvard was home to the world's richest college dropout, Bill Gates, who left to form Microsoft. MIT was a catalyst for such companies as Texas Instruments and Analog Devices.

A top university can look forward to research grants and donations from former students and their respective companies. Universities with a strong graduate program and research capability are still considered strategic to the nation and can count on support from government and industry. There remains a strong, if diminished, consensus that American universities are pillars of the nation's economic and strategic position—fundamental to national identity and security.

In short, the higher learning system can be effective without a clear vision of the nation's competitive strategy because, like other enterprises, it competes worldwide for students, income, research grants, donations, and other important affiliations. And universities can adjust their curricula accordingly.

This is untrue, however, of primary and secondary education. Public and private research dollars are not as readily available at the kindergarten through twelfth-grade level. With the exception of special interest and trade schools, there is far less direct connection to industry. The exposure of secondary students to competition from other nations and cultures is minimal. The curriculum is basically set and relatively rudimentary. Outside of athletics, primary and secondary schools are not viewed as competitive enterprises but conduits that shuffle students from one stage of life to another, propelling students into a university or career. Much of what these students learn—or care to learn—depends on what they think will be expected of them and how they measure their potential for success after graduation. These expectations filter down from the universities, teachers, parents, media, and the world around them. But the level of such expectation implicit in the culture is ultimately a reflection of the nation's political and economic leadership.

Only rarely has the American public school system felt the electric pulse of global competition. During World War II there was little doubt about national purpose or the duties and sacrifices expected of all Americans, old and young. For those in high school, it was hard to avoid the sense that, in the world awaiting them, national need eclipsed self-serving opportunism. In a world at war, high school for most was the entry point to a career in the military or one directly affected by the war effort.

As the dominant world power at war's end, however, the country returned to a peacetime economy and relative complacency about America's technological supremacy. But in 1957, Russia orbited the first artificial satellite, and a panic ensued over the status of American leadership in science and technology, creating a nationwide drive to bolster science in the schools. "No matter what we do now," declared John Rinehart of the Smithsonian Astrophysical Observatory, "the Russians will beat us to the moon. I would not be surprised if the Russians reached the moon within a week."[6] In response to rampant fear that the military and economic threat of the Soviet Union had suddenly taken a great leap, President Eisenhower called for "a system of nationwide testing of high school students, a system of incentives for high-aptitude students to pursue scientific or professional studies," more laboratory facilities, and a program to increase the ranks of science teachers. "For the American people," he added, this is "the most critical problem of all,"[7] ranking "above all other immediate tasks of producing missiles, of developing new techniques in the Armed Services."[8]

Within months, the ensuing congressional hearings produced the National Defense Education Act, providing low-cost loans to college students who would teach in public schools after graduation, and also matching funds for laboratories, textbooks, and facilities used in teaching science, mathematics, and foreign languages, especially Russian. NDEA channeled close to $1 billion toward education—particularly science education—over the next four years; it was a historic break with the long practice of leaving educational spending to states and localities. Four successive "Urgent" issues of *Life* magazine screamed "CRISIS IN EDUCATION" cover to cover, and a book called *Why Johnny Can't Read—and What You Can Do about It* became a smash best seller. Government commissions, senators, admirals, generals, and university presidents poured out articles, books, and speeches comparing U.S. and Soviet education. The result was a full-scale revamping of the American high school science curriculum. Electives were reduced, academic standards were raised, and science, math, and language programs were strengthened. The president presented a clear competitive strategy, and the nation responded.

The massive infusion of resources changed the face of American higher education as well. The number of Ph.D.s in physics awarded by U.S. institutions took off steeply, doubling every 6.2 years during the period 1958–1968. "Stroll through a university campus in the U.S. today and notice the dates of the science buildings," notes a September 2007 article in *New Scientist* magazine celebrating the fiftieth anniversary of *Sputnik*. "Everywhere you look, much of the infrastructure that supports the training of scientists in the U.S. was built in the years immediately after *Sputnik*'s flight."[9]

Another nudge toward a national competitive strategy came in the 1980s, when a debate raged over the threat of losing the semiconductor and display industries and most of consumer electronics to Japan. Sematech, an association of major semiconductor manufacturers and the U.S. government, was formed to bolster the competitiveness of the semiconductor industry. But when the Japanese real estate bubble burst in 1990, much of the concern evaporated, and with it the momentum behind any type of national strategy for competitiveness. Thus America's education system never really received a clear message. Essentially, the country's political and economic leadership signaled a policy suggesting that the education system should stay the course, which it did.

Today there is a major emphasis on monetary returns, less as a means than as a sufficient end. The highest-paying jobs in America are in finance—making deals, running hedge funds, and perfecting the art of leveraged buyouts that can be resold or remarketed at higher prices. Unlike the relatively long-term commitment of money and joint participation associated with venture capital, the publicity regarding the extraordinary remuneration associated with financial transactions is producing an almost surreal environment. An August 2007 article in the *Wall Street Journal* noted that "Mark McGoldrick earned about $70 million last year running one of Goldman Sachs' most profitable units. Turns out it wasn't enough. Now he's planning a hedge fund where he believes he can make more money."[10]

Financial engineering—employing cash and debt to create corporate structures that maximize profits and cash flow—is changing the face of American industry. U.S. companies are also employing an "asset lite" strategy, reducing their dependence on manufacturing and related fixed investment in order to achieve additional management flexibility to meet short-term changes in market demand along with substantial increases in cash flow and profits. For those who can adapt their background to finance and investment banking, the attraction of tremendous compensation in a very short period of time is so great that business schools and even engineering schools have recognized the importance of selling their educational programs as paths to getting into that game. In many respects, it has become a deal economy—stars, cash cows, and dogs taken to its logical extreme.

In the wake of *Sputnik,* Edward Teller, the father of the H-bomb, told a Senate Preparedness Subcommittee that educational reform, particularly in science and engineering, must extend to elementary schools "because by the time a kid is twelve years old, he probably has adopted the mental attitudes which will either make him a good scientist or will definitely get him interested in some field other than science."[11] The message today's schools are receiving from the culture at large is decidedly at odds with what Teller hoped for. For many in secondary school, the message seems to be that to dedicate years to developing a critical skill may no longer be as satisfying, financially rewarding, or easy to achieve as the immediate gains associated with simply buying and selling the equity value in another person's effort. Along with outsourcing, this trend has contributed to a decline in the graduation of American-born engineers and scientists that will be very difficult to turn around.

"Even if action is taken today to change these trends," noted an American Institute of Physics bulletin in June 2004, "the reversal is ten to twenty years away. The students entering the science and engineering workforce in 2004 with advanced degrees decided to take the necessary math courses to enable this career path when they were in middle school, up to fourteen years ago. The students making that same decision in middle school today won't complete advanced training for science and engineering occupations until 2018 or 2020."[12]

The point here is not to make a moral judgment on what strategy is right or wrong for any individual. Every profession has societal value. What is required, however, is a national strategy that helps put these varied business practices in perspective, stresses at least an awareness of what is important to the global competitiveness of the U.S. economy, and motivates America's education system to pursue a plan of action. Meanwhile, as the message of profit over process metastasizes across the nation, competition from Asia, steeped in the exponential growth associated with Moore's Law, garners more and more of the world's technological infrastructure, while America's schools and universities, lacking a national mandate, remain powerless to influence the situation.

COMMITMENT

To be competitive, a nation as a whole must appreciate the exponential acceleration of convergence, infrastructure, and investment. Unfortunately,

on the initial rungs of the educational ladder, the message to students can
be clear—as if a subliminal voice were asking, "Is learning science a necessary evil, or does it have relevance to my life and future?" A significant
part of the answer lies in the will and action of the nation with regard to
its competitive future. Either its leadership understands the principles of
competitiveness and is committed to supporting the long-term investments inherent in the challenges of global competition, or it isn't.

How committed is the United States to the precepts of successful
competition on a global scale? In February 2005, a report from the Task
Force on the Future of American Innovation bore the title "The Knowledge Economy: Is the United States Losing Its Competitive Edge?" The
report was developed with the participation of major American companies and associations, including Agilent Technologies, the American
Chemical Society, the American Electronics Association, the American
Mathematical Society, the Association of American Universities, the
Council on Competitiveness, Hewlett-Packard, Intel, Microsoft, the National Association of Manufacturers, the Semiconductor Industry Association, and many others. The report focused on innovation, and the
introduction put forth a clear warning that everything was not okay:

> For more than half a century, the United States has led the world in sci-
> entific discovery and innovation. It has been a beacon, drawing the best
> scientists to its educational institutions, industries and laboratories from
> around the globe. However, in today's rapidly evolving competitive
> world, the United States can no longer take its supremacy for granted.
> Nations from Europe to Eastern Asia are on a fast track to pass the
> United States in scientific excellence and technological innovation.[13]

Some of the benchmark statistics are revealing. "The ratio of first
university degrees in natural sciences and engineering (NS&E) to the
college-age population in the U.S. is only 5.7 degrees per 100. . . . Japan
awards 8 per 100, and Taiwan and South Korea each award about 11 per
100."[14] In a broader context, in the year 2000 the U.S. accounted for only

25,000 out of 114,000 science and engineering doctoral degrees awarded worldwide. During the seven years between 1994 and 2001, science and engineering enrollment in the United States declined 10 percent, compared to a 25 percent increase for foreign-born students. Approximately 57 percent of all postdoctoral positions in the United States were occupied by foreign-born scholars in 2001. On the other hand, from 1994 to 1998, the number of Chinese, South Korean, and Taiwanese students pursuing a Ph.D. in science and technology in the United States dropped by 19 percent—while the number who opted to pursue similar degrees in their own countries nearly doubled.[15]

According to the report there are significant reasons for the buildup of homegrown scientists and engineers in Asia. Between 1995 and 2001, "China, South Korea, and Taiwan increased their gross R&D investments by about 140 percent. During the same period, the U.S. increased its investments by 34 percent."[16] The significance of these statistics has not been confined to education and research and development. In 1980, the American share of worldwide high-tech exports amounted to 31 percent of the market, while Japan and emerging Asian economies represented 22 percent. Since then the United States has experienced a steady decline in market share, and by 2001, America represented 18 percent of the global market for high-tech exports, while Japan and the emerging Asian economies' share had grown to 35 percent.[17]

The competitive problems cited by the report have spread to other aspects of technological development in America. Regarding nanotechnology, which is fundamental to the development of the semiconductor industry, the report noted that "Asian countries are investing significantly in nanotechnology, and may have already surpassed the U.S. in this promising area of research."[18] In January 2004, the President's Council of Advisors for Science and Technology stated that "in the face of global competition, U.S. information technology manufacturing has declined significantly since the 1970s with an acceleration of the decline over the past five years."[19] The United States is lagging behind in household broadband penetration as well—ranking thirteenth in a list of fifteen highly developed countries. The Task Force's 2005 report cited similar challenges in energy, aerospace, and biotechnology.

In light of these disquieting statistics, what, again, are the status and importance of education in America? The statistics from the President's Council of Advisors on Science and Technology cited at the opening of this chapter suggest that America's university system, like the rest of its educational base, will mirror the political and economic strategy of the nation. As America's orientation toward maximum profit and cash flow reduces its willingness to invest in homegrown advancements in product design and manufacturing in favor of outsourcing, the demand for technological excellence within its universities will also drop. This flagging demand for science and technology degrees is partly compensated by the potential supply of foreign students. But in the long run, they will return to their own countries and their own schools. These students are motivated by the rewards offered for their support of a national strategy dedicated to investment in the design and manufacture of advanced technologies and products. In Asia, this has been a fundamental strategic goal for many years, and their education systems are advancing accordingly. Meanwhile, the relative economic competitiveness of the United States will continue to decline in a world increasingly subject to the ramifications of acceleration in convergence, infrastructure, and investment. This is a problem that America will find difficult to reverse.

In sum, the motivation required to insure that an education system is operating in accordance with its nation's competitive needs assumes that the country has a discernible strategy to be competitive in the first place. The rewards of that strategy encourage the dedication of both students and faculty. If there is no cohesive strategy other than the desire to increase profits or generate cash, then the education system will follow suit. Unfortunately, the concept of stars, cash cows, and dogs can be interpreted in this light. Because of the resources required to take advantage of the exponential growth in convergent infrastructure, with its soaring investment costs—the result of heretofore unimaginable combinations of technologies, products, and markets—America must begin to think about the implications of doing deals that are designed to produce short-term profits and cash flow but may not be consistent with a national strategy of global competitiveness. Either way, the content and quality of America's schools will reflect the decisions of its economic and political leadership. The virtuous circle can easily become vicious.

If the nation continues to jettison "dog" businesses that turn out to be vital to global competition, and those critical jobs move out of the country, the reduced incentive to prepare for waning opportunities will mean a decline of science and technology in the schools. Education is then faced with the same problem as industry. For learning institutions, the prohibitive cost and lack of current-level experience that make it so difficult to get back in the game is measured not only in qualified workers—the short supply of scientists and engineers needed to teach—but in capital expenditures to upgrade laboratories with state-of-the-art plant and equipment that match acceleration in technological advancement. That shortage in turn inhibits significant restoration of strategic industries and perpetuates the schools' lack of emphasis on science and technology. Thus the circle is closed, ensuring that the shortage will continue and perpetuating America's competitive decline. The circle can become a downward spiral.

There are many structural problems affecting America's primary and secondary school system. Classes are often too large, teachers may not have the appropriate educational background, equipment may be lacking, and course material may not be current or applicable. The purpose of this book, however, is not to evaluate the state of education as such but only to argue that it is inextricably connected to the problems of global competition. The emphasis on science and technology—and on the functional aspects of education as a means to livelihood—is not meant to slight those broader aspects of learning that raise awareness and improve the quality of one's life. In this respect, two points are worth noting about what C. P. Snow called the "two cultures." The first is that the humanities and sciences have become ever more interrelated, having undergone their own form of convergence in an increasingly interdisciplinary world. The second is that the vitality of the humanities has always been dependent on that of science and technology in that the latter create the standard of living—the surpluses and freeing from labor—that enable the former.

Because the complications of exponentially accelerating convergence, infrastructure, and investment affect the entire economy, the education system, like the economy it must support, will always have limited resources. As with industry, an education system must have a strategy that can achieve society's goals efficiently yet stay within resource constraints. With the fundamental understanding that America as a nation intends to be competitive in a global economy, a new sense of relevance and necessity will vitalize the education system supporting that end. Otherwise there will be neither the will nor the money to solve its problems.

The ultimate motivation insuring the success of the nation's education system is the conviction of the nation's leadership, as well as its people, that they can and will compete in strategic global markets and share in the benefits of that success. If the United States understands and supports that conviction, America's universities will remain world-class, and its secondary schools, in cooperation with universities and industry, will rise to meet the collective challenges.

CHAPTER 7

It's Not about the Picture:
The Case of HDTV

*Certain technologies, products, and markets are strategic to a
nation's industrial base and ability to compete. Weakness in one
sector may cause weakness in dependent sectors.*

In several 1988 presentations to the American Electronics Association,
members of Congress, and others, I contended that though "high definition television portrays life in vivid splashes of breathtaking color
and sound," the picture "may also reflect the ebbing tide of United States
technological and economic leadership."[1] Contrasting the American
hunger to invest in individual companies bent on high profits in the
short term, I noted that in Japan the entrepreneurial spirit could be defined as the need to push a technological expertise to its logical extreme
in order to integrate it with other technological disciplines and thus
dominate the market. Therefore it was essential for Americans to understand that HDTV was not about the pretty picture. It was the quin-
tessential example of Japan's entrepreneurial spirit. HDTV was about
convergence, infrastructure, and investment.

My talks to the AEA came at an interesting juncture. At the beginning of the 1980s, when the economy was not doing well, Americans

179

began to show concern that the United States was losing its competitive ascendancy in everyday products like cameras, recorders, and television sets. It was also losing its competitive edge in machine tools, robotics, optics, materials, and semiconductors. Japan was seen as the major cause of these losses. Under pressure from the U.S. government in 1978, Japan agreed to open more of its domestic market to American products, but that did not reduce the flow of Japanese exports to the United States. The showstopper of the day was automobiles. Detroit was suddenly having great difficulty competing with Japan. But Detroit carried a big stick. In 1978, automobile production in the United States represented 4.6 percent of the gross domestic product of America. Even in 1998, twenty years later, approximately 10 percent of all U.S. employment was still in some way related to the automobile industry. In 1981, after the U.S. government threatened to impose limits on the number of automobiles Japan could ship to America, Japan announced that it would voluntarily limit its exports of passenger cars to the United States.

After World War II, Japan had been a low-cost provider of products to the United States. For years it posed no economic threat. But over time the quality of Japanese goods improved, designs improved, and perceived value improved. As these strengths developed in the 1960s and '70s, U.S. industry was happy to have such a willing and reliable supplier of goods, one available to take on those tasks that America felt were of lesser value as its industries strove to improve design creativity and achieve higher margins of profit. This approach seemed to work well until the United States woke up to the fact that Japan was developing not only a willing and reliable workforce but a highly motivated and creative technical capability that was shaping totally integrated and sophisticated products second to none. The pressure on America's political leadership began to build. The country needed some type of industrial policy, if not strategy, as protection against what many felt was unfair, unrelenting competition.

The answer came in part from a sector of the U.S. economy able to convince Washington that the strategic nature of its business was fundamental to everything else. That sector was the semiconductor industry. As the 1980s progressed, it became clear that the American semiconductor industry was rapidly losing share to the Japanese, and the Reagan administration eventually ceded to industry pressure and agreed to the formation of an organization, financed in part by the government, that would help plan an industry-wide strategy to maintain American competitiveness in the manufacture of semiconductors. The organization they established was called Sematech.

Though many in the semiconductor industry tried to explain the importance of integrated circuits to the industrial base of America, little concern remained in the nation's capital after the Japanese real estate crash in 1989. "I am more worried that we will have to bail out the economy of Japan than I am about having to protect our technological base," an official in the Office of Technology Policy in the U.S. Department of Commerce said to me at the time. This attitude was expressed in many ways by numerous officials in Washington who disagreed with any policy that might suggest the U.S. government become involved in picking winners and losers. They viewed anyone proposing that certain technologies, products, or markets might be strategic to American economic success as a proponent of "industrial policy." The term is still used to describe direct interference by government through subsidies, tax laws, tariffs, or other regulatory activities that might favor one company or industry over another. More than bad business, such interference is viewed as economic mismanagement and an encroachment on individual freedom.

Sematech continues as an organization to this day. For years it provided the U.S. semiconductor industry a vehicle to discuss and act on strategic issues that affected industry competitiveness. But prevailing sentiment in Washington was unfavorable to any organization that seemed to suggest an "industrial policy." So Sematech's potential was probably limited.

HIGH DEFINITION TELEVISION:
BENIGN INDIFFERENCE

In 1990, there was significant controversy as to whether HDTV, a technology heavily backed by the government and industry consortiums in Japan, would become a threat to America's technological competitiveness. But according to the cynical analysis of those most influential in Washington, the supposed threat of HDTV was nothing more than a political move on industry's part to scare the U.S. government into funding American private enterprise in the design and development of advanced consumer electronics and television products.

I became deeply involved in the debate, having been introduced to HDTV in Japan as early as 1970. I was impressed by a demonstration of the MUSE system, a combination of analog and digital technology. It was my first real exposure to the potential of digital technology, and I was convinced that the Japanese were beginning to capitalize on the potential of digital processing, which could significantly expand the amount of information transmitted from one piece of hardware to another. I felt MUSE would add to the long-term potential of video recording. But I didn't return to the issue until 1985, nearly fifteen years later, when Richard Rosenbloom and Karen Freeze of Harvard University analyzed the fate of the VCR in America. Asked to give a presentation on competitiveness to the American Electronics Association in Santa Clara, California, I used the opportunity to suggest that the industry should begin to think about the impact of a potential loss of certain technologies, products, and markets, particularly consumer electronics, displays, and semiconductors.

It was obvious to most observers by the mid-1980s that the VCR would find its way into almost every household that could afford one. This would mean a majority of homes in the developed world, as the prices for video recorders and related consumer products (largely produced in Japan) were plunging in accordance with the implications of Moore's Law. And since the VCR was a voracious consumer of semiconductor devices, it was beginning to affect the balance of power between the United States and Japan in the semiconductor industry.

Since video recording was an American invention initially commercialized in the United States, the question persisted: Why had it become a Japanese phenomenon? Partly as a result of the Harvard study, I was asked to do an interview on ABC's *20/20*. No sooner had the camera crew positioned themselves in my office than ABC's Lynn Sherr asked the question, "How could the United States have lost the VCR?" The answer, of course, lay in the constant conflict between the American investor's need for short-term profits and the fundamental importance of long-term growth and prosperity for both company and nation. These circumstances would be vividly illustrated when the tactics of stars, cash cows, and dogs encountered the rigors of Moore's Law. But that was a concept difficult to explain in those days. Not until the rapid advance of digital technology and the internet did people begin to realize that something momentous was happening. But that would be over ten years later. In my answer to Lynn Sherr, I mentioned Ampex's lack of resources, serious financial problems, and limited manufacturing expertise. A lot was left unsaid.

After that interview and my presentation to the AEA, I began to reflect seriously on what I had learned from my association with the brilliant engineers at Ampex and in my current position as a member of the founding team of Prometrix. I visualized what might happen as a result of the rapid commercialization and expansion of electronic audiovisual recording. My entry into the semiconductor capital equipment industry made me aware of the rapid technological advancement and increase in spending on semiconductor plant and equipment that were required to support those consumer products. I began to realize that these products, largely because of their semiconductor content, were converging before my eyes. With respect to the growth of technology and capital investment in the semiconductor industry and consumer electronics, it was apparent that both industries were in virtual lockstep and advancing at a pace in line with the exponential projections of Moore's Law.

My conclusions regarding convergence, infrastructure, and investment seemed to me logical and observable, yet many knowledgeable people disagreed. One of those who strenuously objected was Thomas Gale Moore, a member of the Council of Economic Advisors to the President from 1985 to 1989 and subsequently a senior fellow at Stanford's Hoover Institute.

One day an associate called me and suggested I read a policy analysis, "The Promise of High Definition Television: The Hype and the Reality," that Thomas Moore had written in 1989 for the Cato Institute. The direction of the analysis, which countered my thoughts head-on, was evident in the first paragraph of his executive summary: "High-definition television (HDTV) has been described as a technology driver that will determine the future of the computer industry and the semiconductor industry as well as the technological state of our society. However, like many aspects of our political life, this description may be more hype than reality. HDTV has the potential to improve electronic visual displays, but at a cost."[2]

In response to the "several bills that had been introduced into Congress to help foster HDTV," Moore indicated his concern that "government officials have little knowledge or appreciation of the market place." They "often base investment and spending decisions on political considerations. Investments are made to preserve or create jobs, not because they are profitable; governments tend to invest in losing firms. Thus, the best policy is for the government to stay out of the private sector. Its incentives are wrong, its information is inadequate, and its biases are all wrong." To illustrate his point, he added that "while the HDTV industry looks like a winner, it could be the turkey of all time."[3]

At the time that Thomas Gale Moore wrote this article for the Cato Institute, the position of display manufacturing in the United States was still significant, even though, as he noted, the only American company left in the business was Zenith.

Although HDTV probably will not be introduced into the U.S. market in the next year or so, many commentators and politicians are concerned that this market will become another one dominated by the Japanese. As they have pointed out, Zenith is the only U.S.-owned television manufacturer. All video recorders are imported from either Japan or Korea. However, Zenith makes TVs in Asia, while Hitachi, Matsushita, Mitsubishi, Sanyo, Sony, and Toshiba, among others, make color TV receivers in the United States.[4]

Moore was reasonably certain that displays would continue to be made in the United States: "In 1987, almost seventy percent of all color TV sets sold in the United States were made in the United States. Because HDTV sets will be large, they almost certainly will be assembled in the United States."[5]

In presenting his arguments, he referenced comments I had made on the subject:

The fear is that the Japanese, who have a head start on HDTV, soon will dominate this market as well. As Richard J. Elkus Jr., chairman of the Prometrix Corporation, put it, "All markets are linked. Lose one market and you lose others. Lose others and pretty soon you lose your entire technological base." This statement is nonsense. No country has all markets, nor can a country have most markets. The United States does not dominate the coffee market, the banana market, the watch market, the calculator market, the high-speed train market, or the chromium, manganese, and cobalt markets. It does dominate the personal computer, the mainframe and super-computer, the commercial aircraft manufacturing, and the biotechnology markets, among others. A country's dominance of one market implies nothing about its potential to dominate others.[6]

Concerned that proponents of an American strategy to become a player in the HDTV industry were potentially hyping future market opportunities and their effects on America's technological base, Moore declared that

the potential market for HDTV has been grossly exaggerated, with estimates for total sales as high as $100 billion. In fact, the total sales of
color TV sets in the United States last year [1988] amounted to less
than $10 billion. Again, even under the most optimistic assumptions,
HDTV will not capture the entire market. Although HDTV sets will
cost more than the ones that they supplant, the assumption that sales
would be much larger than $10 billion (in 1989 dollars) for any year in
the foreseeable future seems to be more hype than reality.[7]

Moore felt that the government should treat the advent of HDTV
with benign indifference. He concluded that while the success of HDTV
in the marketplace would bring a greatly improved audiovisual experience, it was up to the marketplace to determine if the experience was
worth it.

THE SPECTER OF INDUSTRIAL POLICY

The debate over the future of HDTV continued into the early 1990s.
There were many who agreed with Moore, especially after the collapse
of the Japanese real estate market. Others were against trying to "out-
Japanese" the Japanese; instead of beating them at their own game, they
argued, we should be strategically aware of where the world is going and
get there first. One of the greatest proponents of this philosophy was
George Gilder. As a Harvard student he was a founder of *Advance,* a
journal of political thought. He coauthored (with Bruce Chapman) a po-
litical history, *The Party that Lost Its Head,* and has served as a speech-
writer for several prominent people, including Nelson Rockefeller,
George Romney, and Richard Nixon. According to Ray Kurzweil, "Mr.
Gilder was President Reagan's most frequently quoted living author."[8]
He was presented with the White House Award for Entrepreneurial
Excellence and has been a contributing editor to *Forbes* magazine.

In 1990, I debated Gilder in the Capitol building in Washington,
D.C., about the potential impact of HDTV on U.S. competitiveness. It

was a frustrating experience. Not only did George know his subject and present it well (he suggested that America's technological base was excellent and the future of America's semiconductor industry looked bright, a point aided by the fact that Japan's economy appeared to be crashing), but it was also difficult to explain HDTV when most people had no idea what we were talking about. I'm sure I was able to convince some that the United States was facing a problem. But I felt George convinced many that America's technological base was impenetrable.

Shortly thereafter, he wrote a short book, *Life After Television,* in which he discussed high-definition TV. Acknowledging the potential threat and the concerns that many inside and outside of the high-tech industry had at that time, he noted that "perhaps the most portentous alarm concerning HDTV came from Richard J. Elkus Jr., a 20-year veteran of U.S.-Japan electronics wars. Now a microchip capital-equipment entrepreneur, two decades ago he had worked at Ampex Corporation while it struggled to introduce the world's first successful consumer videotape recorder. Then he had watched helplessly as Sony and Panasonic captured this American market."[9] Quoting my contention that "the Japanese know that when you push a technology far enough it merges with all surrounding technologies, and when you push a market far enough it engulfs all related markets," Gilder added that "HDTV, as Elkus saw it, would engulf the American computer, microchip, appliance, telephone, film and industrial equipment technologies and markets."[10]

Life After Television, though short, was insightful. Gilder suggested that television as we knew it, HDTV or otherwise, was going to become a startlingly different medium, emphasizing interactive relationships rather than a simple one-way propagation of information. He was right. He was pushing for a digital highway in the United States that would take advantage of America's strength in computer technology as a route to dominating a brave, new, interactive world. According to Gilder, television as we knew it was dead. More than anyone else, America had the technology and the intelligence to make it interactive. This would require strategic thinking on the part of industry, the educational system, and politicians.

The problem with Gilder's argument, however, was that the shapers of national political and economic policy did not see in it a competitive issue significant enough to consider defining a national strategy for competitiveness. Moreover, much of the infrastructure of products and markets that the United States needed to fulfill Gilder's dream had been lost. A major portion of the communications infrastructure of products and markets that became interactive just as Gilder predicted were designed and made elsewhere. No one wanted to wait for U.S. industry to catch up. The American consumer already had a plethora of choices.

In 1990, the final report of the High Resolution Systems Task Force Working Committee of the Department of Defense outlined the critical nature of HDTV to national and economic security: "Our report establishes that high resolution technologies are critical in two distinct senses: they are vital to U.S. national security as defined in a strictly military context and they are also vital to the survival of the U.S. industrial base in the economic context of competitive world markets."[11]

A month later, a *New York Times* article by Tom Wicker reported that in "early April, the Pentagon quietly diverted to other purposes $20 million of $30 million allocated by the Defense Advanced Research Projects Agency to high-definition television. About two weeks later, not so quietly, the Defense Department assigned Dr. Craig Fields, the director of DARPA, to another defense position."[12] The explanation, Wicker surmised, was that the actions of Craig Fields and DARPA represented "industrial policy" to which the first Bush administration was strongly opposed. The specter and stigma of industrial policy were everywhere.

Wicker also noted that a Pentagon advisory board had recently urged that HDTV research funds be increased to $100 million yearly for the next five years. He also pointed out that the Congressional Office of Technology Assessment was preparing a report citing HDTV as vital to the U.S. position in the world electronics market. Critics, Wicker added, complained that these recommendations came mainly from the American Electronics Association, while others who opposed the proposed Department of Defense support for HDTV argued that the $30 million from DARPA would be a waste considering how far America was behind the Japanese, who had already spent $700 million on HDTV. But Wicker felt that all these critics missed the point: "The research Craig Fields wanted to sponsor . . . may be important to the survival of the U.S. electronics industry—which is vital to American military strength, even if HDTV may not be. By one estimate, half the total cost of new Army weapons by the year 2000 will be for electronics. Perhaps even more important, high-technology industries will bear the main burden of future American economic competitiveness—on which national prosperity largely depends."

Under the leadership of Roosevelt, Truman, Eisenhower, and Kennedy, things were different. They had to contend with the Great Depression, World War II, the cold war, and *Sputnik*. In those circumstances, national strategic decisions were clearly made, good or bad, that totally shaped American industry, politics, and the economy. Most would agree that the results were basically very good.

But having emerged from depression and world war the richest and most powerful nation on Earth, Americans in the late 1960s began to believe that they could afford both guns and butter—the good life amid costly and sacrificial conflict. It was assumed that the rest of the world would play according to American rules. But American policy has failed to consider the global impact of Moore's Law and the exponential acceleration of convergence, infrastructure, and investment. It simply costs too much for any nation, let alone any company, to do everything on its own. Globalism is not simply a matter of borderless markets with respect to tariffs or other artificial controls to insure the maximum in free and fair trade. Global relationships are essential to all because as technology advances along with the infrastructure of related products and markets, not only companies but countries run out of available resources to keep pace. The technology, infrastructure, and cost requirements move too quickly.

To keep pace with the advancement of technology, and stay abreast of the competition in a global economy, the players need to partner. A successful partnership assumes that each of the participants brings sufficient expertise to the table to insure its long-term value to the relationship while at the same time preserving its independence as a viable economic entity. If each of the participants is competitive in its own right, with sufficient understanding of mutual strategic strengths and weaknesses, the relationship can be of benefit to both, with neither becoming beholden to the other.

In many respects, what has changed the competitive landscape for the United States today was what I viewed in 1970 in Japan: HDTV. Since that time, and in large part because of Moore's Law and the need for co-operative ventures to sustain investment requirements, it's no longer just Japan but all of Asia that is America's competitor. Collectively, Asia soon realized that the amount of concentrated investment required to achieve the infrastructure necessary to exploit the technologies, products, and markets resulting from HDTV would stretch available resources. As a result, joint ventures between companies and countries began to flourish. Unfortunately, much of that infrastructure was developing in Asia (the producer) rather than in America (the consumer).

The United States had opportunities to partner with both Japanese and Korean companies that were increasing their financial and intellectual resources in a strategic attempt to assure the success of an HDTV display industry in their own countries, but America lacked the desire to commit the necessary resources. The United States wanted out, not in. So the Asian nations began to develop large and complex mutual relationships that involved no significant commitment from the United States. Contrary to what many thought was simply a competitive advantage based on low-cost labor riding on the back of a strong dollar, Japan, Korea, Taiwan, and China invested significant amounts of money in the development of technical know-how and production expertise specifically applicable to HDTV. Those investments paid off.

A DOG BUSINESS

The American Electronics Association saw it coming. In 1988 the association's Advanced Television Task Force Economic Impact Team tried to predict what might happen if the United States were not a significant participant in the design, development, and manufacture of high-definition technology and products.

It should be noted that the following comments from the foreword to the ATV Task Force report came eight years before the arrival of the internet as a recognized force in the economy, before DVDs wiped out most of the advantages of the VCR, before wireless communications made the cell phone ubiquitous, before the digital revolution overwhelmed the analog world, and before the semiconductor became as fundamental to communication as water to life.

Economic competitiveness has become *the* national security issue. A second rate economic power will be hard-pressed to be a leader in keeping tomorrow's world peace.

The world is poised on the threshold of a revolution in electronics. In combination with a variety of technical breakthroughs, new technologies will become available which are likely to affect the very infrastructure of the U.S. economy. Advanced Television is a fundamental new imaging technology with enormous capability to affect not only most electronics industry segments but the balance in end-use markets between cable, broadcasters, etc.

There are chilling implications for non-participation. The U.S. needs to gain a proprietary position in key advanced television markets to ensure that technological know-how remains in this country. The end reward for those who design, manufacture, and sell [into] advanced television markets is dominance of computers and telecommunications. Those with access to the means by which ATV-HDTV pictures and voice data are ultimately transmitted to the home, e.g., via fiber optics, direct broadcast satellite, terrestrial broadcast, VCRs, etc., will play a key role in tomorrow's information society where the "smart home" holds center stage. [In reference to the smart home, the report lamented the United States' loss of market share in consumer electronics.]

Total negative impact from the loss of consumer electronics is hard to assess. The U.S. electronics infrastructure is like a biological food chain with many interdependent segments. When one link is weakened or destroyed, other links feel the injury. Many believe competitive problems experienced today by the U.S. semiconductor industry can be traced to this lost segment.[13]

The ATV Task Force stated some projections that seemed unrealistic to many at the time. They projected an explosion in HDTV television set sales in twenty years, forecasting that in 2010 30 million HDTV sets would be sold worldwide and that a total of 208 million HDTV sets would be bought by consumers during the intervening period. These numbers struck those on the other side of the issue as absurdly high. Even more significant was the ATV Task Force projection that this volume of HDTV sets would represent revenues of $18 billion in 2010. The Task Force concluded that the total accumulated revenues resulting from the purchase of these sets for this twenty-year period would reach $170 billion at retail.[14]

But it was obvious from the ongoing HDTV debate that there were two very different points of view. Though some thought that the market might be larger in twenty years than the AEA had concluded, they assumed that the amount of dollars represented by the market for HDTV sets would still be too small to worry about. In a 1990 background paper, "The Big Picture: HDTV & High Resolution Systems," the Congressional Office of Technology Assessment noted: "Skeptics argue that HDTV is likely to be a relatively small market (at most $30 billion in 20 years) compared to the entire world electronics market (which is already $450 billion or more) and can therefore be ignored. . . . Skeptics insist that if HDTV is important, industry will invest in it independently and will do so more wisely than the government could."[15] But the authors of the report were clearly worried:

> If [HDTV] is viewed broadly—as a possible first step back into consumer electronics manufacturing; as a principal driver of High Resolution System technologies (HRS) for future computer and communications equipment; or as a component of a national fiber information network with HDTV or related products serving as the home terminal—then Congress may find that HDTV and related HRS technologies could contribute to several national goals.
>
> HDTV may . . . be an instructive case study of the difficulties facing the United States in reversing the erosion of U.S. leadership in many electronic technologies and in global and domestic electronics markets. The United States is seriously lagging technically and/or in market share in semiconductor materials; ceramic packaging; DRAMs, gate arrays, CMOS and ECL devices generally; LCD displays; optoelectronics; and floppy disk and helical scanning drives (VCRs); to name only a few. The United States will not long remain a world leader in electronics technologies if its technological foundation continues to crumble in this manner.[16]

Yet there was a fundamental problem with the notion that American companies would enter the business *if* and *when* they decided that HDTV was going to be an important industry. In 1990, HDTV was considered a consumer-oriented technology, in spite of its many potential applications to other parts of the economy, and America had been shying away from investments in consumer electronics on the general assumption that it was a low-margin, highly competitive business. This concept was reinforced by the relentless commitment of Japan and other Asian countries to dominate technologically advanced consumer electronics, including displays, and to invest massively in manufacturing expertise—creating a formidable level of competition. The United States decided to exit most of its consumer electronics and display businesses because, in the minds of American business leaders, these had become "dog businesses." Competition was fierce, margins were thin, and there were few clear leaders, let alone one or two suppliers that controlled a major portion of the market.

Though U.S. companies abandoned the game, American demand for consumer electronics and related displays was satisfied by Japan, Korea, and Taiwan. U.S. companies that once produced most of the world's consumer electronics were offered the opportunity to distribute Asian products. What began as an outsourcing of component parts became the purchase of completed products and systems. Though Zenith was still in the display business, all other American producers of TVs were in the process of being sold or shut down. Many economists and political leaders took comfort in the fact that foreign suppliers of television sets to U.S. customers still produced much of their product in the United States. But becoming the home of foreign assembly plants was no guarantee that America would, let alone could, restart its display industry.

In the early 1990s, displays were cathode ray tubes (CRTs) that required relatively little technological investment. Production lines were inexpensive in today's terms, costing a few million dollars per line. That changed with HDTV and the digital revolution. By the time America woke up to the fact that HDTV—virtually inseparable from the display industry—was going to be big business, the cost of getting back in the game had become overwhelming. Few were willing to take that investment risk.

TAKEOFF

The standard for HDTV in the United States was established by the Grand Alliance, a group of companies and research laboratories that included AT&T, General Instrument, MIT, Philips, Sarnoff Laboratories, Thomson, and Zenith. This was the group that Sony founder Akio Morita wanted to help, knowing that a U.S. standard would be instrumental in insuring a market for HDTV products not only in America but also in many other parts of the world. Morita wanted an all-digital standard different than MUSE's analog and digital system, and he was certain that a U.S. digital standard would insure that result. He felt that he could and should contribute to an American all-digital standard because Sony already had a line of digital video-production equipment and display technology that was superior to that available in the United States and readily adaptable to any American-sponsored digital standard.

While a U.S. standard would provide the digital highway for Sony and other Asian manufacturers of digital products, Japan wanted to build the cars—the digital equipment operating on the standard. When I called FCC chair Al Sikes at Morita's request, informing him that Sony would contribute labor, technology, and money to the establishment of an American digital standard, I also tried to warn Sikes of the consequences affecting U.S. competitiveness if America remained indifferent to the concept of supporting domestic participation in the development and manufacture of digital and HD equipment.

Digital television, the foundation for all future HDTV systems, was deemed essential because there wasn't enough broadcast spectrum to accommodate the expected demand for information generated by an analog HDTV signal. Broadcasting a single analog HD signal would use up six megahertz of bandwidth, enough to handle four to five channels of standard analog television. Yet six megahertz can provide up to twenty megabits per second of compressed digital information, enough for one channel of digital HDTV and four additional channels of standard digital television. And with improved methods of data compression, the number of channels could be increased.

But more important, digital television opened a whole new world of communication. The picture is wonderfully improved, providing up to seven times the amount of information available from standard NTSC analog broadcasts on a screen surface many times larger than that available on older CRT displays. Moreover, the electronic system architecture includes sophisticated computer technology enabling interactive digital

TV, the ability to record and play back scheduled or unscheduled program material at the push of a button, the convenience of video on demand, and interconnection with virtually any other digital device, be it camera, recorder, game console, or other video and data source. Above all, digital technology allows the ability to ultimately connect a television system with other systems anywhere in the world, since digital information can be transmitted by wire, fiber, cable, satellite, wireless communication, and the internet.

Political and economic leaders and electronic companies in Japan and other Asian countries knew that with the onset of digital video, HD or otherwise, the entire world of electronic communications would begin to converge exponentially. HDTV would be part of a strategy to build not just a business but a nation. In the United States thirty years ago, however, this was a difficult concept to embrace. Americans dominated most technological development and had a position of consequence in most markets. In the eyes of American leadership, globalism—free and open global markets—was necessary to promote international trade, raise the standard of living, and gain access to markets. Few saw HDTV as essential to the strategic needs of the United States, unaware that in time the acceleration of convergence, infrastructure, and investment would tax the technological and manufacturing resources of any one nation. Most Americans assumed that, compared to the GDP of the United States, future domestic investment requirements just wouldn't cost that much.

In contrast, Japan and other Asian countries developed a series of competitive strategies designed to insure their dominance of the VCR and related consumer electronic products that would ultimately depend heavily on digital displays and HDTV. As a result of Asian companies and nations' concentration of extraordinary investment in these and related products, there are virtually no displays made—let alone designed—in the United States by either American or foreign manufacturers. And as digital electronic products converge, a majority of consumer electronics resulting from that convergence, including cameras, recorders, game consoles, cell phones, and computers, are no longer designed or manufactured in

America. As the source of these products moves to Asia, semiconductor manufacturing is moving right along with them.

The growth of high-definition displays and electronic products necessary to capture, store, and distribute digital information at the speed and capacity required to support the demands of HDTV would have astonished not only the naysayers of the technology but the proponents as well.

In 1988, the American Electronics Association ATV Task Force Economic Impact Team forecast that 24.4 million HDTV sets would be sold in 2008, amounting to just under $16 billion of revenue worldwide with a cumulative total of $135 billion for the period 1990 to 2008.[17] In contrast, in 1989 Thomas Gale Moore thought that the total market for HD sets would not exceed $10 billion for "any year in the foreseeable future."[18] He and other skeptics thought that most of the forecasts for HDTV revenues were basically "hype."

But according to Strategy Analytics, a global research and consulting company, 2007 sales of flat panel LCD and plasma TVs would reach 73.7 million units worldwide and generate revenues of $104.9 billion.[19] Of these flat panel displays, 71 percent would be HDTV ready; 100 percent would be digital. More aggressively, iSuppli Corporation, another industry consulting firm, projected 80.5 million LCD TVs, not including plasma systems, would be sold in 2007 alone, increasing to more than 100 million units in 2008. Strategy Analytics has predicted that flat panel TVs will reach $130 billion in revenues in 2009. If the iSuppli projections are correct, the number of digital LCD displays sold in 2008 alone will equal two-thirds the accumulated sales for the previous twenty years, as forecasted by the AEA in 1988, and four times the number of units the AEA forecast to be sold in 2008. This does not even include plasma displays, which might increase the total sales of digital television sets by another 10 to 15 percent. None of these displays are currently designed or manufactured in the United States.

Not only did the market for sets turn out to be much larger than had been expected twenty years before, but technological advances associated with the move to HDTV turned the world's communications landscape upside down. Consider this: From 1990 to 2006, the digital flat panel display industry grew from approximately $3 billion dollars to $86 billion in annual sales. According to a report by Professor Tom Murtha of the University of Illinois, "Metanational Management and Global Innovation: The Case of the TFT-LCD Industry," considering the growth in sales, increases in substrate size, and cost declines, the rate of change for flat panel displays during this period exceeds the rate of change for the semiconductor industry "by two to eighteen times."[20] The growth of the flat panel display industry was Moore's Law supercharged.

How did this occur? When the AEA was forecasting growth for HDTV, commercial flat screen displays were a distant dream. Digital television existed only in the laboratory. Cell phones were a very limited commodity, and their use of flat screen digital displays that would convey all kinds of data, from simple call number identification and directories to elaborate global positioning systems, belonged to science fiction. Film dominated the camera market, and the DVD did not exist. The internet as we know it did not exist. Yet these products and technologies became not only a reality almost overnight but an integral part of everyday life. The common denominator driving the world of information and its communications infrastructure was the need to store, process, and distribute extraordinary amounts of digital information.

The effort that went into developing HDTV, including the entire infrastructure of technologies, products, and markets necessary to display a magnificent television image, created thousands of products, all variations on a common theme. The explosion of the communications market was all about convergence. Individual components became products, individual products became components, and the sum of the two became electronic systems. The growth has been phenomenal. When the skeptics suggested that HDTV itself would be an insignificant part of the global electronics market—which amounted to $450 billion in 1990—they truly missed the point. If one understands HDTV as the result of learning how to process massive amounts of digital information, as both a convergence and catalyst in the digital revolution, then it should be easy to see that the need to process that information is not limited to the HDTV display and a pretty picture.

The entire electronic ecosystem is driven by the need for speed, for putting a lot of information into a small space. Cell phones and cameras went digital. Miniature digital flat screen displays were developed specifically for cell phones. The storage capacity of solid-state digital memories began to eliminate the need for bulkier, less reliable hard drives, while digital processors tied all the operating components together. The result was a digital cell phone combined with a digital camera, coupled with a central processing unit that allowed it to operate as a small but versatile, portable, high-powered computer on a totally wireless network with internet access. This is the essence of convergence. It would revolutionize telecommunications overnight.

According to the Semiconductor Industry Association, the more than one billion cell phones sold in 2006 had an average semiconductor content of $40 and a flat screen display. This number was projected to rise to 100 million units in 2007.[21] None of these cellular phone displays are manufactured in America.

The global electronics market was forecasted to be slightly more than $2 trillion in 2007, growing to 3.2 trillion in 2012. For the past seventeen years, this market has grown at approximately three times the rate of America's GDP. The largest portion of this market is centered on the processing of digital information. Whether it's DVDs, cameras, recorders, electronic games, modems, computers, electronic instrumentation for aircraft or automobiles, military digital electronics, broadcast equipment, or cell phones, the development and commercialization of HDTV continues to leave its mark everywhere. In November 2007, the *New York Times* reported that "Intel plans to announce a family of microprocessor chips" that "will speed the availability of high-definition video via the internet."[22]

Considering the size of the display industry today, was HDTV destined to be a big business? Virtually every electronics system is somehow attached to a digital display. How could HDTV and digital television not be big business—big enough to build not just companies but countries? The influence of HDTV, initially commercialized in Japan, not only is imbedded in a wide variety of electronic products and markets but has been a significant factor in shifting the technological balance of power between nations.

AN OMINOUS TREND

Along with the move from analog to digital, two major product areas, the display and the semiconductor, have become fundamental building blocks in both the developing HDTV market and the advancement of information systems across the board. The display is indispensable to most communications networks, providing usable information through data, graphics, or pictures. But no electronics system can operate in today's world without a semiconductor, which collects, stores, and processes the information so that the system, with or without a display, can operate as designed. What the display and the semiconductor have in common—besides an evolving architecture that can help differentiate one product from another, as the iPhone is differentiated from other cell phones—is the extraordinary cost of development and fabrication.

Initially, both displays and semiconductors required the investment of millions of dollars to produce a product. Today it takes billions. Anyone who does not stay abreast of the competition is either forced out of the business or left with a highly diminished presence. So it is no wonder that, after LG of Korea purchased a controlling interest in Zenith for $350 million in 1996 and the U.S. abandoned the display industry, American companies had second thoughts about reentry into the business, where the size of a single digital display fabrication facility can easily exceed three million square feet and cost in excess of $3 billion, a sum comparable to the cost of an advanced semiconductor manufacturing facility.

Aside from the cost of manufacturing, when a nation abandons an industry it can easily lose the technology that might have given it the ability to get back in the game. Plasma display technology is one example. In the early 1960s, Donald Bitzer, Gene Slottow, and Robert Wilson of the University of Illinois built the first plasma display panel. It used a single cell. Today's plasma displays use millions of cells. The original plasma display was not competitive with the very thin LCD display and therefore was not commercialized for many years. Then in 1987, Larry Weber, a former student of Bitzer and a research associate professor at the University of Illinois, founded Plasmaco, Inc. Plasmaco attempted to commercialize the plasma display based largely on the patents and technological know-how of the founders. Finally, in 1996, the same year that Zenith was bought by LG, Plasmaco was bought by Matsushita Electric Industrial Company, Ltd. Since that time Matsushita has become the leading supplier of plasma displays marketed under their brand Panasonic.

Displays, like any other electronic system, use semiconductors. The logic and memory of the semiconductor determine how much information is to be displayed, whether it is HDTV or standard digital TV. The semiconductor governs what control the user will have over the television display and what information will be stored for delayed viewing or for viewing simultaneously with another program. Since the semiconductor is equally fundamental to computers, cameras, DVDs, and cell phones, companies that have become principal designers and manufacturers of these end-use products want to achieve as much product differentiation as possible. Therefore the need to be in the semiconductor business as well as the display industry is a given among Japan, Korea, Taiwan, and China, the major producers of consumer electronics. The United States has already exited the display business. What, then, is the case with semiconductors?

In 1979, American companies had 58 percent of the world market for semiconductors; Japan had approximately 26 percent. Yet there was a major concern on the part of U.S. manufacturers and the U.S. government that Japan's markets were not open to the United States for the fair trade of semiconductors. By the end of the 1980s, Japan had achieved a 52 percent share of the market. In 1986, the U.S. government, along with

American industry, negotiated a trade agreement with Japan that many hoped would correct the situation. The negotiation gave American manufacturers some relief; Japan's share of the market dropped to 49 percent, while the U.S. share climbed to 36 percent.

During this period, the position of the American semiconductor industry in world markets caused concern not only in the industry but in the country at large. "The steady erosion of the American position," observed the *New York Times* in January 1991, "has become a matter of concern because semiconductors are considered vital for the nation's economic health and military preparedness. The silicon chips etched with microscopic electronic circuits are the basic building blocks of all electronic machines, including videocassette recorders, robots, missiles, and radar systems."[23]

The United States is expected to spend about 29 percent of worldwide capital expenditures allocated to semiconductor manufacturing facilities in 2007. With this as a backdrop, data prepared in July 2007 by Semiconductor Equipment and Material International is revealing. Semiconductor fabrication facilities, which can cost $3 billion per plant or more today, have two major parts: plant and equipment. SEMI's analysis for the years 2006 through 2008 indicates that investment in capital equipment for semiconductor fabrication facilities in North America represented $6.2 billion or 18.2 percent of the world's total capital equipment investment in 2006, dropping to less than 16 percent in 2007 and 2008.[24] On the other hand, capital equipment investment for semiconductor facilities in China, Japan, South Korea, Southeast Asia, and Taiwan was $31 billion in 2006, increasing slightly to a forecasted $31.5 billion in 2008. Europe is projected to hold relatively constant in equipment investment at $2.7 to $3 billion dollars. In other words, China, Japan, South Korea, Southeast Asia, and Taiwan are projected to receive 77 percent of the funds invested in semiconductor capital equipment in 2008, compared to less than 16 percent in North America.

But funds invested in the facilities that house this capital equipment indicate an even more significant trend. Whereas spending on plant construction in 2006 in North America represented 17.6 percent of semiconductor manufacturing facilities investment worldwide, this number was forecasted to drop to 8 percent in 2007 and 3.7 percent in 2008. Europe is projected to receive exactly what America is planning to receive in terms of new investment in semiconductor facility construction in 2008, just 3.7 percent. If this trend continues, new semiconductor plant and equipment investment in the United States will be only a small fraction of that invested in Asia.

The opening statement from my 1988 presentation to the American Electronics Association remains my prognosis on the impact of HDTV:

> The HDTV market represents a complete merging of technologies essential to the domination of the consumer electronics market and major portions of the telecommunications and computer markets. The nation which becomes the key supplier of production, distribution, and receiving equipment within the HDTV markets will have developed a principal means to control a major portion of the semiconductor chip and equipment business and will have thus achieved a significant step toward technological superiority in the years to come.[25]

Thus the two principles of competitiveness that head this chapter: certain technologies, products, and markets are strategic to a nation's industrial base and ability to compete; weakness in one sector may cause weakness in dependent sectors. America has not lost its ability to compete, but the trend is taking an ominous direction.

CHAPTER 8

Winners and Losers

A substantial loss of strategic infrastructure will ultimately impair a nation's ability to develop meaningful economic and political relationships with other nations.

Significant losses in the infrastructure of strategic technologies, products, and markets reduce a nation's ability to influence its economic and political destiny.

W hy does a nation produce anything? The question is fundamental since it involves the nation's future and the well-being of its people. The answer is deceptively simple. A nation produces something in the hope that its value will entice a customer to give more in return than it cost. Why more? The producer desires compensation not only to cover the time and material invested, but to provide a profit that can be used to purchase the goods and services of others and expand the country's productive capacity. The customers, domestic or foreign, also understand that to afford consumption it is necessary to produce and reap a profit.

The purchase and sale of products and services within a country or between countries are called trade. As trade expands and the growing profits are invested in more products and services, a process begins that is fundamental to the nation's standard of living. An acceptable standard will usually reflect the nation's strategic values—priorities involving the desire for affordable choices in goods and services; transportation; communication; health care; retirement; protection in the form of fire, police, and military security; and, for Americans, the freedom to choose.

The position of the United States emerging from World War II differed from that of all other nations. America had the largest economic and industrial capacity and by far the strongest military force on Earth. It had what most felt were the ingredients essential to comfort and well-being. The relative value of U.S. currency towered over that of any other. The United States could buy the productive output of almost any other country at a fraction of what it would cost other nations to buy goods and services produced in America. Yet because it was usually difficult to buy those products elsewhere, consumers around the world scrambled to be first in line for America's goods and services. For the United States, it was the best of times. America's national strategy reflected its military power, economic strength, and resulting political will.

As the reigning superpower, America feared no one. America and Americans had choices, more choices than anyone else. The United States had the money; it had the military. There was little it didn't have. Americans wanted the good life—cars, clothes, homes, and an education, and above all they wanted peace. Unlike the victors in past wars, the United States wanted dominance but not territory. It wanted others to think like Americans; it wanted democracy in its own image. America understood the disaster that followed World War I. It didn't want Europe, especially Germany, left in ruins to foment another war. So the United States decided to rebuild Europe and looked at Japan in much the same way. The United States allowed the Japanese to retain their institutions but sought to imbue them with the Pax Americana.

Much of the shift in America's position as the world's preeminent manufacturer began in the electronics industry. The willing beneficiary of the U.S. desire to subcontract the production of electromechanical devices, including audiotape and videotape decks, was Japan. Americans wanted to be creative, to invent. When it came to the development of new products, the money and excitement seemed to be increasingly in design—at the front end. The front end encompasses those aspects of the product that the consumer sees and interacts with—the product's look, feel, and purpose, including the user controls. Control loomed large in the American mind, control over the future and the ability to moderate the limits of daily life—the freedom allowed by an abundance of options. This attitude was reflected in the design of its products. Engineers began to design unique product specifications and features that gave the consumer more control. With this approach came a proliferation of knobs and buttons and often a consequent reduction in ease of operation and reliability—a factor that was not lost on future competitors in Asia.

At the same time, America began to feel that the real money was less in routine than in creativity and innovation. "Stars, cash cows, and dogs" was a logical outcome. Because the United States dominated the playing field, "stars, cash cows, and dogs" was simply about picking and choosing winners, making the most out of a situation. American competitiveness settled on what seemed to be a sound strategy. If you've got it all, then the game is about picking out the stars and focusing your efforts and resources on them. What do you have to lose when you already have the rest? In that environment manufacturing began to be seen as merely routine, a necessary evil.

THE POWER OF PARTNERSHIP

Japan's strategy was noticeably different, a result as much of circumstances as of cultural contrasts. Little land, virtually no natural resources, and total devastation from the war led to priorities directly opposite those of the United States. First the Japanese had to eat. Then they had to learn how to rebuild the nation. Because resources were severely limited, it was difficult for Japan to create products and markets in the postwar world. The United States helped by accepting Japanese offers to manufacture American products.

And then an amazing thing happened. Japan's manufacturing expertise, far from remaining routine, began to grow remarkably innovative. At the same time, the Japanese showed an ability to create the front end of new product designs. Products and processes began to converge. As they began to integrate these front-end designs with the electromechanical components resulting from their expertise in mass production, the Japanese were able to introduce a multiplicity of highly desirable, relatively inexpensive proprietary products at an exponential rate. At the same time, as front-end designs and manufacturing expertise converged into integrated systems, reliability and ease of operation became a competitive advantage.

Like any people, the Japanese wanted both individual and collective success. But unlike the United States, very limited resources required an integrated national strategy to gain the leverage necessary to reinvent the country. To succeed, Japan first had to survive and then to grow. In time the rest of Asia, observing what was going on in Japan, assumed a similar model. The strategy of product design, development, and manufacturing began to reflect the national strategies of these emerging economies. Cooperation and competition between companies was commonplace. Within thirty years this group of nations substantially altered the economic balance of power between East and West, particularly in technology. Japan and its followers were riding on the wings of Moore's Law. In very little time, the emerging nations of the world began to sneak up on America. Suddenly the inertia of postwar economic, military, and political strength that the United States had taken for granted was no longer so clear-cut. And if current trends continue, one wonders how much control America will retain over its political and economic future.

In the decades since World War II, the chronicle of American competition includes a long casualty list of products and markets abandoned in whole or part by U.S. companies faced with massive foreign competition. Most of these products saw their first commercial success in the United States. Many of these businesses were abandoned in the face of price competition and inadequate margins relative to other investment opportunities while observers stood by, gravely misunderstanding the strategic nature of these losses.

Consumer electronic products such as recorders, cameras, and television sets were lost piecemeal as American manufacturers transferred the production of key product components, such as tape decks, abroad, principally to Japan. Japanese manufacturers not only offered lower prices but were willing to invest their own capital in plant and equipment. They in turn substantially improved the manufacturing process, including the product specifications of the components. In time, the outsourced manufacturers of the decks decided to produce the other parts of the product, including the front end and controls, integrating all of the pieces into a seamless unit. The result was an advanced product—with improved specifications, features, reliability, and ease of operation— produced at lower cost. Convergence of the parts substantially altered the competitive advantage of the whole. But this was only the beginning. In an environment of accelerating convergence, infrastructure, and investment, the synergism and compatibility of individual products begin to create a multiplicity of new products and markets. The VCR was the best example of this phenomenon.

The loss of the VCR to Japan was not simply the result of Japanese expertise in mass-producing tape decks or their years of experience producing low-cost, limited-performance, reel-to-reel video recorders for schools and businesses. Nor was it due to the millions of dollars the Japanese had invested in the 35mm camera business, including the development of lenses and electromechanical focusing systems. The loss of the VCR was not a result of the significant investment by Japan in robotic mechanisms fundamental to highly elaborate, automated fabrication plants. It did not happen because of the Japanese success in mass-producing television sets and their tremendous investment over the years in display and semiconductor technology. The loss of the VCR was the result of all of this and more. It reflected the convergence of these and other individual products into a highly complex system whose ultimate simplicity opened the door to markets unimagined at the dawn of audiovisual communications. The VCR both catalyzed and epitomized the acceleration of convergence, infrastructure, and investment at the time. The final result was the transformation of a nation with a landmass smaller than California and no natural resources into the second-largest national economy in the world.

The exponential acceleration of convergence, infrastructure, and investment that created the phenomenal success of the VCR was the same process that influenced Roger Smith's decision, as CEO of General Motors, to embark on his massive investment program to reinvigorate GM in 1981. His efforts failed not simply because of bad management but because his company, as big as it was, was relatively alone. Few American electronic companies were the equivalent of their counterparts in Japan. These Japanese companies cooperated with each other, forming a team that became like a company within each company. This team was able to produce state-of-the-art automobiles with integrated electronics at a lower cost and with far fewer defects than those available in the United States. In contrast to American individualism, this cooperation reflected a communal orientation long inherent in Japanese culture.

Though GM had myriad suppliers for the various components of its automobiles, these vendor relationships were more like business deals and unsuited to a seamlessly integrated team. Cost was a large factor. GM's suppliers included Japanese vendors, but the environment was totally different for Japanese companies. What was a supplier agreement in the United States became a structure of long-term relationships in Japan, and in effect those relationships created an extended company. Participants became partners more than suppliers, obligated to support the entire group in both good times and bad. It was this kind of relationship that gave rise to the Toyota production system, now famous for its results in design, cost, and reliability.

And yet the convergence of individual products into a seamless system is only the beginning. Unfortunately, in the world of accelerating convergence, infrastructure, and investment, it's not just components specific to a single product or the integration of products into a complex functioning system that can become a competitive nightmare. Convergence can force a complete change in the competitive landscape as one product morphs into another.

While attempting, in my 1988 presentations, to explain the effect that HDTV would have on the electronics industry, I tried to project the future evolution of video recording. Noting that HDTV was about the processing of vast amounts of information, I suggested thinking of the VCR as "nothing more than a storage device for moving pictures," submitted that "in time the VCR may become a plug-in module . . . and therefore a component part of a computer."[1]

Within a year of those remarks, Toshiba, the former partner of Ampex, announced the introduction of NAND flash, a semiconductor memory device that grew out of technology it had developed four years before, setting a course that would bring my offhand prediction to reality. NAND flash was a solid-state digital device with the ability to store data instantaneously and play it back at will. Its output of information can be viewed on a digital display, reproduced on a fax machine, and transferred electronically to virtually any other digital electronic device. The memory capacity of NAND flash grew rapidly to the point where it could store and reproduce moving pictures and sound. Compared to the relatively large video recorder weighing several pounds with complicated electromechanical functions and a cassette, the NAND flash memory—with many of the same functions—has no moving parts and is just over 1.5 square centimeters with a thickness of less than 1 millimeter.

By incorporating a NAND flash module, the cell phone has become a computer, a camera, and a VCR all in one. The contents stored on a NAND flash module in the cell phone can be transferred to another product, such as a computer, by simply unplugging the NAND flash card and inserting it in another device, or the information stored on a NAND flash in the cell phone can be distributed wirelessly to any digital device anywhere in the world. And as one might suspect, most products using this device are designed and produced in Asia. Considering the potential applications of this technology, one can be sure that the world has seen nothing yet.

LOOKING AHEAD IN
THE REARVIEW MIRROR

What happens if a nation cannot take full advantage of accelerating convergence, infrastructure, and investment relative to its competition? What happens if a nation loses strategic components in its infrastructure of products and markets because it lacks a national strategy for competitiveness? The answer is not always obvious, since the results may not be apparent for years. Meanwhile, the nation's companies can make spectacular profits by taking advantage of the infrastructure and investment of foreign entities. But at what cost? Has the nation simply been mortgaging its future? And if so, how will its debts be paid? In extreme conditions, the result is simple and profoundly disturbing. The nation cedes control of its destiny to others.

A country's economic, political, and military strength is heavily dependent on its competitive position in strategic technologies, products, and markets. The question is which areas of economic activity should be considered strategic. After World War II, Japan had few natural resources and little available land as a base for resurrecting its economic position. To acquire those resources and bring the standard of living in line with other nations, an export-oriented economy was a logical path. Japan needed products that would fit what resources it had—a highly motivated and intelligent population, an understanding of technology, and the educational base to serve its workforce. Electronics was a logical choice.

The manufacture of electronics required neither a large landmass nor, initially, extraordinary amounts of capital. It was an outgrowth of industrial activities remaining from the war effort. Moreover, it was a highly scalable industry. The Japanese understood that electronic products could be manufactured in large quantities from automated facilities that were not labor intensive. A result of far more than hard work and low pay, Japan's extraordinary success grew out of a national dedication, public and private, to concentrating limited resources in industries deemed strategic to the nation's objectives.

The need for a national industrial strategy was fundamental to American policy during World War II. This would change abruptly after the war, when resources were abundant. Strategy shifted toward the opportunistic concept of stars, cash cows, and dogs. As a result of what began as a series of considered decisions on the part of American industry, the United States began to shed key portions of its industrial base, losses extending far beyond electronics. In time, American production lost major, if not dominant, positions—sometimes entire market share—in audio and video record and playback systems, computer monitors and displays, semiconductors, cameras, lenses, television sets, machine tools, and robotics. According to the 2007 *World Machine Tool Output and Consumption Survey,* Japan was the world's largest supplier of machine tools in 2006.[2] The United States was seventh behind Taiwan. In March 2006, *Japan Economic Monthly* reported that its nation represented 46 percent of the world market for manufacturing robots, the rest of Asia 18.5 percent, and the United States 17 percent.[3]

The list goes on. The American automotive industry is having severe competitive problems. The United States long ago gave up leadership in shipbuilding. As of 2006, according to a publication of the U.S. Department of Commerce, the world's three largest shipbuilding nations are Japan, Korea, and China. China is currently building a $3.6 billion shipyard outside of Shanghai, one of the largest ever built.

In May 2006, *Newsweek* featured an article on the design and manufacture of the new Boeing 787 Dreamliner, not just for the uniqueness of its methods but because of the potential implications for the aircraft industry in America.

The prototype of the new Boeing 787 Dreamliner is being built in a virtual factory so big, it effectively spans continents. Engineers in Japan build the wings, Koreans add the raked wingtips, Brits refine the

Rolls-Royce engines, while Italians and Texans fit the horizontal stabi-
lizer and center fuselage. Project managers in Everett, Washington,
watch it all take shape with 3-D glasses that allow them to walk
around the digital prototype and monitor every change made by their
6,000 workers worldwide, just as if the model were being assembled in
a real factory.[4]

Newsweek noted that Airbus is effectively doing the same thing for
reasons of cost, customers, and politics. But putting aside the near-term
benefits to the designers of the next generation of aircraft, the article discussed a potential long-term effect that may not benefit the U.S. aircraft
industry: "The shift east has been quiet, but dramatic. More than thirty-
five percent of Boeing's 787, including the wings (which up until now
Boeing has refused to outsource because their construction requires the
most expertise), is being made in Japan. That's up from fifteen percent of
the 767 in 1982 and twenty percent of the 777 in 1995." On the combined
outsourcing of critical manufacturing tasks by both Airbus and Boeing,
the article quoted aerospace expert David Pritchard, of the State University of New York at Buffalo: "We're transferring lessons learned and
new technology being honed to Asian [companies]. When the next-
generation airplane comes along, we will have no base knowledge of
how to produce it ourselves."

"The endgame is unclear," *Newsweek* concluded,

> but one obvious possibility is the emergence of an Asian rival to Airbus
> and Boeing. The transfer of expertise, technology and money to Japan
> and China is giving Asian aerospace companies the wherewithal to
> dream big—meaning big enough to build their own passenger jets. It's
> happened before. When Shanghai Automotive last month detailed
> plans to launch the first all-Chinese car for the international market by
> next year, the company said the opportunity was ripe because of tech-
> nology and expertise gained from its joint ventures with Volkswagen
> and GM. "There is nothing impenetrable about any duopoly in this in-

dustry," says Richard J. Samuels, MIT's director of the Center for International Studies. "The Japanese government and its heavy industrial firms have openly sought to establish Japan as an aerospace power for generations."

In March 2008, Bloomberg noted a report that Mitsubishi Heavy Industries Limited, Asia's largest aerospace company, is "close to commercial production of Japan's first passenger jet aircraft."[5]

In 2006, outlining its plan for the future of nuclear power, the Japanese Ministry of Economy, Trade, and Industry established "a firm national strategy and policy framework that does not waver over time"[6] as the first of five basic guidelines for future development. This reference to a long-term strategy reflects the essence of Asian business today. It is in it for the long haul, and rightly so. Aside from major opportunities to export nuclear reactors, approximately one-third of Japan's electric power is generated from its fifty-five nuclear power plants.

In October 2006, Mitsubishi Heavy Industries of Japan reached agreement with Areva, the French nuclear engineering group, to design a new generation of nuclear power plants. At the same time, Toshiba agreed to buy Westinghouse Electric from British Nuclear Fuels for $5.4 billion. Using a Westinghouse subsidiary, Toshiba is applying for a license with the Nuclear Regulatory Commission in America to build its new Super-Safe, Small, and Simple (4S) reactor for sale and installation in the United States. Hitachi has a partnership with General Electric. According to the April 2006 *Asia Times*, "the [Japanese] government, which attaches great importance to nuclear power as a key to ensuring energy security, is also considering assistance to help domestic firms in the increasingly intensifying global competition for fuel at nuclear power plants."[7]

China may soon become the largest producer and consumer of nuclear power plants. It plans to build thirty-two new reactors by 2020, receiving technological and construction assistance through agreements with Areva and Toshiba's Westinghouse Electric. This number could balloon to over three hundred units. And these reactors aren't cheap, costing $3 to $5 billion or more apiece. The United States, on the other hand, has not built a single plant in nearly three decades. With the energy bill of 2005, the U.S. Congress finally began to pave the way through tax credits and liability protection to restart the construction of nuclear facilities. Westinghouse Electric, now owned by Toshiba, is the first recipient of new orders. Nuclear energy—the only significant source of power that produces no greenhouse gases and can back up wind and solar systems in the absence of wind and sunlight—may well turn out to be the most efficient source of energy in the face of global warming. If that's the case, nuclear power could become the world's most strategic industry.

PARTNERING WITH THE COMPETITION IN A WORLD OF SCARCE RESOURCES

All of these technologies, products, and markets are affected in one way or another by Moore's Law and the impact of accelerating convergence, infrastructure, and investment. Recording systems, displays, lenses, semiconductors, machine tools, robotics, automobiles, ships, planes, and even nuclear power plants share in the technological advancement of each. And yet at the same time, the progression of Moore's Law has increased investment needs to such a degree that global partnerships, joint ventures, and trade have become essential to provide sufficient resources.

It is difficult for most companies in the semiconductor industry to manufacture their own proprietary products. Giants like Intel, Samsung, Micron Technology, and Toshiba are a few of the dwindling number that can afford their own manufacturing facilities, including process research and development, based solely on their own products. The cost of staying in the game goes well beyond a joint venture between two or more companies. Today, that cost is becoming so great that support from both companies and governments is required to insure a stable environment for the participants. And therein lies the rub. Though the United

States promotes a global economy, it seems unaware of the basic condition now making globalization an absolute necessity. No nation today, not even the United States, can go it alone for very long. There just aren't enough resources.

In the face of scarce resources, global relationships are essential. The cost of national growth in a world tied to accelerating convergence, infrastructure, and investment is ultimately too high for any one country. And what is true for a nation is more so for a company. Both can garner additional resources in several ways. A nation or company can outsource, taking advantage of another's investment or natural resources. It can set up joint ventures that share with others the cost of investment required to design, develop, and produce a product. It can license technology developed by others and use that intellectual property as a base for new products and services. Or it can simply distribute someone else's product.

Just as vital as global partnership is the need to compete globally. Nations and their companies need markets large enough to support the cost of being in the business. The concept of simultaneous competing and partnering is more Asian than American. How is it accomplished? The means to that end lie in what resources, expertise, proprietary products, and services the participants have to offer. To be an acceptable participant in any deal, each party has to have something the other wants. The power to make arrangements beneficial to each of the parties is often proportional to the relative value of what they bring to the table. This can be a very complicated equation.

Enduring alliances require a continued proportional contribution by the participants, assuring that each is in it for the long haul. This involves not only what each is buying but what each is selling. Once one of the participants feels the other is no longer contributing its fair share, the partnership is in trouble. With accelerating convergence, infrastructure, and investment, the world of technology is so dynamic it's not easy to keep a partnership together as the needs of the relationship change. This fast-moving environment requires a clear understanding of the long-term strategy and resulting priorities that drew the participants together. A culture of opportunism, like stars, cash cows, and dogs, can be an impediment. This does not mean that opportunism has no place. But without a set of priorities based on a long-term strategy, opportunistic decisions can become the strategy.

In 1996, there was a latent desire on the part of Korea to continue a relationship in the design and development of displays with the United States. Overtures were made to what remained of the U.S. display industry, but there was no substantive response. This influenced Korea to begin a series of joint venture relationships with companies in Japan. One of the largest is between Sony and Samsung. The result of that partnership was the multibillion-dollar development of an LCD manufacturing capability that made both Samsung and Sony world leaders in display production. Sony needed production capacity and expertise to handle its demand, and Samsung needed intellectual property to expand its technological base. The venture was a fifty-fifty deal between the partners.

As time passes and the investment of both corporations increases, there are two points to keep in mind. First, because of the economic importance of both companies to their respective countries and the amount of money that will ultimately be invested in the venture, the economic and political ties between Japan and Korea will become closer. Second, American makers of panels for flat screen displays are nowhere to be found. There is, however, a glimmer of light. The U.S. company Corning Incorporated established a joint venture with Samsung in Korea called Corning Precision Glass that is also a fifty-fifty deal. Run by Corning, the operation supplies the glass to the Sony-Samsung joint venture. Corning is also establishing a glass manufacturing facility to support Sharp's new $3.4 billion LCD manufacturing plant in Japan. What does America have to offer to attract the cooperation of important potential partners around the world today? Strengths that give the United States bargaining power in the global community include the offer of unparalleled political freedom and the strongest military in the world, able to defend not only the nation but its allies as well. The rule of law in America is another key advantage when potential partners require a high level of political and economic stability. This extends to the protection of intellectual property and the confidence that an agreement made today will be enforced tomorrow.

But the United States has another significant strength, as important as it is large in its impact on the world economy: the American consumer. As a point of comparison, the demand from governments around the world for military products and services amounted to approximately $1.1 trillion in 2005. The United States represented about half of these expenditures. The United Kingdom, France, Japan, and China followed with 4 to 5 percent each. On the other hand, American consumers will spend about $9 trillion in 2007, roughly 70 percent of the country's GDP. In 2007, consumer spending in the United States amounted to nearly 25 percent of the GDP of the rest of the world combined. Why is this so important? In large part because of accelerating convergence, infrastructure, and investment.

LOSING CONTROL

Today the size, growth, and penetration of consumer electronics into virtually all markets make it the primary driver in the expansion and technological advancement of the semiconductor industry. And advances in semiconductor technology drive the entire electronics market. In 1968, when I began my research on what might be the most appropriate configuration for a home video recorder, I determined that the best way to define the product was to prioritize its characteristics according to the market demands it might serve. There were then three basic markets for video recording, two of which were being served and a third on the horizon. The first was the broadcast market, initially addressed by Ampex when it invented video recording. The second was video recording designed principally for closed-circuit use in schools, businesses, governmental agencies, and other commercial establishments. And the third was to be the home market, the one that we all dreamt about from the beginning but that was very elusive because of certain technological limitations.

I decided that certain characteristics fundamental to the design of a video recorder were applicable to all markets. Depending on the intended use—home, closed-circuit, or broadcast—it was not the potential characteristics that varied so much as how they were prioritized. I selected eleven features, including reliability, ease of operation, cost of equipment, size and weight, performance, compatibility (the ability to play tapes recorded for a specific format across the product line and in previous- or next-generation machines), and color capability (recording and playback in color was difficult at the time and considered a luxury).

While the ranking of these features to achieve product definition may seem somewhat arcane, it should be remembered that this was forty years ago and the technology was very new. That things are different now is the whole point. Over the last forty years, one can see the effects of accelerating convergence, infrastructure, and investment through their impact on video recording. The technological capabilities of a video recorder for the consumer market are no longer much different from those desired by other commercial and industrial markets. Color is no longer a luxury— without it you have no product. A small size and low weight, once at a premium if one also wanted high performance, is now standard. Ease of operation and reliability are requirements in any market, whether for broadcast recorders, closed-circuit TV systems, or VCRs. And today, without compatibility within a standard line and between generations of the product—a potential problem at the inception of the VCR—the market for prerecorded tapes and DVDs could not exist, and video recording would have been just another exciting electronics product.

Not only are the demands placed on the development of consumer electronic products often more exacting than those placed upon products designed for more limited commercial markets, but the volume requirements are usually larger by orders of magnitude. The investment necessary to advance the state of the art for consumer electronics is therefore generally much greater than for other markets. It is only the size and growth of the consumer electronics market that has made these investments possible.

Thus consumer electronics today is often the lead indicator of where technology is going. Riding the surge of convergence, infrastructure, and investment, consumer electronics quickly crosses the boundaries of adjacent markets. The demands placed on consumer electronic systems qualify them for a wide range of markets, including entertainment, computing, automobiles, aircraft, commercial and industrial communication systems, and military applications. In the age of information, the $2 trillion market for electronic products, increasingly convergent and heavily influenced by the demands of the American consumer, has become fundamental to virtually every other product and market on Earth. And as the growth rate of this market compounds at a rate twice that of the world's GDP, the power and pervasiveness of electronic products will continue to be a dominant influence on the fate of nations.

For years, America has had the largest consumer market in the world by far. The demands in that market for electronic products made in the United States have paved the way for massive investment in convergent technologies and infrastructure in America. But in the last thirty years a substantial portion of the investment in manufacturing and related design technology has been gradually transferred elsewhere, not only to take advantage of resources unavailable in the United States but to benefit the American consumer who wants lower prices and better quality, the manufacturer looking for greater profits and cash flow, and, above all, the investor seeking a relatively short-term capital gain.

The situation today is tinged with irony. What many feel may decouple American economic problems from affecting Asia and other nations is the rapid growth projected for internal consumption in those countries—their own consumer markets. These home markets in foreign countries may not be large enough to offset a loss of the American consumer now, but they are becoming so. Meanwhile, what powers the accelerated growth in

convergence, infrastructure, and investment in foreign markets today?
The American consumer.

If this trajectory is carried to its logical extreme, the problem the
United States faces becomes clear. As it loses the ability to produce, it ultimately loses the ability to consume—regardless of easy credit—in an
asset-based economy that is long on debt and becoming short on an internal ability to add value. As the United States moves from adding
value to becoming the world's distribution center, its standard of living
will stagnate, as its now robust profit margins move to where the "value-
added" is. Moreover, the nation will become less able to afford the military requirements intrinsic to remaining a world power. America's
power to negotiate deals, let alone control its destiny, will fade as it
brings less and less to the table. Meanwhile, nations interested in taking
advantage of accelerating convergence, infrastructure, and investment
within their own economies will continue their attempts to maintain a
stable—if not growing—U.S. consumer market. What has been one of
the biggest competitive assets of the American economy, its consumer
market, could in the end become the prime competitive asset of everyone
else—that is, until their own burgeoning internal markets lead them to
lose interest and cease funding the American consumer.

CHAPTER 9

Failure Is Not an Option

If the nation as a whole is not competitive, it is difficult for any business or industry within that nation to remain competitive. To be competitive, a nation must have a national strategy for competitiveness.

Nearly four hundred years ago, when the first Puritans were crossing the North Atlantic to settle the wilds of a new continent, their leader, John Winthrop, spoke on the deck of the *Arbella* about what he saw as their mission. "We shall be," he said, "as a city set upon a hill, the eyes of all people upon us."[1] And so it has been, as America has not only raised cities in the wilderness but allowed every citizen the freedom to shape his own future, to perfect her own unique potential. As a result, the unfolding of America's own potential has made it the vanguard, and the eyes of the world are indeed upon us.

The irony is that over the centuries America has fulfilled Winthrop's vision not as a model of separatist religion but as an example of freedom from such theocracies and the best principles of government so far achieved in the evolution of human society.

America is the product of the Enlightenment. The founding fathers preserved what was best in English common law and had the wisdom to understand the necessity for checks and balances among branches of government, a separation of church and state, and a balance between federal power and states' rights. The model democracy they devised prospered on vast physical resources, geographic isolation, and the enterprise, industry, and commerce of generations. By the twentieth century the United States had become the world's richest and most powerful nation.

The spirit of American progress and prosperity lies in its great projects—bridges, canals, skyscrapers, transcontinental railroads, Roosevelt's arsenal of democracy, and Kennedy's mission to the moon. From John Winthrop to John Kennedy, America has always stood at the leading edge of history. But the greatest of all projects has been America itself—the Great Experiment, Winthrop's "city upon a hill," the last best hope of humanity.

The notions that "all men are created equal" and that "the pursuit of happiness" is a vital object of government are still not held to be self-evident in most of the world, or even understood in many parts of it. It is America's task to remain the city upon a hill, but Americans must constantly remind themselves that more is involved than self-indulgence. It is, in fact, a long, difficult, and demanding process that they have been pursuing with ups and downs for over two hundred years. But the result has been an inspiration to peoples all over the world who aspire to the freedom and opportunity Americans often take for granted.

A great nation needs its citizens to feel they have a shared stake in the future. It needs the shared culture, norms, and values that are the essence of nationhood. It must understand that to a certain degree all members have a shared fate. To say my fate is not tied to your fate is like saying, "Your end of the boat is sinking." The irony of short-term opportunism is that it can mistake whose end is doing the sinking.

The so-called "greatest generation" understood this well. Willing to accept risk and sacrifice, they had a vision of something larger than themselves. Raised in the Depression and sent into war, they returned with a work ethic and willingness to invest that outperformed their communist rivals, won the cold war, and built an economic strength unparalleled in the long curve of history. As their last great gesture, they put a man on the moon. It was a generation willing, in Kennedy's words, to "bear any burden, pay any price"[2] to achieve whatever goal it set. No other generation in history has been so adept in its aptitude for science and engineering. Its bridges, highways, tunnels, harbors, and housing projects were the biggest and best in the world. Its educational achievement was the largest one-generation jump in American history. Six in seven reported having fared better than their parents, the highest proportion ever recorded.

We stand on the shoulders of giants. If we balk at the challenges before us, we will betray all those who lifted us into the present. If we are to retain not only our technological leadership but all that we value about America—the sovereignty of the individual, the right to basic comforts and security, the right to education and due process, freedom of speech and religion, freedom to pursue one's dream of the good life—we must find the balance between self-interest and sacrifice required to preserve the system that supports those interests. Without a national strategy to ensure a competitive infrastructure, the fruits of self-interest will be fleeting at best.

And what if we fail? What if we offer up the nation's future for purchase without an understanding of, let alone a regard for, America's long-term interest? It is one thing if other nations rise to America's level of economic proficiency and political stability, but quite another if the parity of nations occurs as a result of America's fall from the power and grandeur of its history. More than a debt to our forebears, we have a duty to ourselves and to the future. Failure is not an option.

STAYING IN THE GAME

In 1999, I attended the annual International Trade Partners Conference, a gathering of executives from the semiconductor capital equipment industry. One of the key organizational meetings where industry leaders can discuss issues affecting the industry and reacquaint themselves with associates from around the world, the conference always has its share of attendees representing semiconductor chip manufacturers, industry suppliers, distributors, and analysts. Each year a keynote speaker provides insight into some important aspect of the industry. Past meetings had featured speakers from companies like Intel, IBM, Texas Instruments, Samsung, and Sony. At this particular meeting, those attending the keynote address were in for a surprise.

The auditorium was filled to capacity. There was no introduction. The lights dimmed, and a large screen was lowered showing a small biplane lifting off a runway, rising nearly straight up, going into a flat spin, then a steep dive, pulling out only a few feet from the ground; then straight up again into a series of barrel rolls and another free-falling plunge that seemed sure to be its last. But up it went again, with colored smoke streaming from its wings, flipped over a few times, and finally landed. The lights went on, the screen went up, and standing on the speaker's platform was Steve Appleton, CEO of Micron Technology and pilot of the plane.

He began by noting that sometimes the engines on these planes quit, and one had to make a quick decision either to bail or to put it in a dive and try to restart. It was a high-risk sport requiring critical, precise decisions with life or death in the balance. But the real reason for showing the aerobatics was to graphically depict the ups and downs of the semiconductor industry. By 1999, Appleton had been on one of the toughest rides the U.S. semiconductor industry had ever seen.

Dynamic random access memories (DRAMs) were considered strategic to the competitiveness of the Asian semiconductor industry. The efforts of Japanese and Korean semiconductor companies to dominate that section of the industry had been relentless. Continually increasing their investment in DRAM memory manufacturing while dramatically lowering prices, they virtually dominated the business. As an American CEO of a major U.S. semiconductor memory company, Appleton was basically the last man standing. American investors had concluded that the memory industry was a dog business; they wanted to bail out, but he had chosen to dive and restart. He stayed in the game. Not only had he kept Micron in the business, but his leadership had made it into one of the largest independent semiconductor manufacturers in the world.

Steve Appleton has never been a stranger to risk or tenacious resolve. As a child he refused to go to the doctor when he had stomach pain and almost died of a burst appendix. The son of a schoolteacher and a donut maker, he earned a tennis scholarship to Boise State University, developing his game through sheer grit. As a nationally ranked player known for his ability to play big points, he learned to play left-handed after breaking his right wrist. His passion for high-risk recreation includes snowboarding, triathlons, and motorcycle racing. He began flying high-performance aircraft after becoming bored with skydiving. A crash in 2004 left him with a gash across his head. "I fly high-performance aircraft," he says, "because I have to do something less risky than the DRAM business."[3] The Micron motto is, "I take my adrenaline straight up."

Appleton went to work for Micron in 1983, working the graveyard shift on the chip fabrication line. Promoted eleven times, he became president in 1991 and CEO in 1994, the third-youngest CEO in the Fortune 500. By 1996, he was in a battle with board members who were concerned, among other things, about the level of Micron investments in capital equipment at a time when the economy appeared to be turning down and pricing from Asian DRAM companies was extremely competitive. Backing a change in management, one of the key board members convinced the major shareholder, J. R. Simplot, to fire Appleton. Simplot complied but reversed his decision only days later when a major portion of Micron management went to Simplot and indicated that without Appleton as the CEO they would leave the company. Appleton was asked to return, and the director involved in the original termination action resigned.[4]

He continued to invest heavily in capital equipment upgrades essential for staying ahead of the technology curve, irrespective of short-term and often violent swings in the memory chip market. He sleeps only four hours a night, and his capacity for work is such that for two years during a downturn in the mid-1980s he worked sixteen hours a day, seven days a week. In 2004, under Appleton's leadership, the company became the world's number-two supplier of memory chips and number-one supplier of CMOS imager sensors. Having purchased a Toshiba semiconductor manufacturing facility in the United States, along with a license to manufacture NAND flash, he has broadened Micron's future into other memory markets. He believes NAND flash memories will eventually replace mechanical hard drives as the way to store data in mobile computers (there are no moving parts, and the boot-up process is instantaneous).[5]

With continued investment in manufacturing technology, Micron has been able to maintain market share worldwide, remaining the only independent DRAM manufacturer in the United States. Micron's position in the industry has allowed the United States to retain a competitive base of manufacturing, research, and development in a broad range of products that are fundamental to the entire electronics industry. Especially important is the fact that Micron helped maintain manufacturing expertise essential to the position of the United States in the production of semiconductors. As a result, Intel, the world's largest manufacturer of semiconductor devices and the dominant supplier of microprocessors, was able to develop a relationship with Micron that has been of great importance to both companies. Over the next three years, the two firms will invest a total of $5.2 billion in their joint venture, IM Flash, to challenge the dominance of Asian chipmakers Samsung and Toshiba in manufacturing NAND for the emerging array of consumer digital devices dependent on flash memory.[6]

This must give Gordon Moore a good feeling. Moore, founder and chairman of Intel, reminisced in 2001 about the competition from Japan that had forced Intel out of the memory business. "Different economics for the Japanese companies allowed them to run their factories and sell their products far below cost. But it still bothers me that we couldn't compete successfully in a business we had created."[7]

Today the integration of microprocessor and memory has become essential to the advancement of computing power. A loss of either Micron or Intel would be a terrible blow to that infrastructure, one essential to America's position in the information age. Maintaining that base of technology and manufacturing expertise in the United States continues to give us an insight into electronic products produced elsewhere in the world. Thus, thanks to Appleton's strategic foresight, determination, and willingness to take risks, we retain a base of technology that will support efforts by the United States to reenter strategic areas formerly abandoned. "For quite a while we had the wind in our face," says Appleton, but "where the company is positioned today, we have the wind at our back."[8]

It seems that with courage, resolution, and, above all, strategic foresight, it is possible to stay the course and not only win but preserve the system that generated productive capacity in the first place. In the case of Micron, that courage extended to the twenty executives who believed in Appleton and backed him at the risk of their own jobs. J. R. Simplot owned 22 percent of the company[9] and therefore was able to make a decision that would be difficult for an angry group of investors to overturn.

The dynamics of Steve Appleton and his management team were essential to what has turned out to be a salutary decision for America. To broaden the base of this kind of effort to the country as a whole, players must understand the importance of staying in the game. This can be accomplished only when one and all know the principles of competitiveness and the ultimate risk of any decision to bail—you might live, but the plane will surely be destroyed.

To survive in the global economy today, one must take risks. Risk has always been the price of any successful venture—whether it be our migration out of Africa into the northern ice, the discovery of the New World, the shaping of a continent, or the preservation of that new freedom. Those who are ready to put themselves at risk to accomplish greater ends, who have a vision of something larger than themselves, will lift our lives to a higher level. The key is to understand those risks.

Sometimes it's essential to save the plane. Without it there may not be an alternate form of transportation, for us or anyone else.

WHO IS THE COMPETITION?

The story of Steve Appleton and Micron is as inspiring as it is instructive. Under slightly different circumstances there might have been no Micron Technology today. Because J. R. Simplot owned such a large percentage of the company, he was able, when confronted by the major portion of his management team, to reverse his decision on Appleton and make it stick. Had the stock been more widely diffused, and stockholder sentiment decidedly against Appleton's decision to invest when the industry's economic future looked particularly bleak, there would almost certainly have been a change of management. That could have been catastrophic for Micron. In the semiconductor industry today, it is well understood that if you miss out on the timing of next-generation investment, the next node, you don't get back in the game. In a meeting I attended at the Center for Strategic and International Studies in the mid-1990s, Robert Galvin of Motorola said that if his family had not held a significant portion of Motorola's stock at the time when its investment in communications didn't look promising, Motorola would not be in the communications business today.

If investors control the corporate votes and insist on short-term profits, high cash flow, and the opportunity for near-term stock appreciation, they will usually get what they want. If companies in the same business vary substantially in profitability, cash flow, and return on investment, investors will often bring pressure on management to equal the best results of the group and improve on them regardless of differing company strategies. Without a national strategy for competitiveness that provides a motivation greater than near-term emphasis on profit margins and cash flow, investor demands will tend to shape management decisions. Stars, cash cows, and dogs then become logical choices. If the infrastructure of technology, products, and markets is dissipated by such decisions, related infrastructure will likewise be slowly lost. The result is an environment that makes any long-term competitive strategy difficult to maintain.

Its management mistakes aside, this situation is what Kodak faced as the world moved from film to digital imaging. By the time Kodak realized the impact of digital photography and image processing, it was not just facing another competitor somewhere in the world. It was effectively surrounded by an army of competitors, all holding pieces of the infrastructure. With so much infrastructure gone, convergence was Kodak's enemy, not its friend.

One of the trends emphasized at the 2008 Consumer Electronics Show was the importance of consumer electronics in the design and marketability of tomorrow's automobiles. As Matsushita suggested in a *Fortune* ad fifteen years ago, large electronics manufacturers were ready to partner with automobile makers, particularly in Asia, as an integrated competitive force.[10] As General Motors' Roger Smith discovered, this has become a competitive disadvantage to American automobile companies that are not similarly privy to local design and manufacturing resources.

The problem goes beyond GM. On the one hand, Ford has been able to develop an onboard information system designed in collaboration with Microsoft. On the other hand, hybrid engine technology has been more problematic. In 2005, the *New York Times* noted that ten years after Toyota introduced a hybrid engine at the Tokyo Motor Show, American automobile manufacturers were in the position of having to license or buy technology from Toyota. U.S. manufacturers now buy parts from Japanese companies "where Toyota has strong influence, either as a buyer or as an investor." Ford officials were complaining that "Aisin AW Company, a Japanese auto parts supplier [owned by Toyota and Aisin Seiki], was placing a low priority on transmissions" the American company had ordered.[11]

In October 2005, Toyota raised its ownership in one of the battery makers, the Panasonic EV Energy Company, from 40 percent to 60 percent. Panasonic EV Energy Company supplies batteries to Honda.[12] At the same time, Toyota bought a large holding in Fuji Heavy Industries, which makes both Subaru cars and a lithium ion battery crucial to the future of hybrid cars. Sanyo also makes batteries and supplies Honda. The complex and highly integrated relationships among companies with expertise in different but related industries is fundamental to the infrastructure of Japan and elsewhere in Asia. These relationships make it more difficult for an outsider to become a true part of the consortium, which assumes, as a matter of course, that the whole is more important than the sum of the parts. The question is always there: Will the customer as both outsider and competitor receive equitable treatment? The answer usually resides in the strength of the outsider's infrastructure.

What are the outsider's options? The *Times* article noted that "Ford, which also buys hybrid batteries from Sanyo, feels uneasy about Toyota's control of some parts, either directly or through pressure on parts suppliers. Ford officials have said that they want to procure more parts from their own factories or from American parts makers." But current data suggests that this has become more difficult: American parts manufacturers have had to look for other markets for their products since U.S. automobile makers, weakened by foreign competition, no longer provide U.S. parts manufacturers with a market that offers the kind of profit demanded by investors.

The political and economic spheres of any nation are highly interrelated. A business cannot stand outside the socioeconomic context any more than an individual can. It is the infrastructure of technologies, products, and markets that gives meaning to the parts. If the nation as a whole is not competitive, it is difficult for any business or industry within that nation to remain competitive. No nation can succeed in a global economy if its greatest competitive problem lies within itself.

GETTING BACK IN THE GAME

The first step toward a revitalization of American competitiveness is the recognition that national competitiveness involves a complex set of interrelated principles. Understanding those principles is essential to any evaluation of the nation's future in a global economy. The process must be as dynamic as the accelerating environment in which it is created.

America must develop a national strategy for competitiveness, one that is responsive above all to the inertia of accelerating convergence, infrastructure, and investment. To put into practice any strategic plan will require patience, sacrifice, and a willingness to persevere when the long-term benefit is not immediately evident. There must be an assessment of the strategic requirements and levels of incentive necessary to insure that participants are not only willing but eager to comply. Since some incentives may seem to reward one segment of the economy at the expense of another, no strategy for competitiveness can succeed if it is not clear to all that the long-term benefits apply to the nation as a whole, not just a select few. Incentives cannot be simply monetary and short-term. The basic incentive must lie in the broader understanding that if the country is not competitive, all who depend on the economic strength of the nation will suffer. On the other hand, improving the nation's competitiveness enhances the future of all. This fundamental philosophy can only be conveyed by strong leadership at the highest levels of government.

For example, when NHK, the Japanese broadcast network, launched HDTV broadcasting in 1984, it became more than a commercial venture designed to sell television sets. HDTV became the centerpiece of a national strategy that would reverberate throughout the world's electronics industry for years to come. The Japanese got it right years ahead of time. HDTV was a logical next step in the acceleration of convergence, infrastructure, and investment. It was about the ability to process, by orders of magnitude, more information. The electronics industry of today is high-definition everything. Viable HDTV required a broad range of technological developments in information and image processing, semiconductors, displays, and electronic systems. The commercialization of HDTV also required a commitment on NHK's part to broadcast programs of interest to the Japanese public in order to stimulate demand for HDTV products. Therefore, well in advance of any international broadcast standard, NHK established an initial Japanese standard for HDTV, supporting it with a regular schedule of high-definition MUSE broadcasts that have continued from the early 1990s to the present.

Though the NHK MUSE system for transmitting HDTV—a combination of analog and digital information processing—was destined to be replaced by an all-digital standard, the technological lead it gave Japan in the design, development, and commercialization of high-definition systems became a cornerstone on which Japan built the strength of its current position in consumer electronics, semiconductors, and display technology. Virtually every Japanese electronics company participated in the development of HDTV technology. As a significant part of its global competitive strategy, Japan never treated HDTV as simply an industrial effort to introduce an exciting new television medium. Seeking public support from the beginning, government agencies even printed educational brochures on the virtues of HDTV.

The solution to America's competitiveness will not come from the grass roots. It won't bubble up from below. It must start with the office of the president of the United States because national competitiveness involves more then a few companies or individuals; it results from the competitiveness of all the nation's economic components. But the president must lead for another reason. Without a broad understanding of exactly what the country wants to accomplish, it is difficult to develop a strategy that will provide the necessary economic foundation for the nation's objectives.

Recognizing that neither the president nor anyone else will always get it right, America must have a set of goals and objectives that form the basis for a competitive strategy. The strategy can always be designed to anticipate a change of plans, but operating with no strategy, or one made without regard to the goals of the nation, will create more confusion than progress.

The following suggestions on how the development of a strategic plan for competitiveness might be approached should by no means be considered complete.

As with Japan's approach to HDTV, a strategy for American economic competitiveness must consider what technologies, products, and markets are strategic to the advancement of industry in the United States. The president of the United States must involve industry and government in a series of dialogues to determine which ones meet that criteria. These dialogues would include individuals from key organizations representing a broad spectrum of American government and industry—electronics, software, communications, biotechnology, automobiles, aircraft, chemistry, materials, space, defense, and institutions of higher learning in science and technology.

This body of people with strong educational and practical background in their respective fields should initially be organized into working groups, each assigned the responsibility of assessing the state of U.S. competitiveness in a relatively narrow area of technological development. These groups should then try to forecast the future competitive position of the nation within these respective areas.

Next, the groups should be amalgamated into one high-level committee to integrate the combined findings of the individual subcommittees. The results of the committee's efforts should then become the basis for recommending a national strategy of competitiveness to the president. The final committee should include two continuing bodies that maintain a constant dialogue with each other, one representing government interests and the other the private sector. Both should remain in existence to insure a continuous update of progress according to the strategic plan as set forth by the executive branch.

Using the ten principles as a backdrop, the technologies, products, and markets under review might be placed in one of three categories: (1) those that require no further action other than to insure their continuing success, (2) those requiring reinforcement of an existing but inadequate position, and (3) those representing areas where the United States must get back in the game.

The entire process rests on a clear understanding of the economic goals and objectives of the nation as determined by the president. If the strategy is to succeed, it needs both congressional and public support. The cost, speed of implementation, and success of the plan will depend largely on the competitive strengths of the country at the time it is put into effect. Because of accelerating convergence, infrastructure, and investment, the plan must be dynamic. It will require continuous reanalysis and adjustment. Progress or delay in one area will affect others, so there must be general agreement on the need for periodic review and adjustment of actions and expectations.

Finally, the basic concept inherent in any strategic plan for national competitiveness is that a long-term view of the country's interests must be widely respected by the nation. Belief in the need to provide long-term benefit to the nation cannot be legislated. It must come from faith in the country's leadership, in clear-eyed appraisals of the country's strengths and weaknesses, and a commitment to provide a foundation that will preserve American freedom and opportunity for subsequent generations.

PLAYING OFF THE NATION'S STRENGTHS

Once it has been determined which industries are critical, America has the ability to influence its strategic direction both internally and externally. Where the United States has little or no strategic presence, it should encourage foreign investment in plant, equipment, and related engineering facilities. This will provide America with exposure to technical and manufacturing know-how currently missing from its industrial base. Establishing foreign-owned manufacturing and research facilities in the United States, either as subsidiaries of the parent corporation or as a joint venture with a U.S. firm, is one of the quickest ways to reeducate Americans about an industry already lost to competition. It is also one of the fastest ways to build a domestic customer base for U.S. industries, many of whose end-use markets are abroad. This is very much the case with the U.S. semiconductor industry.

It is often possible for a nation to build an industrial base where little exists using only its own resources. But depending on the current state of the technological and manufacturing base when the decision is made to reenter the market, the cost and time to accomplish the effort can be daunting at best.

Today foreign industry has many reasons, both economic and political, to invest in America. The United States has the largest consumer market and by far the largest military force in the world. It continues to be a great customer and defender of countries around the globe. It has stable markets and a rule of law. And while there are problems with America's weakening dollar, the falling cost of investment in American assets should encourage foreign manufacturers to invest in the United States, where they may have both a currency advantage and a proximity to the largest consumer base anywhere.

The public must be willing, if not enthusiastic, to accept foreign investment in the United States. Foreign investment in the domestic infrastructure of the United States can be encouraged by local or federal government financial subsidies and tax incentives. The process of licensing for construction can be fast-tracked. Local educational facilities, housing, and attractive communities can be established to draw the required workforce.

The display industry, long absent in America, might be a perfect place to start. The establishment of engineering and manufacturing facilities in the United States by foreign makers of television sets, computer monitors, and other flat screen displays would provide closer access to American computer manufacturers and a closer relationship to the American markets they support. In addition, it would encourage increased investment from other companies important to the supply chain of these display manufacturers. An American company like Corning Incorporated, the manufacturer of glass products used in the construction of flat panel displays produced in Asia, might have interest in supporting a newly established display industry in America.

As the cost of manufacturing a new semiconductor device grows exponentially larger, the ability of individual semiconductor companies to produce their own chips becomes increasingly unlikely. As a result, a large portion of American semiconductor design houses are subcontracting their production to independent foundries (that is, manufacturing-only facilities) mostly located in Asia.

The United States needs one or more independent foundries to support its design-only semiconductor companies, which have few places other than Asia to go for manufacturing process development and production expertise. With the development of an independent U.S. foundry, the integration of the manufacturing process with the design of the semiconductor device becomes easier, more convenient, and cost effective. This has two important by-products. Intellectual property is retained within American borders, while a greater and more integrated team approach between the fabless semiconductor company and its foundry manufacturer should become an asset in the development of state-of-the-art proprietary products.

The investment necessary to create an independent U.S. foundry will be several billion dollars. This can be accomplished by a joint venture between U.S. companies that would benefit from such a relationship or by the spin-off of a manufacturing arm from an existing American company. It could also occur by attracting investment from a foreign foundry seeking an American subsidiary.

Finally, an assessment must be made as to the competitiveness of American manufacturers in strategic end-use markets such as consumer electronics. To be no more than a distributor of someone else's product provides little in the way of research and development, let alone manufacturing expertise. If the United States is to be simply a component manufacturer for other nations' end-use products, it will find this a difficult formula for success. Ultimately, the nation that produces the end-use product will prefer that its component requirements be manufactured domestically. Because the convergence of components and end-use products is happening so quickly—often completely altering the competitive nature of both—having a domestic supplier makes the process more efficient. The producer of the end-use product wants to be in control of its future. At the very least, the foreign manufacturer of end-use products will pressure remote suppliers of components to locate component manufacturing—and possibly design facilities—in the vicinity.

The revitalization of U.S. industry in the production of globally competitive end-use products (particularly in consumer electronics) will help offset current infrastructure advantages in other countries. By reestablishing or reinvigorating the domestic design and production of end-use products, U.S. companies can help rebuild their supporting industrial infrastructure—one that not only counters the competitiveness of other nations but also may entice them to partner with America and share in the advantages of U.S. infrastructure.

It is imperative that the United States reassess its position on antitrust laws. The most important change in emphasis should be an understanding that the impact of global competition on American manufacturers and the U.S. economy is just as important to U.S. competitiveness as the economic consequences of relationships between American companies. At some point, the cost of being in a high-technology business becomes so expensive that it is difficult for one company to do it all. Thus there is a need for Americans to learn how to combine competition with cooperation without destroying each other or the purchasing power of the American consumer. The value of industry cooperation, joint ventures, and other relationships must be viewed in terms of America's global competitiveness rather than simply as restraint of trade.

During the time when IBM dominated the computer market, it spent an inordinate amount of effort trying to insure that the Justice Department didn't dismantle the company rather than strategizing how to remain competitive in a global market. Though this was not the only factor in its loss of position in the computer business, it didn't help. Industry in America has a responsibility to avoid restraint of trade that is at the expense of the consumer. But the government must also understand the importance of a strong industrial base in a world of accelerating convergence, infrastructure, and investment. The country must be fair to itself and to others, but it must also be competitive. If American industry is not competitive globally, the United States will become predominantly a country of consumers and distributors, as its base of technology and products becomes uncompetitive in world markets—a situation unsustainable at best.

STRATEGY IS EVERYTHING

A significant degradation in the competitiveness of an economy as large as that of the United States can have serious side effects that result in other crises. This is particularly true for America, given that the world's reserve currency is the U.S. dollar, the world's largest consumer is the United States, and America spends half of the world's military budget. As an example, the global economic problems in the wake of the 1929 market crash were instrumental in precipitating the Second World War a decade later. When the crisis comes, it is easy to recognize and respect a leader who faces the enemy and emerges victorious. It is far more difficult to recognize and respect a leader who, while not facing an obvious crisis, understands the threat and is able to explain the seriousness of problems underlying the decline in U.S. competitiveness. It is essential that these problems be understood, explained, and resolved before the nation reaches the point of no return and some other crisis develops. The current decline in American competitiveness requires a leader who can rise above politics, understand the problem, and communicate it with a force and clarity that bring action. It is this kind of leadership that deserves the nation's respect.

It is the responsibility of the office of the president to set in motion a process that motivates Congress and the nation to understand America's strategic competitive needs in the context of its goals as well as existing U.S. laws, rules, regulations, tax codes, and economic policies. The purpose of a national competitive strategy is not to pick winners and losers but to enhance what is lacking in the nation's strategic technologies, products, and markets. Picking winners and losers is the strategy of stars, cash cows, and dogs.

For years Washington politicians have given the concept of industrial policy a bad reputation. Yet in an environment of limited resources and global competition, every law, rule, regulation, or tax code is a form of industrial policy that affects the nation's competitiveness. Developing a competitive strategy makes it easier to assess how well the industrial policy conforms to the country's needs.

Without a national strategy for competitiveness, industrial policy can produce results that may meet certain criteria but are unfortunate in retrospect considering what might have been. In 2006, President Bush signed the Deficit Reduction Act, which included the Digital Television Transition and Public Safety Act. For many valid reasons, not the least of which is the desire to open up the broadcast spectrum to provide for additional communications channels for homeland security, the DTV Act will end all analog TV broadcasts from full-power TV stations in the United States in 2009. Anyone without a digital TV receiver—or an analog to digital converter—will not be able to receive live television broadcasts. The D/A converter may cost $40 to $50 and will most likely be made in Asia.

Though of obvious value to the nation and the consumer, the many benefits of going digital will not extend to the design and manufacture of television sets in America, for that industry no longer exists. The United States could not even implement this law—this industrial policy—without the design and manufacture of displays made in Asia. America's current account deficit will be increased accordingly. As a result of the DTV Act, foreign producers of displays and related digital electronics will receive orders for some eighty million TV receivers as the old analog systems are replaced. In reality, America is beholden to its foreign suppliers of flat panel displays designed and manufactured in Asia. This situation—the total dependence of the United States on the output of a foreign industry—might be seen in a different light were the nation's defense perceived to be at stake.

In 1999, the *New York Times* obituary for Akio Morita, noting that he had been quite vocal in his criticism of U.S. business practices, recalled comments he had made in the 1980s, a time of rapid growth in the Japanese economy and of American angst about what many in the United States felt was an unfair competitor. American managers were financial paper shufflers, he said, who could "see only ten minutes ahead" and were not interested in building for the long term. And because American companies were losing interest in manufacturing, the United States was "abandoning its status as an industrial power."[13]

These comments were made when Japan was becoming an economic powerhouse. When it later suffered economic reversals, these and similar comments were taken less seriously. My own discussions with Morita in the 1990s made it clear to me that his message had even deeper implications. A nation's strength lies in its ideals and intent. The backbone of resources that gives those ideas and purposes credibility is a nation's economic base—the power of its technology, products, and markets. When the nation speaks from the strength of that backbone, others listen. My concern is that in a world governed by convergence, infrastructure, and investment, if America loses its infrastructure, few will listen.

With a loss of manufacturing expertise in strategic industries such as displays, semiconductors, and consumer electronics, America is losing the ability to commercialize its own products. *All of America's technological industries and institutions are linked.* When one of those links is broken, America loses some of the technical knowledge and economic incentives necessary to innovate, and thus some measure of its ability to compete. As markets become larger elsewhere, the United States needs to know that it can produce what others want. America must be able to compete successfully in markets that will someday be much larger than its own and to do so in the face of rapidly growing, highly sophisticated, indigenous competition in those very same countries.

Eventually, American consumption will no longer be the economic force that it is today. The greater amount of financial resources that emanate from consumer demand for the world's technological developments, products, and markets will come from somewhere else. To meet this challenge, America must improve its balance of trade: it must make the products that others want while it can still take advantage of the financial resources that come from America's extraordinary consumer base.

On Christmas Eve 1968, three Americans became the first men to circle the moon. At the end of a dark and violent year of war, riots, and assassinations, it was a collective triumph for all people on Earth, who were given a glimmer of hope in America's greatness. *Time* magazine dropped plans to feature the dissenter as "Man of the Year" and instead put the three astronauts on its cover. Exactly thirty-eight years later, on December 25, 2006, *Time* put a mirror on its cover—the person of the year was "you."[14] The reference was to the undeniable importance of user-generated content and self-expression on the internet. But the United States, mesmerized in many ways by individual power in the moment, needed caution in taking that cover to heart. It may not be all about "you."

In the largest context, the suggestion that both a nation's economic infrastructure and the global economy must be seen as an ecosystem of independent parts is in line with the whole conceptual thrust of the last half century. The move from a mechanical, reductionist view of the world to a systems approach has infused almost every area of theory and practice—from sociology, medicine, ecology, and evolutionary biology to quantum physics and the new sciences of chaos and complexity. As the mechanistic themes of isolation and permanence give way to the holistic concepts of connection and change, the overarching motif for the twenty-first century reflects astronaut Ed Mitchell's epiphany as he gazed out at the surrounding cosmos during his return from the moon: "Everything is connected."[15] What is true of the cosmos is no less true of economies. These connections provide the exponential power of convergence, infrastructure, and investment. We ignore them at our peril.

Asserting that America is becoming less competitive in the global community is in no way a suggestion that there aren't world-class

American companies, institutions, technologies, and products. The United States is a leader or major player in software development, computer design, biotechnology, pharmaceuticals, the practice of medicine, semiconductor design, development of media content, aircraft design, and agriculture, to name a few. Our institutions of higher learning are still the best in the world. But the national infrastructure in the broadest sense is becoming less resilient to the competitive position of others.

The United States must begin to view its role as a net exporter of goods and services. To change the competitive direction of the United States will take many years and potentially cost hundreds of billions of dollars. Those dollars will not come from government subsidies—there just isn't enough money. Those dollars will have to come primarily from the strategic direction of American industry and a resulting considered application of its resources. Therefore, America needs a national competitive strategy now. Strategy is everything.

Acknowledgments

Sitting in the center of the room amid three hundred members of the press and investment community when I introduced Instavideo at New York's Americana Hotel on September 6, 1970, was my wife, Helen. At 2 A.M. the next morning in the studios of *Life* magazine, she watched the photographers try to capture the essence of the VCR for their center spread: "Cassette TV: The Good Revolution." Through that entire period Helen witnessed what we both thought might well turn out to be one of the world's most successful failures. She was there when I closed the deal transferring the Instavideo technology to Toshiba in Japan. Helen was witness to every significant event that led to this book. Without her devotion, support, and encouragement, this book could never have been written.

Helen was there when I joined the founding group at Prometrix and was formally introduced to the semiconductor industry. Though the manufacturing of video recorders is no longer an American enterprise, the semiconductor industry is. It remains one of the most strategic businesses on Earth, one fundamental to the creativity and productivity of the United States. America owes a special debt of gratitude to those gifted, diligent, and above all, persistent people whose inventions and contributions built America's competitive position in the world of the semiconductor—the industry at the heart of the information age.

Acknowledgments never do justice to the contribution of others. No amount of words can match the permanence and power of ideas and expertise. In the case of Wyn Wachhorst this is particularly true. The poetic style that he used to tie history and ideas together in chapters 3, 4 and 9 were indispensible to the book. As a matter of interest, Chapter 3 was based in part on his biography of Edison.

Clyde Prestowitz was a constant source of support when it came to tying my thoughts to the economic conditions facing America and its trading partners. It was his invitation to provide the Economic Strategy Institute with my principles of competitiveness, published in 1991, that led me to consider writing this book.

The person I credit most in helping me formulate my views on how the world works is Akio Morita, founder of Sony Corporation and one of the smartest men I have ever met. My conversations with him in the 1990s led me to the understanding that there was a direct connection between the strategy of Sony and Moore's Law.

If one finds value in these pages, much of it is owed to my fortuitous relationship with my partners at Prometrix, Tencor, and KLA. In that regard, four men: Ken Levy, founder of KLA, Jim Bagley, Chairman and CEO of Lam Research Corp., Stan Myers, CEO of the Semiconductor Equipment and Materials International, and George Scalise, President of the Semiconductor Industry Association, have been particularly helpful along the way as a sounding board for ideas and conclusions.

One of the most important opportunities I received many years ago came from Robert White, former undersecretary of Commerce for Technology and a true patriot. Bob offered me membership on the selection committee of the National Medal of Technology and an insight into the minds of the greatest American technologists of our time. There are so many others to thank, names too numerous to mention. But all represent the best America has to offer because they all strove to add value.

Finally, I would like to thank my editor and boss through this process, William Frucht. I can't imagine anyone else putting up with me.

NOTES

INTRODUCTION

1. Michael L. Dertouzos, Richard K. Lester, and Robert M. Solow, *Made in America: Regaining the Productive Edge* (Cambridge, Mass.: MIT Press, 1989), 132.

2. "Global Market for Electronics Slated for High Growth through 2012 according to BCC Research," December 16, 2007, http://www.bccresearch.com.

3. Charles J. Murray, "Semiconductor Capacity Decline Will Have Impact: Drop Foreseen in Research and High-End Engineering Jobs," *Design News,* November 20, 2006, http://www.designnews.com/article/CA6390338.html.

4. Associated Press, November 2, 1988, http://ils.unc.edu/~viles/172i/users/big/docs/AP881102-0297.

5. YahooFinance.com, January 24, 2008.

6. Richard J. Elkus Jr., "The Seamless Product," *Automobile Magazine,* November 1991.

7. Joseph B. White, "Toyota to Detroit: We Will Bury You," *Wall Street Journal,* September 25, 2006, D5.

8. "General Motors—A Corporate Governance Case Study," http://www.ragm.com/books/corp_gov/cases/cs_gm.html.

9. Alex Taylor III, Alicia Hills Moore, and Wilton Woods, "Can GM Remodel Itself?" *Fortune,* January 13, 1992, http://money.cnn.com/magazines/fortune/fortune_archive/1992/01/13/75996/index.htm.

10. "General Motors—A Corporate Governance Case Study."

11. Jonathan Sidener, "Who Needs Fabs Anyway? Chip Developers Have Found Success Without Manufacturing Capabilities," *San Diego Union Tribune*, February 8, 2008, http://SignOnSanDiego.com/news/business/20080208-9999-1b8fabless.html.

12. Carl Freire, "Sharp to Create New Flat Panel Center: Sharp to Create New Flat Panel Base in Western Japan, Reportedly with Corning, Others," Associated Press, http://www.abcnews.go.com/print?id=3431319.

Chapter 1

1. Michael A. Cusumano, Yiorgos Mylonadis, and Richard S. Rosenbloom, *Strategic Maneuvering and Mass-Market Dynamics: The Triumph of VHS over Beta* (unpublished manuscript), March 25, 1991, 6.

2. Richard S. Rosenbloom, ed., *Research on Technological Innovation, Management and Policy,* vol. 2 (Greenwich, Conn.: JAI, 1985), 165.

3. "Tape-It-Yourself TV," *Life,* September 17, 1965, 56–60.

4. Cusumano, Mylonadis, and Rosenbloom, *Strategic Maneuvering and Mass-Market Dynamics,* 30.

5. Robert Lubar, "Five Little Ampexes and How They Grew," *Fortune* (April 1960): 116.

6. Ampex Corporation Publications Department, *March Activity Report*, April 8, 1971, 1.

7. Extrapolated from Ampex Corp./DE, Results of Operations for Three Months Ended 1996, 10Q, filed on May 1, 1997, SEC file 0-20292, accession number 903112-97-639; Ampex Corp./DE, Consolidated Statement of Operations and Comprehensive Income (Loss) (Unaudited) Nine Months Ending September 30, 1999, 10Q, filed on 11-15-99, SEC file 20292, accession number 1012870-99-4246.

8. Rosenbloom, *Research on Technological Innovation, Management and Policy,* 175–176.

Chapter 2

1. "The Kitchen Debate," July 24, 1959, http://TeachingAmericanHistory.org/library/index.asp?documentprint=176.

2. Ibid.

3. Sony Corporation, "Sony History: Establishing Tokyo Tsushin Kogyo," http://www.sony.net/Fun/SH/1-1/h2.html.

4. Sony Corporation, "Sony History: A Letter from the United States," http://www.sony.net/SH/1-4/h4.html.

5. Sony Corporation, "Sony History: The UN Building Radio," http://www.sony.net/Fun/SH/1-5/h5.html.

6. Sony Corporation, "Sony History: Is 'Pocketable' Japanese-English?" http://www.sony.net/Fun/SH/1-6/h2.html.

7. Richard J. Elkus Jr., "Towards a National Strategy: The Strategy of Leverage," presentation at the conference "Compete or Concede? CEOs Respond to the High-Tech Challenge," sponsored by Rebuild America, American Electronics Association, Congressional Clearinghouse on the Future, July 13, 1988.

8. Ibid.

9. Richard J. Elkus Jr. et al., "High Definition Systems in Japan," Japanese Technology Evaluation Center Panel, February 1991, http://www.wtec.org/loyola/ar93_94/hds.html.

10. Ibid.

CHAPTER 3

1. *Scientific American* editor Beach relates the entire incident in George S. Bryan, *Edison: The Man and His Work* (Garden City, N.Y.: Doubleday, 1926), 86–87.

2. The events surrounding the phonograph are from Robert Conot, *A Streak of Luck* (New York: Seaview Books, 1979), 107–113.

3. Quoted in Tom Farley, "Tom Farley's Telephone History Series," http://www.privateline.com/TelephoneHistory1.htm.

4. The Edison story is taken from Wyn Wachhorst, *Thomas Alva Edison: An American Myth* (Cambridge, Mass.: MIT Press, 1981).

5. On Meucci, see "Antonio Meucci," Italian Historical Society of America, http://www.italianhistorical.org/Meucci.html.

6. John H. Lienhard, "Who Invented the Telephone?" *Engines of Our Ingenuity* no. 1098, University of Houston, http://www.uh.edu/engines/epi1098.html.

7. On Ford, see Allan Nevins and Frank Ernest Hill, *Ford: The Times, the Man, the Company* (New York: Scribner's Sons, 1954), and *Ford: Expansion and Challenge, 1915–1933* (New York: Scribner's Sons, 1957); also Douglas G. Brinkley, *Wheels for the World: Henry Ford, His Company, and a Century of Progress* (New York: Penguin Books, 2003).

8. PBS, "Transistorized!" http://www.pbs.org/transistor/album1/index.html.

9. "Guglielmo Marconi," http://en.wikipedia.org/wiki/Guglielmo_Marconi.

10. On the development of the transistor, see the many articles at "Transistorized!" http://www.pbs.org/transistor/index.html.

11. On William Shockley and Silicon Valley, see Michael Riordan and Lillian Hoddeson, *Crystal Fire: The Invention of the Transistor and Birth of the Information Age* (New York: Norton, 1998), and Christophe Lécuyer, *Making Silicon Valley: Innovation and the Growth of High Tech, 1930–1970* (Cambridge, Mass.: MIT Press, 2007).

12. Wyn Wachhorst, "Ten Days that Unexpectedly Changed America: Einstein's Letter," *Journal of American History* 93 (December 2006): 983–984.

13. "Memorandum by the Chief of Staff, U.S. Air Force to the Secretary of Defense on Long Range Detection of Atomic Explosions," in "The Decision to Drop

the Atomic Bomb," Harry S. Truman Library and Museum, http://www.truman
library.org/whistlestop/study_collections/bomb/large/index.php.

Chapter 4

1. "Men of the Year," *Time*, January, 3, 1969, 9, 12–17, and cover.

2. Jeffery Sonnenfeld, *The Hero's Farewell: What Happens When CEOs Retire*
(New York: Oxford University Press, 1988), 181.

3. Ryan Lizza, "The Mission: Mitt Romney's Strategies for Success," *New Yorker*,
October 29, 2007, http://www.newyorker.com/reporting/2007/10/29/071029fa_
fact_lizza.

4. "BCG History: 1966," http://www.bcg.com/about_bcg/history/1966.html.

5. Bruce D. Henderson, "The Experience Curve Reviewed, IV: The Growth
Share Matrix or the Product Portfolio," Boston Consulting Group, 1973, http://
www.bcg.com/publications/files/Experience_Curve_IV_Growth_Share_Matrix_
1973.pdf.

6. Gordon E. Moore, "Cramming More Components onto Integrated Circuits,"
Electronics 38 (April 19, 1965): 114–17.

7. Richard P. Rumelt and Olivier Costa, "Gordon Moore's Law," paper for the
Anderson School at UCLA, 2003, http://www.anderson.ucla.edu/faculty/dick
.rumelt/Docs/Cases/MooresLaw.pdf.

8. Colleen S. Spiegel, "Global Electronics: High Growth Products and New
Markets," a research report by BCC (Business Communications Company), November 2007, http://www.electronics.ca/reports/technology/new_markets.html.

9. Joel Garreau, *Radical Evolution: The Promise and Peril of Enhancing Our
Minds, Our Bodies—and What It Means to Be Human* (New York: Doubleday,
2005), 88–106.

10. Chang-Gyu Hwang, Address to the Association of Pacific Rim Universities
presidents' meeting, July 6, 2006, http://www.ferret.com.au/c/Samsung-Electronics-
Australia/Secrets-of-Samsungs-innovation-success-n687251.

11. Yoshiko Hara, "Toshiba Forecasts NAND, OLED Expansion," *EE Times
Online*, April 12, 2007, http://www.eetimes.com/showArticle.jhtml?articleID
=199000591.

12. Giovanni Gavetti, Rebecca Henderson, and Simona Giorgi, "Kodak and the
Digital Revolution," Harvard Business School, November 16, 2004, 2.

13. Albert Abramson, "The Invention of Television," in *Television: An International History*, ed. Anthony Smith and Richard Paterson, 2nd ed. (New York: Oxford University Press, 1998), 9–22; R. J. Reiman, "Who Invented Television?"
http://inventors.about.com/gi/dynamic/offsite.htm?site=http://ieee.cincinnati.fuse
.net/reiman/10%5F1994.html. On Campbell-Swinton, see J. D. McGee, "The Con-

tribution of A. A. Campbell Swinton, F.R.S., to Television," *Notes and Records of the Royal Society of London* 32 (July 1977): 91–105. On Baird, see Iain L. Baird and Malcolm H. I. Baird, "Baird Television," http://www.bairdtelevision.com. On the Farnsworth-Zworykin debate, see Paul Schatzkin, "The Farnsworth Chronicles," http://inventors.about.com/gi/dynamic/offsite.htm?site=http://farnovision.com/chronicles/tfc%2Dwho%5Finvented%5Fwhat.html.

14. Gavetti, Henderson, and Giorgi, "Kodak and the Digital Revolution," 2–4.

15. Ibid.

16. Paul Carton and Jim Woods, "Shot Out of a Canon: A Snapshot of Our Latest Findings on Digital Cameras," ChangeWave Alliance, January 23, 2007, http://www.changewave.com/freecontent/viewarticle.html?source=/freecontent/2007/01/alliance-canon–012307.html.

17. Lyra Research Press Room, "Lyra Believes Digital Camera Worldwide Shipments Will Exceed 130 Million by 2010, a 10 Percent CAGR, Despite Market Saturation and Camera Phone Competition," Lyra Research Industry, January 10, 2007, http://www.lyra.com/PressRoom.nsf/a6df7dce4a0ca65f85256d160061e4eb/d616063 68aed17018525725f004d323d?OpenDocument.

18. Steve Hamm and William C. Symonds, "Mistakes Made on the Road to Innovation," *Business Week*, November 27, 2006, http://www.businessweek.com/print/magazine/content/06_48/b4011421.htm?chan=gl.

CHAPTER 5

1. Cybertelecom Federal Internet Law & Policy: An Educational Project, "Universal Service," http://www.cybertelecom.org/usf/.

2. "IT Industry History," Caslon Analytics, http://www.caslon.com.au/itindustry/itdates6.htm; "The 1960s (Into a New Age of Technology)," Webb & Associates, Telecommunications History Timeline, http://www.webbconsult.com/hist-time.html.

3. Sheldon Hochheiser, "The American Telephone and Telegraph Company (AT&T)," 1989, 4, http://www.porticus.org/bell/pdf/tattc.pdf.

4. David Massey, "Bell System History: The Bell System," http://www.porticus.org/bell/bellsystem_history.html.

5. "Claude E. Shannon Obituary," IEEE Information Theory Society, http://www.itsoc.org/shannon.html.

6. "Hoover's Profile: Cisco Systems, Inc.," http://www.answers.com/topic/cisco?cat=biz-fin.

7. Audry Selian, *3G Mobile Licensing Policy: From GSM to IMT-2000; A Comparative Analysis*, Office of the Secretary General of the International Telecommunication Union, 6, http://www.itu.int/osg/csd/ni/3G/casestudies/GSM-FINAL.doc.

8. "Toshiba Will Reportedly Invest 6.6B in New NAND Plant," *EE Times*, http://in.reuters.com/article/asiaCompanyAndMarkets/idINT14241320080206.

9. Bolaji Ojo, "Did You Know?: R&D Drives a Giant's Self-Reinvention," *EE Times*, June, 18, 2007.

10. Mark LaPedus, "Sixteen IC Makers Join $1B Capex Club," *EE Times*, June 19, 2007, citing IC Insights and company reports as sources.

11. *Nikon Annual Report*, 1999–2000, 17, http://www.nikon.co.jp/main/eng/portfolio/ir/ir_tool/ar/pdf/1999/99annual_e.pdf.

12. "GCA Reports $116M Loss in 4th Quarter," *Electronic News*, April 21, 1986, http://www.iirusa.com/upload/wysiwyg/M1839_Images/M1739_Grabowski_Article.pdf.

13. Douglas A. Irwin and Peter J. Klenow, "Sematech: Purpose and Performance," *Procedures of the National Academy of Science, USA*, vol. 93 (November 1996): 12739–42.

14. CNET News.com, "Corning Buys Tropel for $190 Million," http://www.news.com/Corning-buys-Tropel-for-190-million/2100-1033_3-251371.html; Dan Holden and Peter Dunn, "GS Sets Ultratech Buyout; GCA Slims to Lure Suitors: General Signal to Sell Ultratech Stepper Unit to Management Group, GCA Corp. Unit to Lay Off 16 percent of Its Employees," *Electronic News*, January 25, 1993.

15. Paul Kallender, "ASML Acquires SVG for $1.6B: Company Business and Marketing," *Electronic News*, October 9, 2000.

16. Thayer Watkins, "The Bubble Economy of Japan," http://www.sjsu.edu/faculty/watkins/bubble.htm.

17. Daniel P. Burbank, "The Near Impossibility of Making a Microchip," *Invention and Technology Magazine* 15 (Fall 1999), http://www.americanheritage.com/articles/magazine/it/1999/2/1999_2_44.shtml.

Chapter 6

1. Richard M. Jones, "White House S&T Council Discusses IT, Workforce, Nanotechnology," *FYI: The AIP Bulletin of Science Policy News*, October 10, 2003, http://www.aip.org/enews/fyi/2003/132.html.

2. "Leisure Class," VC Confidential (http://www.vcconfidential.com), quoting analyst Marc Faber, April 2006. See also "GlobalHigherEd: Surveying the Construction of Global Knowledge/Spaces for the 'Knowledge Economy,'" http://global highered.wordpress.com/2007/11/22/graphic-feed-us-dependency-upon-foreign-science-and-engineering-phds–2006/.

3. Christine M. Mathews, "CRS Report for Congress: Foreign Science and Engineering Presence in U.S. Institutions and the Labor Force," June 21, 2007, 2, http://fas.org/sgp/crs/misc/97-746.pdf.

4. Vivek Wadhwa, Gary Gereffi, Ben Rissing, and Ryan Ong, "Where the Engineers Are," *Issues in Science and Technology*, Spring 2007, http://ssrn.com/abstract =1015843; "Leisure Class," VC Confidential.

5. Timothy Aeppel, "More Parts Producers Give Up on Auto Industry," *Wall Street Journal*, July 29, 2007, http://online.wsj.com/article/SB118575161039881718.html.

6. "Great Aviation Quotes," http://www.skygod.com/quotes/predictions.html.

7. President Dwight Eisenhower quoted in "Answer in Oklahoma," *Time*, online reprint, November 25, 1957, http://www.time.com/time/printout/0,8816, 891802,00.html.

8. Dwight Eisenhower, "Our Future Security," radio and television address, November 13, 1957, http://www.eisenhowermemorial.org/speeches/19571113%20 Radio%20and%20Television%20Address%20on%20Our%20Future%20Security.htm.

9. Ivan Semeniuk, "How *Sputnik* Changed the World," *New Scientist*, September 8, 2007, 44.

10. Monica Langley, "Why $70 Million Wasn't Enough," *Wall Street Journal*, August 21, 2007, http://online.wsj.com/article/SB118740076313301636.html.

11. Edward Teller, "What We Must Do," in *The Challenge of the Sputniks*, ed. Richard Witkin (New York: Doubleday, 1958), 77.

12. National Science Board, *An Emerging and Critical Problem of the Science and Engineering Labor Force*, January 2004, http://www.nsf.gov/statistics/nsb0407/ nsb0407.pdf.

13. Taskforce on the Future of American Innovation, "Benchmarks of Our Innovation Future: The Knowledge Economy: Is the United States Losing Its Competitive Edge?" February 16, 2005, 1, http://www.futureofinnovation.org/PDF/ Benchmarks.pdf.

14. Ibid., 3.

15. Ibid., 3–5.

16. Ibid., 9.

17. Ibid., 11.

18. Ibid., 13.

19. Ibid.

CHAPTER 7

1. Richard J. Elkus Jr., "Towards a National Strategy: The Strategy of Leverage," presentation at the conference "Compete or Concede? CEOs Respond to the High-Tech Challenge," sponsored by Rebuild America, American Electronics Association, Congressional Clearinghouse on the Future, July 13, 1988.

2. Thomas Gale Moore, "The Promise of High-Definition Television: The Hype and the Reality," Cato Policy Analysis No. 123, August 30, 1989.

3. Ibid.

4. Ibid.

5. Ibid.

6. Ibid.

7. Ibid.

8. Ray Kurzweil, "George Gilder," http://www.kurzweilai.net/bios/frame.html?main=/bios/bio0004.html.

9. George Gilder, *Life After Television* (New York: Norton, 1994), 2.

10. Ibid.

11. U.S. Department of Defense, Defense Science Board, High Resolution Systems Task Force Working Committees, Excerpts from Final Report, March 6, 1990.

12. Tom Wicker, "In the Nation: The High-Tech Future," *New York Times,* May 24, 1990, http://www.nytimes.com/.

13. ATV Task Force Economic Impact Team, "High Definition Television (HDTV): Economic Analysis of Impact," American Electronics Association, November 1988, i.

14. Ibid., section 2, 3–4.

15. U.S. Congress, Office of Technology Assessment, *The Big Picture: HDTV and High-Resolution Systems* (Washington, D.C.: U.S. Government Printing Office, 1990), 11.

16. Ibid., 1–2.

17. Robert Cohen, *The Consequences of Failing to Develop a Strong HDTV Industry in the U.S.* (Briefing Paper #9), 6, http://www.epi.org/briefingpapers/1989_bp_consequences.pdf.

18. Moore, "The Promise of High-Definition Television."

19. Strategy Analytics report cited in "Will Flat Panel Sales Reach $100 Billion In 2007?" *Retail Bridge*, October 15, 2007, http://www.mbc-thebridge.com/archives/view/?publication_id=2&release_id=240.

20. Tom Murtha, *Metanational Management and Global Innovation: The Case of the TFT-LCD Industry*, Research Institute of Economy, Trade and Industry, Policy Symposium, Tokyo, March 14, 2007.

21. "Global Chip Sales Hit Record $247.7 Billion in 2006," Semiconductor Industry Association, February 2, 2007, http://www.sia-online.org/pre_release.cfm?ID=426.

22. John Markoff, "Intel to Unveil Chips for Improving Video Quality on the Web," *New York Times*, November 12, 2007, http://www.nytimes.com/.

23. Andrew Pollack, "U.S. Chip Gain Is Japan's Loss," *New York Times*, January 3, 1991, http://www.nytimes.com/.

24. Semiconductor Equipment and Material International, "Capacity Report: January 2007 to December 2008," July 2007, personal communication from the company.

25. Elkus, "Towards a National Strategy."

CHAPTER 8

1. Richard J. Elkus Jr., "Towards a National Strategy: The Strategy of Leverage," presentation at the conference "Compete or Concede? CEOs Respond to the High-Tech Challenge," sponsored by Rebuild America, American Electronics Association, Congressional Clearinghouse on the Future, July 13, 1988.

2. Joe Jablonowski, "Global Metalworking Factory Investment Grows: The World Machine Tool Output & Consumption Survey," 2007, http://www.mmson line.com/articles/040702.html.

3. Japanese External Trade Organization, "Trends in the Japanese Robotics Industry," *Japan Economic Monthly* (March 2006): 8, http://www.jetro.go.jp/en/market/report/pdf/2006_15_c.pdf.

4. Emily Flynn Vencat, "A Boeing of Asia?" *Newsweek International*, May 15, 2006, http://www.newsweek.com/id/47636.

5. Masumi Suda, "Mitsubishi Heavy Gains After Report on Regional Jet," Bloomberg.com, March 21, 2008.

6. Japanese Ministry of Economy, Trade, and Industry (METI), *Nuclear and Industrial Safety Agency Development of Recent Five Years and Future Issues*, November 2006, http://www.nisa.meti.go.jp/english/index.html.

7. Hisane Masaki, "Japan's Appetite for Uranium Is Growing," *Asia Times Online*, April 20, 2006, http://www.atimes.com/atimes/Japan/HD20Dh01.html.

CHAPTER 9

1. John Winthrop, "A Model of Christian Charity," http://en.wikipedia.org/wiki/City_upon_a_Hill.

2. John F. Kennedy, Inaugural Address, *Public Papers of the Presidents of the United States: John F. Kennedy; Containing the Public Messages, Speeches, and Statements of the President, January 20 to December 31, 1961*, Washington, DC.: U.S. Government Printing Office, 1–3.

3. Christopher Smith, "High-Risk Hobbies Keep CEO's Skills Sharp," *Seattle Times*, January 15, 2006, http://seattletimes.nwsource.com/html/businesstechnology/2002740825_appleton15.html.

4. Steve Appleton, presentation to International Trade Partners Conference, 1999.

5. Ibid.

6. Smith, "High-Risk Hobbies."

7. Gordon E. Moore, "The Accidental Entrepreneur," December 3, 2001, http://nobelprize.org/nobel_prizes/physics/articles/moore/index.html.

8. Thinkexist.com, "Steve Appleton Quotes," http://thinkexist.com/quotes/steve_appleton/2.html.

9. Peter Burrows, "Micron's Comeback Kid," *Business Week*, May 13, 1996.

10. Richard J. Elkus Jr., "The Seamless Product," *Automobile Magazine* (November 1991).

11. James Brooke, "In the Hybrid's Wake, Trying to Catch Up," *New York Times*, October 20, 2005, http://www.nytimes.com/.

12. Ibid.

13. Andrew Pollack, "Akio Morita, Co-Founder of Sony and Japanese Business Leader, Dies at 78," *New York Times*, October 4, 1999, http://www.nytimes.com/.

14. Lev Grossman, "Time's Person of the Year: You," *Time*, December 25, 2006, 40–41.

15. Marshall Master, "Interview with Edgar Mitchell," *Cut to the Chase*, no. 84, http://www.yowusa.com/radio/cttc/2008/cttc-0208-84/1.shtml.

Index